Fred Allen's
Radio Comedy

AMERICAN CIVILIZATION

A series edited by Allen F. Davis

Fred Allen's Radio Comedy

ALAN HAVIG

TEMPLE UNIVERSITY PRESS
PHILADELPHIA

Temple University Press, Philadelphia 19122
Copyright © 1990 Temple University. All rights reserved.
Published 1990
Printed in the United States of America

Library of Congress Cataloging-in-Publication Data

Havig, Alan R., 1940–
Fred Allen's radio comedy / Alan Havig.
    p.   cm.—(American civilization)
    Includes bibliographical references.
    ISBN 0–87722–713–6 (alk. paper)
    1. Allen, Fred, 1894–1956.   2. Radio programs—United States—
History.   3. Comedy programs—United States—History.
4. Comedians—United States—Biography. I. Title. II. Series.
PN1991.4.A6H3   1990
792.7'028'092—dc20
                             89–20566
                                 CIP

To my parents
Harold R. Havig, 1899–1989, and
Blanche S. Havig

Contents

Acknowledgments

I wish to thank those whose support helped make this book possible. Nancy Walker, a former colleague at Stephens College and now at Vanderbilt University, generously shared her knowledge of American literary humor. Many students who enrolled in my "Popular Culture in 20th Century America" course through the years, and in "Humor in America," which the Center for Conceptual Studies at Stephens sponsored in the spring semester of 1986, were helpful associates-in-learning as I explored radio comedy in a broader cultural context. My special thanks go to colleagues Amy Harvey and David Edens, co-teachers of the Conceptual Studies course. Stephens College not only offered me teaching opportunities but also financial support for my research: a summer study grant in 1977, a Firestone-Baars Faculty Development grant in 1982, and a sabbatical leave in the fall of 1983. I am grateful to the staff of the Hugh Stephens Library at Stephens College for essential assistance, specifically Director Marguerite Mitchel, Joanna Todd, Jean Nauert, Carla Conley, and Margaret Faust. Sherry Hunter and Laura Ellis, friends and former students, served as long-distance research associates at a crucial time when I could not be in New York, and I thank them.

I am most happy to express public appreciation to

Allen Davis, editor of the American Civilization Series in which this volume appears. Davis began easing my work into final form nearly twenty-five years ago, and he has not lost his touch. In countless ways, not all of which I know about, the capable and kind professionals at the Temple University Press made publication of my research and writing possible. Thanks in particular to Janet Francendese, Senior Acquisitions Editor, Mary Capouya, Senior Production Editor, and Irene Glynn, copyeditor.

I also express appreciation to those who permitted and facilitated my use of materials essential to a study of Fred Allen's radio comedy. The Manuscripts Division of the Library of Congress has microfilm copies of Allen's radio scripts, which I read. David Wigdor of the Manuscripts Division has subtly encouraged my interest in radio comedy and the popular arts over the years. The Trustees of the Boston Public Library, who hold the literary rights to Allen's scripts, have graciously granted permission to quote from them and other Allen materials. I appreciate the help of Jane Manthorne, the Library's Curator of Publications. Sheila Ryan, Curator of Manuscripts, granted permission to use some of Fred Allen's letters in the H. Allen Smith Papers, Special Collections, Morris Library, Southern Illinois University–Carbondale. Letters, memos, and reports in the National Broadcasting Company Collection, located at The State Historical Society of Wisconsin, Madison, helped me to understand Allen's relationship with that network, and I thank the staff of the Society for facilitating my use of those materials in this study. The materials are used by courtesy of the National Broadcasting Company, Inc. I am grateful to Gene M. Gressley, Director of the Archive of Contemporary History, University of Wyoming, Laramie, who made available copies of newspaper clippings on Allen's career from the Al Durante Collection, and copies of several of Fred Allen's letters from the Arnold M. Auerbach Collection.

And finally, I give thanks to spouse Bettina and daughter Kirsten, who permitted me to spend untold hours with

Fred Allen; and to Allen himself, who made those hours worthwhile. His comedy made this scholarly project so enjoyable that there is loss, as well as obvious benefit, in its completion.

I had completed two drafts of this study before Robert Taylor published his biography, *Fred Allen: His Life and Wit* (1989). I have chosen not to swell my notes further with references to this first book-length treatment of Allen's life and professional career. Taylor's fine volume and mine are complementary, and I urge interested readers to consult both. Mr. Taylor has written a biography. This study analyzes Allen's radio comedy within the contexts of American radio as an institution during the 1930s and 1940s; American popular entertainment during the nineteenth and twentieth centuries; and American humor, as expressed in literature as well as in performance. Taylor's approach and method are those of a journalist, mine of a scholar. Careful readers will discover the value of each treatment.

One final note: in 1953, fred allen told his friend goodman ace why, for years, he had typed his letters and other writings in lowercase. "i have never been able to shift for myself," was the excuse of this wordplayer.* i have honored mr. allen's shiftless habits in what follows. conscientious readers need not mentally correct seeming errors of capitalization. simply sit back and enjoy the idiosyncracies of a humorous man.

*Goodman Ace, "f.a.," *Saturday Review* 36 (August 1, 1953): 26.

Fred Allen's
Radio Comedy

An Introduction

The ear is the poet's perfect Audience.
                    ARCHIBALD MACLEISH,
                    The Fall of the City, 1937

Humor reflects and gives expression to social change. In the early twentieth century, as the frontier closed and Americans concentrated in commercial and industrial cities, rural comic types gave way to urban ones in the nation's popular literary and stage presentations. The mighty deeds and brash confidence of the mythical Davy Crockett, and the "humor of audacious exaggeration—of perfect lawlessness" that characterized Artemus Ward's platform performance, yielded to the nervous imaginary triumphs of Walter Mitty under the impact of twentieth-century change.[1] Some observers have identified a "new humor," which emerged around the turn of the century. Reflecting urban pressures, responding to heightened ethnic and gender tensions, the voice of the new humor spoke in sharper and more frenzied tones than had nineteenth-century native humor. As expressed on the vaudeville stage, in the mass-circulation print media, and on silent movie screens, brief, hard-hitting verbal and visual jokes replaced rambling tales rendered in dialect as the most common form of American humor. In more formal literary circles, authors discovered the new psychology during the World War I era. When "serious" humor absorbed Sigmund Freud's or John B. Watson's views of human nature, it left behind more optimistic eighteenth- and nineteenth-century modes of comic expression.[2]

This book is about a twentieth-century medium of entertainment: radio. And it is about Fred Allen's place in broadcast comedy during the 1930s and 1940s. But just as an evolving tradition of American humor is an essential context in which to understand Allen's career, so also must a broader perspective reveal the unique nature of radio comedy. A basic premise of this study is that the electronic media of the twentieth century have helped shape American comedy writing and performance. Broad historical forces such as immigration and the growth of cities, plus the emergence of issues like women's rights and black liberation, certainly help mold a nation's humor, but the media through which comedians communicate it to an audience also impose a style of humorous expression and influence its content. When the movie screen embraced comedy, the motion picture medium established a set of boundaries for expression that was at once more liberating and more restrictive than those encountered in publishing or in live performance. Although the evocative word picture of a novel or the witty dialogue of a vaudeville sketch were beyond the silent film's technological potential, the moving picture between 1907 and 1927 opened up hitherto unimagined possibilities for visual humor.

So it was with other new media. In some ways, new means of presentation transcended the limitations of the old, but at the same time, new means of communication possessed their own constraints. Each medium of comic expression established a novel framework for the creation and transmission of humor. As a new instrument of mass communication appeared, a brief but critical transition period occurred, as creators and performers struggled to adapt older styles and traditional content to new circumstances. Sir Herbert Beerbohm Tree, an accomplished stage performer, learned how inappropriate his theatrical acting techniques were during the filming of *Macbeth* in 1916. "Do you think you could teach me something about this new medium?" he pleaded with director David W. Griffith.[3]

Radio, too, demanded appropriate techniques of its writers and performers. Perhaps no other mass medium demanded so much of its audience; unable to see the programs, audience members had to be persuaded to use their imaginations, to visualize what the stage and screen previously had depicted. Not surprisingly, some creators of radio fare did better than others in perceiving and utilizing the new medium's unique potential and limitations. Vaudeville comics dominated radio comedy, broadcasting's most popular form of entertainment. Busy meeting production schedules, few comedians or their writers thought seriously about the aesthetic parameters of the aural medium. But some in radio consciously attempted to develop techniques and shape material appropriate to a listening audience.

The silent motion picture is an instructive example of humor's adaptation to a new medium, in this instance a visual one. Perceptive film directors soon recognized that, as Cecil B. DeMille stated in 1914, "Photographing a stage play 'as is' won't make a good picture . . . we waste the possibilities of the screen."[4] What the silent camera could best exploit was what the stage could not contain: motion, continuous and exaggerated. Thus the premiere achievement of American silent movies was their violent, frenzied, physical—and therefore eminently visual—comedy. Mack Sennett comedies for the Triangle and Keystone companies, writes Kalton Lahue, developed the silent screen's successful comedy formula: "a race-track tempo with gags flying fast and furiously, one pushing its predecessor aside without leaving time for analysis or second thoughts."[5] In 1924, the critic Gilbert Seldes noted that for a decade Sennett had been "doing with the instruments of the moving picture precisely those things which were best suited to it—those things which could not be done with any instrument but the camera, and could appear nowhere if not on the screen."[6] Sennett's exuberant improvisations occurred on the streets of Los Angeles. They were as inappropriate to the live stage's restricted space as they would have been to the primitive sound stages of 1927 to 1930, with their crude and immovable microphones, or to the live television studios two decades later. It is no coincidence that Sennett and other directors of silent comedy exploited the automobile, for the mechanical mobility possible only on streets and highways was basic to their comic achievement.[7]

Working in a silent world, comedians Charlie Chaplin and Harold Lloyd employed the art of mime to create a distinctive visual humor. Their comedy was both subtle— Chaplin's walk—and broad—the stunts of Lloyd.[8] Action, rather than dialogue, communicated humor. Or, as Vachel Lindsay put it in 1915: "Moving objects, not moving lips, make the words of the photoplay."[9] "The lift of an eyebrow," Chaplin wrote after the advent of sound, "may convey more than a hundred words." While the acceptance of the sound motion picture was culture bound because of its dependence on spoken language, the silent comedy's language of movement made it universally understood. Its broad appeal made silent comedy "more satisfactory entertainment for the masses than talking comedy," Chaplin maintained. Others agree. "The greatest comedians in terms of impact on the public have been those working in an essentially visual medium," one film historian writes; "a visual experience is the most nearly universal in understanding and appeal." Without debating the relative merits of visual and aural comedy, it is clear that successful silent screen comics turned their artistic medium's major limitation into an advantage.[10]

William K. Everson maintains "that the sound motion picture was an entirely different medium from the silent motion picture, and not merely the extension of it."[11] By adding another sensory dimension, talking pictures in the late 1920s changed comedy just as silent movies had altered stage conventions. Although Chaplin continued to create a uniquely visual humor, he was virtually alone in rejecting dialogue, as silent film scenarists yielded to scriptwriters and diction coaches joined studio staffs. William deMille recalled the difficult years of transition from the silent screen to the "talkies." Rudimentary recording technology dictated "that the screen, in order to speak, had to lose its freedom of movement . . . it talked its head off."[12] By the time a new comedy style emerged in the 1930s, comic action appeared less in the form of physical movement than in the fast-paced, zany dialogue of the Marx Brothers, the distinctive voice inflections of W. C. Fields and Mae West, and the sophisticated repartee of Clark Gable, Katharine Hepburn, Cary Grant, and others in the decade's "screwball" comedies. As comedy's physical action slowed, the pace of verbal wit accelerated, and popular stage plays such as Charles MacArthur and Ben Hecht's *Front Page* became appropriate for film presentation. Andrea S. Walsh has called the career women films of the 1940s, such as *His Girl Friday* (1940), "quintessentially verbal," and the characterization applies broadly to the comedies of the first postsilent era.[13]

During the same years, broadcasting reversed the motion picture's sequence of sensory innovation. As motion pictures began to talk in the late 1920s, radio became a widely popular vehicle for aural humor. (Two decades later, television would add broadcasting's visual dimension.) Radio writers and performers created their material in a medium whose sensory demands ran counter to long-term trends in the fine and popular arts, trends that reflected changes in the larger culture. The theater historian Benjamin McArthur argues that "the late nineteenth century marked the transition from one kind of sensory dominance to another: from an aural orientation that predominated in the mid-nineteenth century to a visual orientation of the turn of the century."[14] The nineteenth century sought entertainment and edification in speeches from the pulpit and platform: it made national heroes of orators

Daniel Webster and Henry Ward Beecher; and it immortalized the storytelling of Abraham Lincoln and Mark Twain. The twentieth century preferred visual presentation. The theater historian A. Nicholas Vardac demonstrated that directors in Europe and America deemphasized dialogue and featured visual realism and spectacle during the final pre–motion picture decades.[15] Film could and did capture these qualities far better than the stage; the Broadway revue and musical also appealed more to visual than aural appreciation. Television's dominant place in the national culture since the 1950s is further evidence of the prevailing visual orientation. In our time, the celebrity looks beautiful; the product that sells is one that advertising can present as visually attractive; and the successful individual dresses correctly, communicates effectively, through body language, and carries a trim, healthy figure. Or so some claim. Music videos even allow fans to see interpretations of rock songs.

This visually oriented world intensified the challenge that broadcasters would have faced in any event: to develop a language of radio to communicate effectively with unseen listeners. The language had to consist of spoken words, of course: of fictional dialogue, of news reports, of announcer narration. But the language of radio was to encompass much more. Actors utilized voice inflection to signify a change of mood or even to assume the roles of multiple characters. Talented adult voices played children, whites depicted blacks, and men performed female roles in radio's illusory world. Radio sound technicians could reproduce, with amazing accuracy, practically any sound from the "real" world, sounds that greatly multiplied the vocabulary of radio's language. The studio audiences' responses, often prompted and manipulated, were elements of this language. Applause and laughter effectively cued the home audience's response to program content. And, finally, music constituted an essential complement to voice and sound-effect communication. Music provided transition bridges from one comedic or dramatic scene to another, and it established mood or helped create imaginative settings, from a busy street corner to an isolated farmstead, from nineteenth-century Wyoming to twenty-fifth-century outer space.

During its brief reign as the major source of in-home entertainment, from the mid-1920s to the early 1950s, radio suffered from a serious inferiority complex. Even *Variety* and other trade papers often criticized its programming as unimaginative and excessively commercialized; creators, critics, and consumers of the fine arts held network radio programming in contempt—a conclusion rarely based on careful listening. But there was another side to radio.

By the late 1930s, the commercial networks' experimental production units, especially at the Columbia Broadcasting System (CBS), had achieved what some dared to call a "radio art." Radio showcased sustaining dramatic anthologies, which pioneered the development of plays uniquely crafted to the aural dimension. The dramas of Orson Welles's "Mercury Theater on the Air," of "Columbia Workshop," and of individual writers like Norman Corwin and Arch Oboler, suggested that the discovery of a radio aesthetic, one that would ensure radio's artistic if not commercial future and find application in comedy programming as well as in serious drama, was at hand.[16] A few media prophets—David Sarnoff and Lee De Forest among them—preferred to leap beyond radio's future to its replacement by a superior form of broadcasting. De Forest predicted during World War II that television, through its visual impact, would create "deeper, more engaging, better understood and longer lasting" programs than radio. But others preferred to see radio fulfill its own promise.[17]

Radio's more ambitious dramatic anthologies had convinced thoughtful observers that broadcasting's mass audience was an advantage, not a cause for apology. *Variety's* radio editor, Robert J. Landry, wrote in 1942 that "for the first time in history a near-universal audience" existed for drama. Landry and CBS's Douglas Coulter, who worked with the "Columbia Workshop," were among those who believed that radio presentations were qualitatively as well as quantitatively different from those in other media. The radio "art form" was more than "a stripped-down, concentrated, one-dimensional, aural version of stage drama."[18] As "the newest form of literature," wrote Carl Van Doren in 1941, radio plays challenged writers in a way that stage drama and movie scripts did not. Nothing could be "left to the actor's gestures and movements, which will not be seen." Dramas such as Corwin's "are plays fundamentally for the ear."[19] Archibald MacLeish's *The Fall of the City: A Verse Play for Radio* was one of the most successful experiments in serious radio drama. The poet firmly believed in the artistic advantages of the "mechanism which carries to an audience sounds and nothing but sounds." Lacking visible actors and stage sets, radio plays relied on "the spoken word" and

> the word-excited imagination—a theater in which poets have always claimed peculiar rights to play. Nothing exists save as the word creates it. . . . Over the radio verse has no visual presence to compete with. Only the ear is engaged and the ear is already half poet. . . . The ear is the poet's perfect audience, his only true audience. And it is radio and only radio which can give him public access to this perfect friend.[20]

Comedians were not poets, but, like MacLeish, they sought access to "this perfect friend."[21]

We need not restrict our recognition of radio's unique accomplishment in sound to experimental programs. The comedy and drama series that filled radio's daily schedule also represent that achievement. Walter Kerr's interesting and important observations about silent film comedy help us to understand and appreciate radio's aesthetic of sound. "Logically," Kerr writes in *The Silent Clowns*, art begins in a taking away. No painter or poet or dramatist in his right mind ever attempts to reproduce the abundance of life in toto. . . . He limits the frame, sacrifices a dimension, chastens color, looks for absences, refusals, self-imposed limitations that will enable him to suggest more with less. . . . The more of life, the less of art.

Radio, limited to the aural stimulation of its listening audience, necessarily applied the creative reductionism of which Kerr speaks. In the process, its most skilled and insightful practitioners created a genuine popular art. Lacking the visual, radio demanded more of its listeners than television would of its viewers, just as the silent film made its audiences work harder than the "talkies" did.

The less complete the canvas, the more there is for the viewer [or listener] to contribute. He must work with hints, and the more he must do for himself, the more deeply engaged he becomes in the work. . . . When the artist, in whatever medium, provides *all* the stimuli necessary to keep his audience awake and fully informed, the audience, having nothing to do, goes limp.[22]

Perceptive contemporaries recognized the unique challenge and the original achievement of this one-dimensional medium. Their own words best amplify Kerr's theme. The exiled European aesthetician Rudolph Arnheim, who never acquired the comfortable familiarity with America's commercial mass culture that Paul Lazarsfeld, Herta Herzog, and some other refugees from Nazism displayed, marveled at radio's novel creative setting: "Broadcasting has constituted a new experience for the artist, his audience, and the theoretician: for the first time it makes use of the aural only, without the almost invariable accompaniment of the visual which we find in nature as well as in art."[23] Another observer who placed radio in a broad comparative context also practiced the "art of radio writing," as he called it. In 1940, Arch Oboler praised the freedom radio offered to its dramatists.

> The most flexible form in the history of artistic expression, radio offers great, exciting opportunities. There are no limitations of stage or movie set, there are no boundaries of time and space; a word, a sound effect, a strain of music, and in a split second the listener is emotionally a part of the dramatic thought of the author.[24]

The actor Don Ameche, whose many years of radio performance began in 1930, recognized as well how audience involvement contributed to broadcasting's effectiveness. "It was far and away the greatest medium of all. And the reason behind that is very simple. The listener had to make a contribution, and his enjoyment depended totally upon the *amount* of contribution he made."[25]

One radio actor, Joseph Julian, agreed that radio's "audience experience was unique." Movie, theater, and television audiences "are essentially passive," he argued in his memoirs.

> They watch and wait for something to be "done" to them. . . . But radio is "Theater in the Mind," and the audience must earn its reward. It must always expend energy, reaching out to embellish, to supply what is not there. . . . No other art form ever engaged the imagination more intensely. Even bad radio shows were better than their equivalent in other media, the listener's imagination providing more reality than could be shown on a screen or stage. This creative expenditure of energy made the listeners collaborators in the truest sense.[26]

And Arnold Auerbach, a writer familiar with several branches of the entertainment and publishing business, joined in praising radio precisely *because* it lacked certain sensory dimensions.

> What if they [radio heroes] *were* only voices? A voice, intimately cherished, can take on as much dimension as a 23-inch picture. And possibly, since we didn't see our idols, we tired of them less quickly. Sometimes the lack of video was even an advantage. . . . If we had *seen* Orson Welles, could his *War of the Worlds* have panicked us into believing in a Martian invasion? Doubtful, terrifying though Mr. Welles may be.[27]

Radio's greatest comedic and dramatic advantage was its boundlessness; paradoxically, that creator and audience freedom flowed from its sensory limits.

Fred Allen was among those who understood the special qualities of radio as a popular art. One reason for Allen's success was his recognition that radio demanded an adaptation of the comedian's heritage—most of all the conventions of vaudeville humor—to the radically different setting created by broadcasting. "The radio listener saw nothing: he had to use his imagination," Allen recalled. "It was possible for each individual to enjoy the same program according to his intellectual level and his mental capacity." The low quality of television programming confirmed for Allen the advantage that radio enjoyed precisely because it lacked visual cues. In television, "a writer is restricted by the limitations imposed upon him by the scenic designers and the carpenter. . . . There was a certain type of imaginative comedy that could be written for, and performed on, only the radio."[28]

These remarks appear in Allen's memoirs. But his earliest programs, broadcast for a product called Linit Beauty Bath from late 1932 into the spring of 1933, suggest that he recognized the requirements of the radio medium from the start of his broadcasting career. Allen designed his show with the "blind" home audience in mind, although he did not ignore those present in the studio. The stage comedians Eddie Cantor, Ed Wynn, and Will Rogers, all of whom preceded Allen in radio, had already established the studio audience as an unavoidable feature of comedy programming.[29] Allen tried to distinguish himself from comedians who played only to that immediate audience. As he explained a "new idea of presentation" to his first radio audience, "The show is designed for both a seeing and hearing audience." Convinced that distant listeners would easily follow and develop loyalty to programs unified by a theme, Allen focused each week's "series of episodes and comic situations" on a loose "plot," set in a specific business or institution: a manufacturing firm, a courtroom, a department store.[30] On the Linit and other early series, Allen developed numerous techniques, including a script-writing style that I call verbal slapstick, which took advantage of radio's unique, sound-only properties. The last three chapters of this book study and illustrate that style.

The challenge of adapting older traditions of stage comedy to radio fell largely to vaudevillians, and so observers have asked how successfully they accomplished that transition. Many writers praise vaudeville as a perfect school for radio comedy. Years of appearing before audiences in all regions of the nation and in communities of all sizes taught vaudevillians what made Americans laugh. When a national audience turned to radio listening, no group could better entertain it than the veterans of vaudeville. John E. DiMeglio found that Allen himself endorsed the idea: vaudeville trained the comedian "to judge audiences and to adapt himself to any group and adjust himself to meet assorted conditions."[31]

This view is somewhat misleading. Some well-traveled actors did understand the common denominator of regional taste in comedy; the knowledge and experience gained from working before thousands of live audiences could be helpful in radio and in other entertainment media. Nevertheless, radio created a radically new context within which comedians prepared and delivered their material. Vaudeville humorists knew the difference between what played in Columbus, Mississippi, and Columbus, Ohio, but many of them had no clear understanding of what would please members of both communities who listened simultaneously to radio programs issuing from New York studios. Too, in radio, as Fred Allen's experience dramatizes, comedy material fell victim to more frequent and authoritative interference than was the case in vaudeville or other stage entertainment. And then there was the problem of the bifurcated audience, a problem that Allen began to grapple with in 1932. Vaudeville could never fully train the comic performer and writer—and Allen was both—for a medium that lacked a visual dimension. Vaudeville was a school that only partially prepared its graduates for careers in a medium that required a comedy crafted to remote, unseeing, but imaginative listeners.

Students of American humor often assume the reality and importance of distinct and largely self-contained categories of comedic expression. Literary study has custody of the comic spirit in formal writing: novels, plays, short stories, poetry, and essays. Captured in print and therefore readily subject to analysis, as well as available for reader pleasure, that portion of humorous literature judged to possess lasting significance is included within the "serious," or fine, arts. The academic respectability accorded humorous writing follows from judgments about literary merit—use of language, characterization—as well as cultural and social significance: the work's effectiveness as satire, parody, and so on. Since it requires the mastery of language and recognition of historical and social references, literary humor is the domain of educated, sophisticated readers and critics.[32]

A second category of American humor is less formal, less "serious." Authentic in that it arises spontaneously from a people, an expression of folklore or modern "joke-lore," it is part of our culture's oral tradition. Folk humor is the domain, not of literary critics or historians, but of cultural anthropologists, folklorists, and others contributing to cultural studies and the social sciences. Only when a serious writer—a Mark Twain or a William Faulkner—draws on vernacular speech or native humor does literary study take account of this tradition. Students of such varied forms as Navaho legends, Polish and other joke cycles, and public bathroom graffiti seek an understanding of the structure and function of humor in past and present cultures.[33]

A third tradition is more popular and ephemeral than literary humor, and more self-consciously manufactured to please a paying audience than folk humor. It consists of a wide variety of forms, among them the performance of a stand-up comedian, a television situation comedy, and a paperback collection of cartoons. Historically, its audience sat in nineteenth-century minstrel or vaudeville theaters, and later purchased tickets to see motion pictures. Twentieth-century critics and advocates label it "mass" or "popular." As "show business," it carries a stigma that allows both the custodians of art and the collectors of lore to dismiss it. Since its creators are often anonymous, its content profit motivated, and such texts as scripts inaccessible in printed form, until recently few have studied or preserved this comic tradition.

One aim of this book is to join others in American Studies, popular arts, and mass communication scholarship to subvert the rigid boundaries presumed to separate the three comic traditions in American culture. One method of exposing the inadequacy of categories is to deny their uniqueness. The sociologist Herbert Gans, who points out the many features shared by popular culture and high culture, provides a model of this approach. He argues, for example, that if businesses shape culture as they seek maximum profits through the mass production and distribution of entertainment and art, profit-seeking firms also distribute, and shape, "much of high culture, at least in America, where government subsidies and rich patrons are few." Gans also denies that traits such as cultural diversity and creative innovation apply exclusively to the fine arts.[34]

Mark Twain illustrates how supposedly discrete levels of culture share characteristics and creators. Undeniably, Twain's best work represents lasting literary achievement. Yet his art drew on the everyday life of common people, employed their vernacular, and mined the rich reserves of their folk culture. Twain the author sought commercial as well as aesthetic success. Lecturing for generous fees and promoting his books' sales, he was a Gilded Age cultural huckster.[35] The same applies to other writers, from public lecturer Artemus Ward to television talk-show guest Norman Mailer. Scholars honor the humorous columns of Kin Hubbard, Finley Peter Dunne, Ring Lardner, George Ade, and Dorothy Parker, among others, as an important part of the nation's humorous art. Humorous journalism, of course, assisted entrepreneurs to market copies of advertiser-financed, mass-circulation newspapers or magazines. H. L. Mencken and George Jean Nathan, critics who influenced the direction of serious writing in America during the early twentieth century, founded the pulp magazine *Black Mask* in 1920. In its pages, Dashiell Hammett and others developed the popular, commercially successful hard-boiled detective story, a mass cultural formula of enduring influence.[36]

Other examples abound. While S. J. Perelman was one of the *New Yorker* crowd, he also wrote screenplays for the Marx Brothers during the early 1930s. Hollywood, the world capital of despised, vulgar culture in the pretelevision era, attracted the talents, often misused, of such serious writers as F. Scott Fitzgerald, William Faulkner, Nathanael West, Aldous Huxley, James Agee, Dorothy Parker, Ben Hecht, P. G. Wodehouse, and Donald Ogden Stewart.[37] Robert Benchley and Alexander Woollcott, drama critics and original members of the Algonquin Round Table (named for the literary luncheons of New York writers at the Algonquin Hotel) exploited the commercial mass media as outlets for their humor. Benchley wrote and performed in forty-eight short films during the late 1930s and early 1940s, made appearances in about forty feature films, and starred in a radio comedy show. Woollcott's radio program, "The Town Crier," was a commercial success on the CBS network during the 1930s.[38] William Lyon Phelps, retired Lampson Professor of English at Yale, starred in a commercial radio program in 1934–1935, a program that also featured conductor–composer Sigmund Romberg.[39] The versatile Woody Allen has brought laughter to a later generation through the pages of the *New Yorker*, stand-up comedy routines before live audiences, and in Hollywood motion pictures. Ruth R. Wissen writes: "The Jewish fool" of folklore and literature—the schlemiel character Allen and many others have interpreted—"made the transition from Europe to America at the level of popular culture and did not flourish in serious American Jewish fiction until the postwar period."[40]

Fred Allen worked in the mass medium of radio, and he learned his craft while performing in big-business–dominated vaudeville and New York's commercial theater. At the same time, he was a writer and performer who had to fight to preserve his artistic independence and freedom of expression in a way that novelists and painters do not experience. Because he had to defend it, artistic freedom meant more to him than it could to those who had never encountered censorship and efforts at control. Allen wrote not only his own stage and broadcast comedy but also short fiction and casual essays—a minor literary output that this study utilizes. Had he achieved his dream of becoming a full-time writer, we today might know him as an "American humorist" rather than a "radio comedian." His talents made either achievement possible. Allen was a student of nineteenth- and twentieth-century literary comedy. As a young actor during this century's second decade, he read works by classic British and American humorists: Charles Dickens, Mark Twain, Artemus Ward, Bill Nye, Eli Perkins, and Josh Billings among them.[41] In his radio scripts, along with vaudeville influences appeared traces of important and enduring American comic elements, including the personae of the oral storyteller and the "little man" of the twentieth century. A performer whose vaudeville act made a lasting impression on the youthful S. J. Perelman, and on whose radio program appeared literary humorists Robert Benchley, Franklin P. Adams, and H. Allen Smith, should be assessed in a broad context of intent and achievement.

Herman Wouk was one of Allen's young assistant scriptwriters before World War II. Wouk later called his boss "a classic humorist, one of those rare spirits who see the world as it is, and who laugh in order not to weep."[42] The Austrian philosopher Ludwig Wittgenstein called humor "a way of looking at the world," and as Wouk's comment suggests, that may be a sufficient theoretical framework within which to place Fred Allen's career as a twentieth-century comedian.[43] In 1954, James Thurber wrote: "You can count on the thumb of one hand the American who is at once a comedian, a humorist, a wit, and a satirist, and his name is Fred Allen."[44]

Fred Allen's reputation as a respected humorist who was able to work in a commercial mass medium remains high several decades after his radio program left the air. This book intends to enhance a later era's knowledge and appreciation of Allen by offering a more complete understanding than others have attempted of the roots of his comedy and the themes it exploited. The comedy style Allen developed in smalltime vaudeville from 1912 to 1922, and in Broadway revues between 1922 and 1932, shaped the man who first stepped before a CBS microphone on October 23, 1932, and it continued to influence the maturing radio comedian until his retirement in 1949. Chapter 2 analyzes these years of apprenticeship. A survey of Allen's programs in Chapter 3 precedes two chapters on the con-

text within which the humorist-as-radio-comedian functioned during the 1930s and 1940s. Chapter 4 treats the
problems and challenges that faced the radio comedy
writer, while Chapter 5 discusses the organizational structure that inhibited comedic expression in broadcasting. A
careful reading of Allen's texts, the hundreds of radio
scripts he and his assistant writers created between 1932
and 1949, furnish the primary source for understanding Allen's humor.[45] Chapter 6 shows that, while he employed
conventions of American comedy not fully appropriate to
the broadcast medium, Allen also made important innova-
tions in the new field of aural comedy. Allen was a satirist,
an acute observer and acid critic of some of the values and
institutions of his time, and Chapters 7 and 8 discuss his
contribution to that form of humor, one not common on
radio. Chapter 8 also pays a visit to radio's most important
byway, Allen's Alley.

A final caveat, which falls into the category of "it goes
without saying," must indeed be said. All humor, perhaps
most emphatically commercial comedy that must speak
immediately to a live, mass audience, is rooted in a particular time and a specific place. The radio scripts that preserve Allen's comedy amount to the skeletal remains of a
once-living thing, radio comedy's meaningful integration
with the lives of the generation that survived the Great
Depression and went to war in 1941. Radio comedy was
not mere escapism. As Andrew Bergman has remarked
about mass moviegoing during the 1930s: "People do not
escape into something they cannot relate to."[46] Instead, radio comedy, as Kalton Lahue commented about comedy in
general, was "contemporary and spontaneous in origin,
having meaning and rendering humor only in terms of a
specific environment or circumstance."[47] David Marc has
observed that comedy "cannot take place without a context, without a relationship to what people believe about
themselves and the world."[48] While some of Allen's work
has a timeless quality, most of it is time and place specific.
One task of this volume is to suggest the meaning that his
work had for his times.

By way of introducing the "star" of our presentation, as a radio announcer might have said it, Ladies and Gentlemen, here is Fred Allen. We approach him at a crucial moment in his professional career, as the Great Depression forces many stage comedians to attempt the transition from stage to studio.

On the eve of America's most devastating Depression winter, Allen, an unemployed vaudeville and Broadway actor, obtained his own network radio comedy show. Debuting on October 23, 1932, just as the Hoover–Roosevelt election campaign was drawing to a close, Allen joined a growing number of broadcast comics who injected interludes of laughter into the lives of demoralized and confused Americans. Public morale was of little concern to him, however. Of far greater immediacy was the challenge of establishing himself in a medium whose comedic potential was still undeveloped, in the wake of vaudeville's collapse and Broadway's morbidity.

The economic crisis of the early 1930s did not strike each branch of the entertainment industry with equal effect, and therein lies the explanation of radio's appeal to many performers. The historian Andrew Bergman points out that the Hollywood motion picture studios "suffer[ed] badly" from 1930 until the autumn of 1933, when their recovery began. During the remainder of the Depression decade "the automatic movie-going of the late 1920s was no more; theater managers had to work for their patronage" with such gimmicks as free dishes and Bank Night.[49]

The live stage, in New York and across the nation, including vaudeville, the legitimate theater, musicals and revues, suffered a precipitous audience decline beginning in 1930. The show business weekly *Variety* reported that mid-1932 was "Broadway's dullest summer in modern show times."[50] The modern times against which commentators measured the early Depression years were the free-spending, entertainment-hungry 1920s, of course, but by any standard the live stage's economic difficulties translated into large-scale unemployment. Vaudeville, which had featured thousands of performers on national and regional circuits at the height of its success between 1895 and 1925, experienced multiple ills even before the Depression hit. Both the sound motion picture after 1927, and radio, whose major national networks formed in 1926 and 1927, drained vaudeville of its material, its performers, and its patrons. The economic crisis merely finished what these electronic forms of mass amusement had begun.[51]

Radio alone was Depression-proof. Among entertainment forms, only broadcasting would "emerge from 1932 with an increase of business over the previous year and show a substantial profit," *Variety* reported at the end of that year, and the medium's success continued unbroken into the post–World War II years. The opening of the National Broadcasting Company's (NBC) Radio City in the RCA Building, a part of the fourteen-structure Rockefeller Center complex in midtown Manhattan, symbolized radio's success story. That a business could celebrate growth by dedicating lavish facilities during the subdued Christmas season of 1932 was a telling fact not lost on listeners or performers.[52]

By the early 1930s, although he had acquired limited experience in motion pictures and on the radio, Fred Allen remained a stage comic vulnerable to the theater's decline. As had other vaudevillians between 1928 and 1931, Allen performed one of his acts in a Vitaphone short for Warner Brothers, the first studio to profit from the "talkies."[53] But his unsuccessful movie career, when it began in earnest in 1935, grew from radio rather than stage prominence. The broadcast historian William McKinley Randle discovered what may have been Allen's first radio appearance: in January 1923, radio station WGM [?] featured the touring company of *The Passing Show of 1922*, of which he was a cast member, on several programs.[54] Traveling east from California in 1928, Allen and his wife and partner, Portland Hoffa, performed on the "WLS Showboat" program in Fort Wayne, Indiana.[55] A year later, Alexander Woollcott's first "Town Crier" radio broadcast on New York station WOR featured as guests the stars of Broadway's *The Little Show*, one of whom was Allen.[56] Although, by the late 1920s, guest appearances occasionally led to radio careers, Allen's did not. According to columnist Jo Ranson, CBS gave the comedian an audition sometime in 1929, but the potential sponsor exercised his veto: Allen would "never do for radio."[57] He experienced the early Depression years outside radio's economic security.

From October 1930 until the early summer of 1932, Allen shared top billing with Libby Holman and Clifton Webb in the revue *Three's a Crowd*. As early as the spring of 1931, the show's critical acclaim proved stronger than its box-office revenues. The stars agreed to work for a percentage of the net to help keep the production afloat, but little money remained after the cast and crew received their wages. That fall, the revue went on tour, a tactic that so dismally failed to generate audiences that producer Max Gordon abandoned the show in Chicago early in 1932.

In his personal correspondence, often hastily written backstage and from hotel rooms while on tour, Allen revealed a capacity for humor in the midst of personal disappointment and professional disaster. (His later letters also reveal Allen's dislike of capital letters and disregard for punctuation, which the reader will become familiar with as the book progresses and Allen's opinions are quoted on many subjects.) Allen fantasized about Depression infants who "are being weaned on aspirin to fortify them for the economic headaches" that would plague their lives. He noted that the hyenas at a New York zoo had ceased to laugh. The city hired men to tickle them, hoping to raise at least a chuckle "out of respect to the Republican Administration" in Washington. But flights of fancy were no solution to the impending collapse of *Three's a Crowd*. In a last-ditch effort to save it, Allen and others in the cast took over the show, presenting an abbreviated version in motion picture theaters between showings of feature films.[58] But the revue closed permanently in St. Louis, and by June 1932, Allen was writing comedy scenes for a new Broadway show in which he had been promised a role. That show, as he learned on his return to New York in September, would never open. Allen had always enjoyed performing before stage audiences, but his experience with *Three's a Crowd* had made less acceptable the liabilities inherent in theatrical life: "uncertainty, broken promises, constant travel and a gypsy existence." To Allen, radio offered a stability and permanence that the theater could not. "There may have been other advantages but I didn't need to know them." Fred Allen was ready for radio.[59]

This time, a sponsor was ready for him. In his radio memoirs, Allen recalled the birth of his first series during the fall of 1932. His agent and friend, Walter Batchelor, brought together the comedian, who was already at work developing ideas for a show, the Corn Products Refining Company, an experienced radio sponsor, and the firm's advertising company, which took charge of production. By September 27, less than a month after his return to New York from a summer in Maine (and earlier than his memoirs imply), the comedian had signed a contract with Corn Products to star in a twenty-six-week series for one of their retail products, Linit Beauty Bath. Originally marketed as a starch, Linit, one of the older brand names for which imaginative advertising executives found new and sophisticated applications during the 1920s, was now being used to serve the beauty of stylish women.[60] The Linit program ran from October 23, 1932, through April 16, 1933, appearing on Sunday evenings from 9:00 to 9:30, Eastern Time. Sixty Columbia stations carried the show, which originated in Studio B of WABC, CBS's flagship station. The studio accommodated a live audience, admitted free of charge, and within a month of its debut, Allen's show received more requests for tickets than any of the network's programs.[61]

So began a career on radio that would last until June 26, 1949, when broadcasting had already begun a transition to television that Allen would not successfully negotiate. The audiences for Allen's Linit programs, as far as anyone in the early days of listener measurement could tell, were large. When the Corn Products Company decided not to renew Allen's contract at the end of the twenty-six weeks, it was not out of dissatisfaction with the comedian. An afternoon program seemed a better investment of scarce advertising dollars for a product seeking a market among women purchasers. In addition to a satisfied sponsor and ample audiences, Allen enjoyed praise from professional critics during his first series of programs.[62] And he would continue to enjoy all these signs of success throughout his long career.

Why, then, would Edwin O'Connor, Allen's friend, argue that the comedian "felt no particular affection" for radio and that, in it, in contrast to his years in the theater, "he had no fun at all?"[63] If there is truth in this statement, it omits an important consideration, one to bear in mind as our discussion unfolds. Allen had a consuming pride in his work. He found the Linit programs demanding and exhausting, especially so because he wrote as well as delivered the comedy. Throughout his radio years, Allen complained of the burdens he discovered during the Linit series: "there is no time for anything but the broadcast," he wrote; he was "at the mercy of the sponsors"; he was "all in."[64] Allen predicted that "the first bad program" would find Portland and himself "flying up Madison Avenue with the Linit people right behind us."[65] "Still," he reflected, "it isn't bad." He was proud not only of the response to his programs and what he felt was the quality of their comedy but also of the fact that success resulted almost solely from his own efforts. "I have been living by my own wits for years," while Al Jolson, Eddie Cantor, and "the others have to rely on writers and they're at the mercy of whoever provides the material for their assorted ventures."[66] Personal and professional pride in his individual comic achievement sustained Allen on the radio treadmill. The story of his apprenticeship reveals how Allen learned to live "by my own wits."

The World of
a Smalltimer, 1894–1932

an actor who has opened the show in Elyria
knows what trouble is.

FRED ALLEN, 1944

John Lawrence Sullivan, the champion prizefighter
and idol of Boston's Irish, once called his home city "the
greatest Sullivan town in the whole world." Without the
Sullivan listings, he added, "the Boston Directory . . . 'ud
look like the Bible would if it didn't say nothing about
God."[1] Sullivans lived in the city and in its streetcar sub-
urbs, and their number increased by one with the birth of a
son to Cecilia (Herlihy) and James Henry Sullivan at their
Somerville home on the last day of May 1894. Christened
John Florence Sullivan by parents who admired the boxer,
the future Fred Allen had made his debut. When he took
the name Fred Allen years later, John Florence was not es-
caping the stigma of a female name, although he once
joked that when you grow up in a rough neighborhood
"and your mother gives you the name Florence—she's trying to get rid of you."[2]

Johnny Sullivan, in fact, had no adult memory of his
mother, who died of pneumonia in 1897. His father, a mo-
rose man deeply affected by the death of his wife, "was a
stranger" to John and younger brother Bob. A bookbinder

25

employed by the Boston Public Library, James Sullivan
worked and drank to excess. Years later, Fred Allen recalled the small family's ritual Sunday visits to his Sullivan
grandparents in Cambridge. Leading their inebriated father
home in the evening, he and Bob "looked like two sardines
guiding an unsteady Moby Dick into port."[3] The Sullivans
lived with Elizabeth Herlihy, the boys' "Aunt Lizzie," and
her disabled husband and assorted kin and boarders in a
"sort of community project," located initially in Allston
and later in the Savin Hill section of Dorchester. This
"generous and charitable" woman became John and Bob's
surrogate mother. For twenty years, Fred Allen sent a portion of his stage earnings to Aunt Lizzie; after he began to
share in radio's prosperity, his support included such presents as a trip to Ireland.[4] The Irish in Aunt Lizzie's home
could not be classified as "lace curtain," those who "have
fruit in the house when no one's sick," as Allen later defined them.[5] But there the Sullivan boys found the affection and security that their father was unable to provide. In
1909, when James remarried, Johnny chose to remain with
his aunt. That the father meant little to the son, and that
his drinking was a source of family tension, is evident to
readers of Allen's autobiography, which provides more detailed and more affectionate characterizations of friends
and acquaintances in Boston's theatrical district than of
James Henry Sullivan.

The strain of pessimism evident in Fred Allen's outlook undoubtedly grew out of his bleak family relations.
His remark to an interviewer in 1946 was typical: "Life is
an unprofitable episode that disturbs the otherwise blessed
state of nonexistence."[6] Allen once shouted at a boy whom
he had just rescued from the traffic of a busy New York
City street: "What's the matter? Don't you want to grow
up and have troubles?"[7] Some called his mood dour, his
view of life cynical; others thought of Allen as a "sourpuss."[8] Perhaps the word melancholy best describes his
outlook, a melancholy that was his less by virtue of his
Irish heritage or youthful poverty than by the absence of a

mother and the broken relationship with his father.[9] As a comedian, Fred Allen later created his unique versions of the "little man," a persona employed by many twentieth-century writers. Allen's little man could be termed the smalltimer; whether a vaudevillian or not, this character of limited ability, narrow vision, and joyless personality was continually at the mercy of forces beyond his control. Although it was natural that Allen would explore one of his era's most familiar humorous devices, he may have gained his vision of the hapless, frustrated, and inadequate little man as much from James Sullivan as from the conventions of American comic writing and performance. Although Johnny Sullivan left his father, his memory of the man who lacked the inner resources to deal with life's tragedy remained with him. That memory was one element of Fred Allen's experience that prevented his comedy from descending into pure cleverness or silliness; it was a memory that kept his humor in touch, as all good humor must be, with life's melancholy realities.

Poor but bright boys of John Sullivan's generation occasionally attended Harvard. Harold E. Stearns, of the class of 1913, was one Boston area student from a destitute, single-parent family who found the financial support to study there.[10] But John, whose family saw no reason to encourage the pursuit of learning unrelated to vocation, found his contact with Cambridge's most famous institution limited to walks across Harvard Yard.[11] In later years, Allen occasionally ridiculed the impracticality of "Harvard men"; the Irish outsider made this bastion of Yankee cultural and economic power the butt of radio jokes.[12] Harvard and other universities had begun to nurture humorists—one example is Robert Benchley, who edited the *Lampoon* in 1911–1912—but John Sullivan's formal schooling ended with his graduation from the Boston High School of Commerce in 1911.[13] As a writer and performer of comedy, his most important school would be the stage.

John might have followed his father's example. He might have become a smalltimer in more than the narrow vaudeville sense, rising through the ranks of the Boston Public Library's staff, which he joined on his fourteenth birthday as a part-time book runner so that he could contribute to Aunt Lizzie's household income. Or he might have applied his high school business training to a position with an area firm, such as the Colonial Piano Company on Boylston Street, where he worked in 1911. But he did neither. Instead, he turned to the entertainment industry and its promise of social mobility. In vaudeville he tested his ability to live by his wits.

The vaudeville historian John DiMeglio writes that "the lure of the stage was an overpowering one for countless ghetto children and for restless youths from the hinterland" in the early twentieth century. "The offer of riches and adventure was too much to resist."[14] Youths in Boston, especially if they were Irish, had particular reason to find vaudeville and other stage entertainments attractive. The great national demand for commercial amusement in the early decades of the century, which Robert C. Toll says provided "abundant entry level opportunities," offered a bright contrast to Boston's sluggish economy and stratified social structure.[15] While working in the public library, John Sullivan read books on comedy, and on Saturdays he "squandered" enough of his $4.80 weekly earnings to attend a vaudeville show. During the summer of 1911, following his high school graduation, John performed a comic juggling routine in an employee's talent show. The favorable response of co-workers pointed to a career, especially the comment of one girl: "You're crazy to keep working here at the library. You ought to go on the stage."[16]

The vaudeville stage attracted John. While working at two jobs, he also developed a presentable juggling act, and in 1911 he found an outlet for it. "Amateur contests were . . . the door into vaudeville" for many performers, according to one theater historian, and amateur nights were highly popular in Boston before World War I.[17] Fred Allen later recalled that "actors, warblers, hoofers—all kinds of would-be entertainers—went to any length to get a laugh

or to win the sympathy of these rowdy audiences" at amateur nights.[18] Usually one night a week in small neighborhood theaters, amateur entertainers took the stage after
the regular vaudeville bill and moving picture had ended.
Although John Florence Sullivan's first performance in one
such amateur night did not win the contest, his act was
good enough to obtain other amateur appearances through
agent Sam Cohen. The dollar John earned for his debut performance at the Hub Theatre on Washington Street, plus
the excitement and fellowship of theatrical life, "finished
my interest in the library" forever. During subsequent
months, he appeared in most of the city's smalltime theaters. By 1912, he helped Cohen run the amateur booking
agency.[19] No doubt recalling his apprenticeship, Fred Allen
later created an opportunity to assist another generation of
aspiring performers when his broadcast joined radio's rage
for amateur contests during the Depression-scarred mid-
1930s.

Vaudeville was not a new phenomenon. Emerging in
the 1880s, it had become the most popular form of amusement in America's cities by the turn of the century. Even
before 1910, however, it faced a serious rival for patrons in
the first electronic amusement, the motion picture. Yet
the appeal of vaudeville was strong. Albert McLean writes
that vaudeville "reached its full maturity" by 1915, during
the years in which young John Sullivan learned his craft on
its stages.[20] In 1900, the two thousand theaters that featured only vaudeville attracted half of the nation's theatergoers. Thirteen years later, the *New York Times* reported that 2,973 theaters in the United States "get regular
bookings," and most presented vaudeville. Thirty thousand
performers, earning an aggregate annual wage of $30 mil-
lion, found work in these theaters.[21] In Milwaukee, an average of more than 75,000 people saw a vaudeville show each
week in 1911. Comparable figures for Kansas City, Mis-
souri, in 1912, and Detroit in 1913, were 31,000 and 37,260
per week. In San Francisco, according to statistics com-
piled in 1913, vaudeville theaters with a seating capacity of

12,334 offered 218 performances each week to an estimated audience of 141,977 customers.[22] In lavish "palaces"
and modest opera houses, located in towns and cities knit
together by railroad-defined circuits that spanned the nation, vaudeville served a vast public.

One of the birthplaces of clean, family-oriented
vaudeville, Boston remained in 1911 "a very active vaudeville town."[23] John Sullivan could only dream about appearing in the top Boston theaters, one of which, the Colonial,
was the first of Benjamin Franklin Keith's and Edward Al-
bee's lavish palaces and "the capital of their [vaudeville]
empire."[24] But the city's amusement audience supported
dozens of modest theaters in inexpensive downtown loca-
tions as well as residential neighborhoods, theaters that
commonly combined movie showings with live acts. The
Hub Theatre, where John Sullivan first performed on amateur night, offered "three acts of cheap vaudeville and a
feature picture, three shows a day," plus the weekly amateur contest. Turning professional in 1912, John played in
establishments such as Winthrop Hall at Upham's Corner
in Dorchester, an upstairs movie house. "The Winthrop
Hall," Fred Allen recalled years later, ran one two-reel
comedy, a feature picture, and three acts of underpaid
vaudeville" to neighborhood residents each evening. Anx-
ious for work, and for advancement, John accepted numerous one-night stands in outlying Massachusetts towns
between 1912 and 1914, traveling as far as Sanford, Maine,
and Norwich, Connecticut, for engagements. A struggling
smalltimer just beginning to refine his act and make contacts with bookers, he performed in private clubs and before summer amusement park crowds as well.[25]

From the start, John Sullivan combined jokes with his
juggling, at first billing himself as "Fred St. James—Comedy Juggler." Later he changed the name of his act to
"Freddy James—Almost a Juggler," and still later to
"Freddy James—The World's Worst Juggler."[26] As the evolution of titles suggests, John gradually recognized that his
strong suit was the manipulation of words and ideas, not
airborne objects. Inspired by a British actor named Griff,

who had made mediocre acrobatic and juggling skills serve his humor, John "started to study comedians" instead of jugglers. By early 1914, he had lengthened and improved his monologue and retained only a few juggling tricks as entrees to verbal comedy. He burlesqued juggling, building his career on a parody of something serious. The decision to exploit his comic talents in effect launched the career of Fred Allen. Since "laughter was the foundation of vaudeville," John Sullivan aspired to become one of the "monarchs of the vaudeville stage," the comedians. That decision, to give up a visual juggling act for wordplay, also would make possible a broadcasting career.[27]

Had John Sullivan, vaudeville actor, remained in Boston, he would have only the limited opportunities of a "coast defender," the theatrical booking agents' term for local talent who played only Boston theaters. Outside acts from, say, New York readily found work, and bookers used the familiar faces and talents of coast defenders when nothing fresher was available. Knowing that opportunity lay in vaudeville's capital, New York City, and already an experienced actor at the age of twenty, John was ready to leave Boston by the fall of 1914. As a hedge against failure, he deposited $40 of his $100 savings in a bank, arranged to have a friend send him return fare should he run out of luck and cash, and left home. "I had forgotten Johnny Sullivan," Fred Allen wrote of that day, September 18, 1914. "Freddy James—The World's Worst Juggler," was "heading for New York on the old Fall River Line."[28]

Although he performed successfully in bigtime vaudeville during the late 1920s and became a headline comic in Broadway revues between 1922 and 1932, the stage experience that most shaped Fred Allen's career was that of smalltime vaudeville.[29] In outlook and temperament he shared much with the thousands of smalltimers who toured the Poli, Loew, Sun, Pantages, and other circuits during the half century when vaudeville was the "entertainment of the masses." He fondly recalled these intrepid performers in his autobiography, particularly in its overview chapter, "The Life and Death of Vaudeville."[30] These were actors who never played the Palace Theatre—the acrobats, singers, dancers, and comics who lived out of theatrical trunks, raised their children in dressing rooms and cheap hotels, invested their savings in diamonds that doubled as signs of status among other actors, and dreamed of retiring to a chicken farm on Long Island. With them, Fred Allen (John Sullivan settled on the name he would thereafter use in 1918) "spent a hundred nights curled up in dark, freezing railroad stations in the Kokomos, the Kenoshas, and the Kankakees," waiting for predawn journeys to bookings in "the Danvilles, the Davenports, and the Decaturs" of America.[31] Like the smalltimers he described, Allen focused almost obsessively on his career. His arrival in New York City coincided with the start of the Great War in Europe. He spent almost a year in wartime Australia in 1916–1917 and then, enjoying a draft deferment as the sole supporter of his Boston relatives, toured the United States during the months of America's participation in the conflict. Through it all he was apparently little affected by the war that transformed so much of the national experience. Allen did read the newspapers, for as a vaudevillian he acquired the habit of drawing comedy from current events, but like the typical smalltimer who "thought and talked only about his act and about show business," Allen's perspective was rather restricted.[32]

As did many smalltimers who experienced long stretches of unemployment, Allen doggedly pursued financial security. On several occasions he chose the certain employment and comfortable income (he earned $275 a week in 1919, for example) of an established smalltime monologist over the fleeting popularity of the bigtime acts and the risk of failure in a different medium in Hollywood.

"A bird in the hand may soil your sleeve," but, according to Allen, that bird saved you the "worry about where your next meal is coming from."[33] In about 1920, Allen refused to accompany fellow vaudevillian Harry Langdon to Hollywood, where Langdon found great success for a time. Always skeptical about the film capital, Allen believed that fame in the movies "is as fleeting as any fragment of a second"; Langdon, who slipped into obscurity after the advent of sound motion pictures and died in poverty in 1944, might well have reached the same conclusion.[34] Allen's caution was also behind his postponement of marriage to Portland Hoffa, a chorus girl he had met in 1922 and had courted since 1924, until he could offer her a certain future. As he put it, "I had seen enough insecurity at home" as a boy. The couple married in May 1927 and soon toured as a male–female comedy act.[35]

In the highly conventionalized world of vaudeville, comedy performers marketed themselves as variations of types, only marginally different from other Yiddish monologists, dumb Doras, or rube comics. Genuinely fresh material or a truly unique delivery was rare; the business was rife with the wholesale theft of material.[36] An original joke told in a New York theater on Tuesday could appear in several parts of town on Wednesday, and become a classic by week's end. Working in this formulaic and imitative medium, Fred Allen necessarily shared much with fellow comedians, but he also succeeded in developing a style of comic expression distinctive enough to attract the notice of major Broadway producers by 1922 and of radio talent hunters ten years later.

Allen used standard presentational formats and a common style of comic expression. For the major part of his vaudeville and revue career, Allen performed as a single, as did many monologists, often appearing "in-one." In front of the curtain while the crew prepared for the next act on the full stage behind it, he faced the challenges of providing a transition from one featured act to another. In the Shubert brothers' revue *Artists and Models* in 1924,

Allen twice appeared "in-one" after nude tableaux. He later called his routine, which the audience largely ignored, "an antidote for sex."[37] In *The Greenwich Village Follies* of 1925 Allen began to write and appear in comic sketches as well as perform monologues.[38] He also wrote two-acts for himself and veteran comic Jimmy Savo in the revue *Vogues of 1924*, and vaudeville routines with partners Bert Yorke in 1926 and Portland after their marriage.[39]

The descriptive term "nut act" further defines Fred Allen's place in vaudeville comedy. Nut comedians, such as Joe Cook, Ed Wynn, and Allen's good friend Doc Rockwell, combined "outrageous distortion, noisy satire, and mad humor, adding up to an insanely imaginative entertainment," according to Douglas Gilbert.[40] Gilbert and the trade publication *Variety* categorized Allen as a nut comic.[41] Nut comics were improvisers. Their impulsive, unpredictable quest for laughs delighted audiences, but their unreliability made theater managers nervous. Some nut acts veered into levels of scatological humor, which vaudevillians labeled "jazz," "hokum," "jasbo," and "gravy" in order of ascending censorability. Allen did not exploit sexual themes, nor did his stage behavior fit the 1917 description of nut comedians, who "have been known to leap through the bass drum in the orchestra pit or to dash headlong through an expensive piece of scenery."[42] Instead, Allen's typical improvisation was the ad-lib, a spontaneous remark prompted by some item in the day's news or, more likely, some object or occurrence in the theater. He once asked how much a member of the orchestra would charge to haunt a house, a line that biographical accounts cited for years as evidence of Allen's spontaneous wit.[43] As a radio comedian, Allen's ability as an ad-libber and his frequent departures from scripts caused consternation among broadcast executives who, for their own good reasons, opposed on-air deviation from the approved text.

As a single or a partner, nut comic Fred Allen employed what the historian Albert F. McLean has called the "new humor," a comedic style that vaudeville did much to

popularize.[44] Reflecting America's decisive shift from a pre-
dominantly rural to an urban nation, the new humor replaced the rambling tales of the rustic storyteller with a
string of jokes fired off by a monologist at a tempo appropriate to explosive and chaotic city life. Vaudeville routines such as Allen's were compact, carefully crafted, and
packed with hard-hitting lines designed to elicit an uproarious response. Although the comics relied on numerous visual elements, from wild costumes to pratfalls,
the new humor was essentially verbal.[45] Monologues and
dialogues vibrated with the "fluid, living language of the
cities," and the comedians reveled in wordplay. Provoking
laughter with the unexpected and incongruous, the stac-
cato jokes of the vaudeville stage were filled with "dialect,
. . . boners, . . . slang, and other surprises of sound and
syntax."[46] Allen's comedy reflected the new humor's critical stance in its irreverence, exposing the powerful and
pompous, laughing at marital relationships and the family,
and poking fun at public officials, ethnic peculiarities, and
such novelties as the "new woman." "Through humor,"
McLean observes, "the mass man, in the midst of urban
flux, did his criticizing and judging."[47]

Allen's borrowings from fellow vaudeville comics
were obvious to Sime Silverman, *Variety's* editor, whose
reviews of the acts appearing in New York's numerous
vaudeville theaters praised originality and discouraged tiresome repetition on the stage. In January 1918, just after
Allen had returned to the city from his extended tour of
Australia, parts of Canada, and the American West, Sime
saw his sixteen-minute performance as a "talking juggler"
at the American Theatre. The reviewer was not favorably
impressed. Although Allen "may think he has an act,"
"the very familiarity of it must push him back on the
small time." Referring to humorous concepts more than
specific jokes, Sime concluded that Allen "is merely a copy
of other and better acts," and the young comic's jokes
themselves showed little individuation.[48] In 1917, for example, Allen told of the woman who "used to be a school

teacher, but she has no class now." In a 1922 revue act that presented ancient gags carved on headstones in an "Old Joke Cemetery," Allen used the line: "She broke my heart, so I broke her jaw."[49] Both jokes enjoyed general circulation, appearing, in fact, in a widely sold 1925 jokebook.[50] Though unoriginal, Allen's jokes did draw on the fundamentals of vaudeville humor, like wordplay: "Summer is going—Winter draw[ers] on." He joked about family relationships: "He's a good boy—everything he steals he brings right home to his mother." And Allen wrung laughs from current preoccupations such as Prohibition: "You don't need gasoline nowadays to rub out beer stains—they put it in the beer." Other jokes cut authority figures down to size, as Allen would do to NBC vice-presidents in the 1930s and 1940s: "I could tell he was a policeman—he had his hat off and the woodpeckers were starting to congregate."[51]

If Allen shared so much with other comedians, what made his talent unique? What accounted for his continued success in a new medium, while vaudeville's decline forced hundreds of his contemporaries into retirement? Of course, the reception given a performer is only partly a matter of personal taste, and audiences often enjoyed what professional critics like Silverman did not. In 1921, for example, young S. J. Perelman and a high school friend caught Allen's act in Boston. The comic's "saucy tomfoolery" captivated the boys, although the fundamentals of his act probably had changed little since Silverman saw it three years earlier. "So unbridled was our laughter," Perelman later recorded, "so resonant our applause, that the head usher twice appeared to threaten us with expulsion. No comedian . . . had ever equalled him. . . . Idolatry could go no further."[52]

A performer's comedic skills were bound to improve with stage experience. By 1920, *Variety* reported that Allen "scored the laughing hit of the bill" at New York's Alhambra Theatre "with one of the most original monologues seen in vaudeville."[53] Six years later, the paper evaluated the two-act he performed with Bert Yorke at the Palace Theatre: "Allen's running fire of comment [was] probably the brightest talk ever heard on a vaudeville stage." Calling him "unique," *Variety* noted that Allen wrote "his own ultra-smart material" and had "a keen sense of comedy and a big league delivery."[54] If reviews accurately reflect stage performances, Allen must have improved measurably as a comedian since *Variety's* deprecatory assessment of 1918.

What distinguished Fred Allen from most other vaudeville, and later radio, comedians was his ability to create humorous material. Best known as a performer, Allen also became a skilled writer. Many vaudeville performers depended on professional comedy writers, but Allen enjoyed the freedom of one who imagined and shaped at least some of his own material. Many of his routines revealed the originality that *Variety* praised. Allen valued his experience in vaudeville not for teaching him the common denominators of the national taste (which his radio programs one day would try to please) but for making him skilled in creating and adjusting material to audiences whose comedy preferences differed. His years of traveling the smalltime circuits in the United States and three other English-speaking nations forced Allen to adapt to different tastes, to be flexible, talents that would prove as necessary in live radio as on the live stage.

Allen studied the history of humor to improve his ability to write comedy. In Australia in 1916 he began reading Charles Dickens and Mark Twain in order to learn "the methods two famous authors had used in developing characters and comedy situations," and his reading broadened to many other writers as it extended through the years,[55] strengthening his desire to write. During his years on the stage he wrote his own material, sold acts to other performers, and gained a reputation as one who could improve the comedy material in weak revues. By the time he stepped before a radio microphone to deliver aural comedy, Allen had developed considerable skill in manipulating words for humorous effect, and throughout the 1920s his comedy, like vaudeville's in general, was primarily verbal.[56] As a student of humor and as a creator of verbal comedy whose stage experience placed a premium on flexibility, Allen unknowingly prepared himself for a career in radio.

Allen's experience in vaudeville shaped his style of radio comedy in several other ways. Vaudeville "entertainment was largely topical fun. The trend of its humor was the march of those times."[57] Daily immersion in a humor that was immediately responsive to current news stories and popular fads unquestionably influenced Allen's early introduction and long use of a news-of-the-week segment on his radio programs.

The current scene for vaudeville audiences was largely urban, although many rube comics and other acts with a rustic flavor were featured.[58] As Michael M. Davis, Jr., of Manhattan's People's Institute noted in 1910, the vaudeville theater was the modern city in miniature: members of the audience, unknown to one another, passively watched a string of unconnected acts that lacked the development of a play, before disappearing into the crowd on the streets outside. "Vaudeville is adapted in many ways to cosmopolitan audiences," the progressive reformer wrote, "whose members have few common sentiments, or common ideas."[59] This urban orientation was as characteristic of Allen's radio humor as it was of his vaudeville acts and revue routines, notwithstanding favorite characters such as Titus Moody, the New England farmer who resided on Allen's Alley, and the small-town illusion that framed the "Town Hall Tonight" shows of the 1930s. Allen's radio programs reflected their origin in New York City; he refused to follow the lead of other radio comedians, and of network programming generally, and broadcast from Hollywood. His personal experience with life in Boston, New York, and other cities where he performed joined with the city values of the vaudeville medium to make Fred Allen perhaps the most urban of radio's comedians.

Douglas Gilbert has noted that the comedy performed in variety theaters, which were vaudeville's predecessors in the 1880s and earlier, was heavily "racial," that is, ethnic in the broadest sense.[60] Drawing on traditions older than the mid-nineteenth-century minstrel show, comics elicited laughter from the stereotyped appearance, behavior, and speech of German, Irish, Jewish, and other immigrants, as well as southern blacks.[61] The vaudeville of Allen's era drew liberally on this heritage. Nathaniel Benchley once commented that, in the early twentieth century, "a joke wasn't considered funny unless it was about an Irishman, Negro, or a German"; and Gerald Weales adds that "dialect comedians were rampant in vaudeville."[62] Although Fred Allen was not an ethnic comic, he occasionally employed an ethnic joke in his stage acts. But when he told of the "big-hearted Scotsman who donated $200 to the widow of the Unknown Soldier," for example, he made automatic use of one of his profession's most successful laugh-producing devices.[63] Allen's radio career, as Chapter 8 illustrates, reflected the persistence of dialect humor and ethnic characters long after vaudeville's demise.

To focus on broad influences such as ethnicity and urbanism on his comedy is to depersonalize what for Allen and many other performers was a quintessentially personal experience. Allen articulated, at the time and for years after he left vaudeville, a unique interpretation of the bittersweet world of the smalltimer. As long as he lived, the comedian fondly recalled warm and humorous incidents from his two decades on the stage. To his readers and listeners, it often seemed as if the vaudeville associations were uniformly dearer, the performance conditions always more humane, than those in the corporate world of radio entertainment. Although the passage of time surely softened unpleasant memories of unresponsive audiences and midnight train travel, his vaudeville years were clearly a very positive period in Fred Allen's life. In contrast, in short fiction published between 1924 and 1945, Allen revealed the darker side of the smalltime vaudevillian's life, presenting a bleak portrait of the smalltimer as the little man. Allen carried both perspectives into his radio years.

As he became a recognized figure on Broadway during its glamorous post–World War I era, and a writer who published short humorous pieces in magazines as prestigious as the *New Yorker*, Allen might have cultivated the city's literati.[64] In fact, he did become a close friend of James Thurber later in life.[65] But Allen did not find his intimates among the Algonquin Wits or other cultural arbiters who shared, as he did not, a university education and a reputation for urbanity and sophistication. His later characterization of Alexander Woollcott as "a bloated poseur" correctly suggests that he had little in common with most of the humorists associated with the *New Yorker*.[66] Allen's closest friends came from his early Boston years, his later radio career, and among his vaudeville associates. The latter group included Doc Rockwell, a fellow New England nut comic; John Royal, one-time manager of the Keith-Albee Theater in Cleveland and later an NBC executive; and Jack Haley, a boyhood friend from Boston who also established a career in vaudeville and who played the Tin Man in *The Wizard of Oz* in 1939.[67] Throughout the 1930s and 1940s Allen provided financial support to many down-and-out vaudevillians he had known years earlier on the smalltime circuits. In spite of his complaints about being victimized by panhandlers, Allen's sense of obligation to former associates was strong.

Allen found humor in the smalltimer's existence. In late 1920, he wrote to agent Sammy Tishman about a recent performance in Centralia, Illinois. That town's audience, which had been slow to appreciate his jokes, was "so low that a dwarf takes tickets to make them feel at home." The theater manager enjoyed harassing visiting actors. Allen thought him "so narrow minded if he fell on a pin point it would stick in both of his eyes."[68] Years after he played Bayonne, New Jersey, Allen recalled the theater there, where a cat had delivered a litter of kittens in the aisle during his act. Topping the cat's performance was difficult, but Allen managed to quip: "I thought my act was a monologue, not a catalogue."[69] Allen, like other smalltimers, stocked such incidents in "his store of memories . . . to escape from the unhappy present into the happy past."[70] He also drew on such recollections several times each radio season, as he hosted guests who shared vaudeville backgrounds. Although most of the nostalgia was pure fantasy, the funny "remember when" encounters with Jack Haley, Jack Benny, Ben Bernie, Maurice Evans, Doc Rockwell, Tallulah Bankhead, Ted Lewis, and others revealed the effectiveness of vaudeville as a source of comedy. Between January 1937 and June 1948, Allen wrote twenty-nine vaudeville reminiscences into his radio scripts. On these programs, audiences learned of such acts as Mahatma, the tightrope walker, who was also frequently drunk. "One night Mahatma was tight and the rope wasn't," and a career promptly ended.[71] In 1938 Allen recalled his juggling act: "two minutes of juggling and eight minutes of picking things up." On the same radio program, he told of a female impersonator he had recently met. "He hasn't worked for two years. It's made a man out of him."[72] Listeners who had never seen a vaudeville show got something of its flavor from these radio spots.

Although Fred Allen wrote many bound volumes of radio scripts, thousands of letters worthy of publication, and numerous pieces of humorous commentary, he deprecated his literary achievement. As he remarked on a 1941 broadcast: "Radio shows are transient. . . . You do a radio show, it goes out into the air, sparrows step on it, it's forgotten. A man who writes a book leaves something for posterity."[73]

In 1925, Allen had hopes of becoming a full-time writer. The previous November, Tommy Gray, the author of *Variety's* humor column "Tommy's Tattles," had died at the age of thirty-six. Given that the paper had never employed another humor columnist in its two-decade history and that Gray had a large and loyal following among vaudeville's professional comics, editor Sime Silverman's invitation to replace the late writer was a distinct honor for the thirty-year-old Allen.[74] Between January 21 and March 11, 1925, Allen published eight weekly installments of a column entitled "Near-Fun," after the "Near-Beer" of Prohibition.[75] Filled with quips and jokes, the column probably served some traveling performers as a source of stage material. Allen's goals were to amuse vaudevillians and to gain experience as a writer. Show business insiders could appreciate comedy about actors like themselves, told in the argot that was the vaudevillians' own. While writing the column, Allen continued to perform in the road-show edition of *The Greenwich Village Follies*, but when it closed in the spring of 1925, he faced a decision. Sime had not paid him for the material already published, and while Allen was working in the show, that was fine; but now Allen needed employment. And he wanted to become a writer. Still seeking security and a "more satisfying life" than acting, he proposed that Silverman place him on full-time staff at $60 per week. "A writer at sixty can be a Steinbeck, a Faulkner, or a Hemingway," Allen wrote years later. "An actor at sixty can make a funny face or do a creaky dance." When Silverman rejected the proposal, Allen returned to vaudeville.[76]

If Silverman's decision helped ensure that one day there would be a Fred Allen radio show, it also provided the comedian with a valuable apprenticeship that intensified his desire to write about, as well as for, vaudeville and other media of mass amusement. Allen had published two short vaudeville fantasies in *Variety* before he began doing "Near-Fun," and five more followed over the next two decades.[77] These stories describe a vaudeville that contrasts with most published depictions of it and that reveals another side of Allen's interpretation of the smalltimers' world. For it was of smalltimers that he wrote—marginal performers living a marginal existence—not the well-publicized success of bigtime celebrities. Filled with puns and other language play, given authenticity by the use of stage slang, and pervaded by the black humor that Allen would later interject into radio scripts, these stories suggested the desperate, sometimes grotesque lives of the "little men" of the nation's itinerant entertainment industry.

Allen's brief stories affirm that human sympathy and generosity usually prevailed among vaudevillians. In his first effort, "The Acrobat's Christmas," Mortimer Kneecap of the Flying Kneecaps turns down a desperately needed booking on Christmas Eve so that his tights can hang by the fireplace. In the absence of a stocking, the leotard alone can hold the gifts that his little daughter Phoenix expects from Santa Claus. Other tales illustrate less benevolent human traits and less enriching experiences. Trained animals, for example, play key roles in the tragic deaths of has-been smalltime performers. One of these is Myer, "The Vaude Elephant That Didn't Remember," who swallows his master, Epstein, by mistake. After seven years without work, the pachyderm forgets to place Epstein back on the stage after balancing the man in his huge mouth. In "The Confession," Moe the Talking Dog steals the meat ration coupons from Waldo, his master, after Waldo selfishly tries to starve him. In the jungle of the smalltime, Waldo, who had once depended on his dogs for a living, dies of malnutrition.

Revenge and retribution play roles in the violent demise of another smalltimer, the rotund singer Pansy Flannigan. Under attack by a four-legged fugitive from the trained animal act Madam Odor's Hyenas, Pansy's only hope of survival is that Bull's-Eye Aspinwall, a sharpshooter, can kill the animal with his last cartridge. He misses. For the first time in his career, he misses. Why? Because Pansy's husband, agent Launcelot Fineberg, had denied the marksman a booking for years. "At last I have had revenge Launcelot Fineberg. . . . You kept me out of work so long that I can't even shoot straight." Unconscionable exploitation occurs in the smalltimer's world: Waldo, the dog trainer already mentioned, eats his act after vaudeville's decline leads to unemployment and chronic hunger. Some of Allen's characters are grotesque eccentrics. Sylvester Prebble, "gripped by a mania for entertainment," does more than fall in love with the theater in "Don't Trust Midgets." He lives in a theater for years, suggesting that media addiction predates television. In the story about a *Variety* reporter, or "mugg," ace vaudeville critic Fing is a jounalistic sadist. "I panned hell out of that show at the Hamilton yesterday," he brags to the office boy. "None of them acts will get another date after my notice gets to the bookers. It's a great life."

To the specialized professional audience for which they were designed, Allen's stories undoubtedly were funny. Show business people had encountered cynical critics and self-serving booking agents. They had known unemployment, disappointment, and even hunger. Allen helped them laugh at such experiences. To those interested in Fred Allen's prebroadcasting career, the vaudeville short fiction is also important because it reveals Allen's insights into the smalltimer's life. The world of the smalltimer could be harsh and brutal, the actors themselves "little men" and women with limited control over their lives. Their helplessness when pressed by adverse circumstances exposed the selfishness and cruelty that is the potential of humans everywhere. In some of his radio scripts, as well as in the vaudeville short fiction, a streak of literary naturalism combined with Allen's ability to perceive comic potential to produce a variety of black humor that was uniquely his own.

Radio's talent hunt probably would not have identified Allen's broadcasting potential on the basis of his vaudeville background alone. His success in a series of Broadway revues beginning in 1922 was the key to a future in broadcasting. For a rising smalltimer like Allen, the move from vaudeville to the revue format signified a gain in professional status and increased recognition among show business producers, agents, critics, and theatergoers. New opportunities for contacts and publicity were now open to him. While performing in *The Little Show* in the summer of 1929, for example, Allen wrote nonsensical "autobiographical" fragments for the *New York Times* and *Theatre Magazine*, and in 1930 a major magazine did a feature article on his life.[78] Allen's revue career gave him more than a format for the Linit programs. In the city that had by 1926 become the nation's broadcasting center, the revue had given him a place in the talent pool that would supply radio with comedians after the theater's collapse.

The theater historian Margaret M. Knapp distinguishes among three categories of Broadway revues. Fred Allen became a featured performer in all three types between 1922 and 1932. Allen performed as a monologist and with partners in several shows that imitated the famed and successful Ziegfeld Follies. The major purpose of *The Passing Show of 1922*, *Artists and Models* (1923), and *Vogues of 1924* was to display beautiful women in lavish surroundings. Comedians were important components of the program because they held the audience's attention during set changes and because they provided genuine entertainment, but women were the main attraction.[79]

Allen performed in the 1924 edition of *The Greenwich Village Follies*, which represents for Knapp the topical revue, unique as "a subtle brand of satire thus far unknown to the revue form." Late in the decade, the topical revue spawned a variant, the best examples of which became Fred Allen's greatest Broadway successes: *The Little Show* (1929) and *Three's a Crowd* (1930). These revues also dealt in satire and parody, much of it of the theatrical world, but they made greater use of song and dance and "a more opulent style" than had earlier topical revues. David Ewen notes that these "intimate revues" added a measure of "sophistication and . . . adult intelligence" to their musical and dance numbers.[80] From his several years' experience in creating and performing bitingly humorous commentary on topical subjects, Allen moved directly into radio, a medium in which he would also find abundant opportunities for satire and parody.

It was with *The Little Show* and *Three's a Crowd* that Allen joined productions whose consistently high quality equaled his own comedy material. His performances pleased the critics. *Theatre Magazine*, which characterized *The Little Show* as "fresh as a May morning," found "the gifted Mr. Allen . . . continuously funny." Brooks Atkinson of the *New York Times* wrote that Allen was "not merely an ingratiating comedian, but a deft one, with an extraordinary talent for making his points at a skimming pace."[81] Such praise continued as Allen and Portland performed in *Three's a Crowd*. The comic hit of the show was Allen's "hilarious travesty," as Atkinson called it, of Admiral Richard Byrd's South Pole expedition. Dressed in a moth-eaten fur coat, Allen delivered the routine with masterful timing and understatement. Writing almost a decade later, Max Wylie recalled the Byrd lecture "as one of the great burlesques" of its era. In the 1950s, Ben Gross referred to it as "one of the wittiest" comic bits ever heard on Broadway.[82]

By the time Fred Allen began his series of radio programs for Linit in October 1932, he had developed his comedy skills on hundreds of stages over a twenty-year period. Along with other fugitives from the collapsing stage, however, he would find that the stage was inadequate preparation for radio. The new medium would present veteran comedy writers and performers with unfamiliar demands, in an environment often hostile to their art.

The Fred Allen Shows, 1933–1949

This drudgery, this sham . . . this gold mine.
"TEXACO STAR THEATER," 1942

Thirty minutes before airtime, uniformed ushers filled the large studio with a mixed crowd of New Yorkers and tourists, eager to participate in a major network radio show. Although he had performed radio programs in auditoriums seating several hundred visitors, during the late 1930s and again in the late 1940s Fred Allen broadcast from NBC's huge Studio 8-H in the RCA Building in Rockefeller Center. Twice each Wednesday in the late 1930s—at 9:00 P.M. for most of the nation, followed three hours later by a rebroadcast for the West Coast—a throng of 1,318 curious radio fans crowded into that studio for Allen's hour-long program. Minutes before the start of the show, the star comedian strolled onto the stage to warm up his audience. Covering the genuine pride he felt in his work with a comfortable cloak of self-depreciation, Fred Allen addressed the instant but fleeting community. "For those of you who got caught in the crowd and swept in here," he announced on one occasion, "I would like to say that this is the Fred Allen show, and you still have eight minutes before we go on the air to get the heck out."[1] The

chuckling fans remained fixed in their chairs. Allen wel-
comed them "to the never-never land of radio . . . a land of
curious specimens—and I, a species of comedian, am the
most curious of all."[2] Inviting his visitors to participate in
the next sixty minutes of entertainment, the comedian encouraged laughter. People stifled laughter at their own risk,
he added impishly. A suppressed snicker, grown to a mature laugh, might emerge, full-voiced and awkwardly, during a tax audit; another could lurk "in your lower colon to
laugh at the food as it passes through."[3] Having advised his
audience to give free rein to its humorous impulses, Allen
went to his position on the stage. The warm-up over, Allen's company was ready to present another hour of comedy and variety entertainment to an audience not of hundreds but of millions, in homes throughout Manhattan and
across the continent, in Canada as well as the United
States. Soon Allen would know, and only he would deeply
care, whether the labor of writing, cutting, conferring
about, and rehearsing this week's script had produced a
worthy program.

As the broadcast progressed, the studio observers' experience contrasted dramatically with that of the home audience. The program's entertainment compelled each
home listener to create "a little world of make-believe"—
to "visualize" each sidewalk interview with imaginary
characters or the scene of a murder mystery in the English
countryside.[4] Those present in the studio heard and saw a
different order of fantasy: an experienced team of professional performers and technicians matter-of-factly execut-
ing directions printed in a forty-page script. Yet surviving
accounts of the studio scene, both verbal and photographic,
suggest that it was as fascinating as the worlds imagined
by radio listeners.

Allen's program opened with a musical fanfare and
the familiar theme song. The all-male orchestra wore uni-
forms whose outstanding visual feature was a red coat. Although no cameras captured the scene for listeners, Allen's
orchestra leader, singers, and supporting comedy players

dressed for the two weekly broadcasts. Fred Allen's only personal concession to informality was a loosened tie and collar. His chewing tobacco inappropriate to a public stage, Allen substituted a three-stick wad of gum during the broadcasts. As his part of the dialogue ebbed and flowed, he alternately stored the gum in a rear recess of his mouth or brought it forth for use. While they worked, members of the cast largely ignored the studio audience, intent on making scheduled appearances at the microphone to read their lines, then withdrawing to a row of chairs until cued. Other equipment picked up the musical numbers, and cast members with speaking roles clustered around a single microphone, with Allen so positioned that the studio audience usually saw only his back. The musicians intently followed the comedy dialogue. They had rehearsed in a different studio from the actors and heard the comedy for the first time during the broadcast. Often the most spirited laughter came from the orchestra, a response Allen relied on to help convey a sense of spontaneity in case the studio audience was unresponsive. Despite well-timed comedy bits, commercial copy, and musical numbers, the star's ad-libs or the studio audience's unexpectedly sustained laughter often caused frantic time-is-short signals from the control booth. But usually the cast performed all that Allen and his director had planned for the program, and the announcer signed off shortly before 10:00 P.M. His work temporarily finished, Allen lingered with members of the studio audience who sought autographs, wished to shake his hand, or recalled the comedian's appearance at a hometown theater years earlier.[5]

Thirty-nine times each year, for fifteen and one-half broadcast seasons, Fred Allen's workweek culminated in such a broadcast. But over the years from August 4, 1933— when he quit the "self-imposed exile from radio" that followed the Linit series—to his final broadcast on June 26, 1949, Allen's shows evolved.[6] This chapter explains that evolution, discussing a number of program features and the functions performed by supporting cast members.

During his years on the air, Fred Allen's "show" consisted of hundreds of individual programs. Under various titles, the programs were presented in seven separate series for five major corporate sponsors; they were produced by the radio departments of four large New York advertising agencies; and they were broadcast over two national networks. These numbers suggest impermanence and discontinuity. But, in fact, Allen's comedy style and a continuing basic format brought important unities to these fifteen years of varied program features, numerous cast members, and an assortment of assistant writers. That Allen wrote and thus controlled his scripts assured a continuity of humorous concepts through the years of Depression and war.

The conventions of the comedy–variety show format, a broadcasting formula that Allen adapted to his purposes, also lent coherence to his programs.[7] *Fortune* magazine's assertion in 1938 that "variety is the backbone of current programming" continued to describe Allen's potpourri of skits, guest interviews, and music for more than a decade.[8] A recent graduate of Broadway when he began in radio, Allen characterized his series of programs for Linit as revues, and he persisted in applying that word to his shows through the years. "Why, we do a little revue here every week," he remarked during the 1947–1948 broadcasting season. "You could take away the scripts from the cast, cut the best parts out of a few shows, and make a good Broadway revue out of them."[9]

Over an eleven-month period that began in early August 1933, Allen completed three brief series of programs. All appeared on NBC's Red network, on which Allen would spend most of his radio years, and exhaust much of his patience and health. The first series, the "Salad Bowl Revue," illustrates early radio's practice of building a product association into the program's title. The maker of Hellmann's Mayonnaise, Best Foods, Inc., sponsored the thirty-minute show on Friday evenings at 9:00 P.M.; it continued on the air through December 1, 1933.[10] Allen's sponsor on the two other series was the Bristol-Myers Company. From January 3 to March 14, 1934, the comedian created a weekly half-hour show named after the drug firm's laxative: the "Sal Hepatica Revue." Since network radio's largest advertisers included pharmaceutical manufacturers, Allen the smalltimer remarked that he had "achieved radio big time" through Bristol-Myers sponsorship.[11] He also achieved a degree of security under this company's patronage. Bristol-Myers, a pioneer in network radio advertising as early as 1925 with its popular musical group the Ipana Troubadours, remained Allen's sponsor through the 1939–1940 broadcasting season.[12]

Although audience measurement and program ratings would become increasingly important to broadcasting's decision makers as radio matured, Allen's "discouraging failure" in the numbers game apparently explains the brief history of his "Sal Hepatica Revue" in 1934. Bristol-Myers purchased the entire 9:00 to 10:00 P.M. hour on Wednesdays from NBC Red, and preceded Allen's 9:30 show with a musical program. Neither program's audience figures impressed executives of the sponsoring company and the advertising agency, but clearly they were more disappointed by Allen's failure to attract a large audience. "In the ten or twelve weeks we've had this show on the air, we've made little if any progress cutting into the Burns and Allen audience." That was the conclusion of William B. Benton of Benton and Bowles, the Bristol-Myers advertising agency, and by mid-March the sponsor ordered the agency literally to double its efforts to win listeners from Columbia's (CBS) popular George Burns and Gracie Allen program. The idea was to unite the two thirty-minute Bristol-Myers offerings into a one-hour show starring Fred Allen, which would continue to promote both Ipana toothpaste and Sal Hepatica. The title of the new production announced Allen's challenge: to create and sustain an "Hour of Smiles."[13]

The concept of dual-product sponsorship was untried in 1934 and therefore was a source of anxiety among the radio advertising fraternity. In an era unfamiliar with the

spot announcement and multiple-sponsor programs, the
agencies trained listeners to identify products with programs and their stars. Clearly, the agency and its client
were nervous about their new, more lengthy broadcast. According to *Variety*, Bristol-Myers officials feared "that the
identity of the two products would be lost in the shuffle"
of creating a single program from two. Recognizing that he
was "violating orthodox advertising practice," Benton
pressed NBC to make a special effort to promote the new
hour-long show and its featured comedian, whom he called
"one of radio's finest entertainers." Without that promotion, "I'm afraid our progress against Burns and Allen may
be too slow to satisfy the client."[14]

The crisis, if there was one, quickly passed; perhaps it
qualified as one of the manufactured mountains raised by
the "molehill men" whom Allen found infesting the industry's executive offices. He took over the 9:00 to 10:00 P.M.
slot on Wednesdays beginning on March 21, 1934, with his
new "Hour of Smiles." The commercial copy made a careful distinction between the two Bristol-Myers products for
a public apparently bright enough to observe the differences between a paste imprisoned in a tube and granules
stored in a bottle.[15] And *Variety* soon judged the expanded
program a success and its comedian "stronger than ever."[16]
Based on audience measurement, Allen's success with listeners was satisfactory to the sponsor, and it continued to
fund his hour until 1940.

On July 11, 1934, the fifteen-week-old "Hour of
Smiles" quietly became "Town Hall Tonight," the five-
season series of programs that earned for Allen the reputation as "the greatest natural comedy genius in radio."[17]
And notwithstanding such later comic achievements as
the Allen's Alley feature of the 1940s and the show's top
ranking in the Hooperatings after World War II, a long perspective on his entire career reveals the "Town Hall" years
to have been Allen's most creative ones.[18]

On Wednesday evenings Allen invited listeners to join
a noisy, good-natured local crowd in a mythical village

meeting hall for Ipana's "smile of beauty" and Sal Hepatica's "smile of health." If, as noted, Allen's programs manipulated the illusion of a revue, on the "Town Hall" series they also played with rural and small-town images. The comedian himself seems to have promoted the Town Hall label out of a concern for audience demographics. "It seemed to me," he later recalled, "that if we had a title that would interest people in small towns, our program would have a wider appeal."[19] Perhaps he took for granted a sizable urban listenership and wished to capture more rural Americans, who might shun a program that did not mix a rustic flavor with its urban elements. Ironically, some listener surveys found that "Town Hall Tonight" was more popular among urban than rural listeners. A Cooperative Analysis of Broadcasting (CAB) survey reported in June 1937, for example, that it was the fifth most popular program among a sample of urban listeners, while it did not appear on the list of the top-ten rural American favorites. Comedians Jack Benny, Eddie Cantor, and Phil Baker appeared on both lists.[20]

To generate a listening audience for "Town Hall," Bristol-Myers spent from $20,000 to $25,000 weekly. One reliable estimate placed the program's "production costs" at $10,000 per week in 1938, from which amount Allen took his and Portland's salary after paying the other employees: actors, assistant writers, and some production personnel. This sum was $4,500 less than the average production costs of the ten highest-rated programs (Allen's was among them) at the time. The cost of network time for Allen's full-hour program in 1938 was only about $1,200 above the average cost of time for the top-ten shows, some of which were only thirty minutes long.[21]

After a half-dozen years of stable sponsorship, schedule, and format, Allen's program underwent some changes in the fall of 1940. For a time he continued to broadcast from 9:00 to 10:00 on Wednesday evenings, but now it was in the name of Texaco and on CBS, the network of his radio debut in 1932. In the early months of 1940 the Texas

Company began negotiations to lure Allen to its "Texaco Star Theatre" when his contract with Bristol-Myers ended, and by the third week of May the comedian agreed to terms for the fall. But the rival network may have been more determined than his new sponsor to sign Allen. An NBC official observed on May 6: "Columbia quite obviously is breaking its neck to get this [Allen's] show whether for Texaco or for some other advertiser." Broadcasting from a CBS theater at 1697 Broadway, originating on New York station WABC, and reaching listeners over eighty-seven CBS affiliates, Allen's program was in direct competition with NBC's new Bristol-Myers comedy program featuring his replacement, Eddie Cantor.[22] Allen made the change for sensible professional reasons; *Variety* reported that he would enjoy both an increased salary and greater creative freedom than had been true at NBC. Allen tells a more amusing tale of how he came to be sponsored by Texaco. In 1940, the oil company faced a financial crisis. With people glued to their home radio sets, few drove their cars. Texaco's gasoline sales plummeted until company executives hit upon a solution. "We have got to put a man on the radio who will drive people out of their homes and into their cars." According to Allen, he was their man.[23]

Allen's program switched to Sunday nights beginning on March 8, 1942, again broadcast from 9:00 to 10:00 P.M. For the remainder of his radio career, Allen was a fixture on Sunday, the most popular radio listening night of the week.[24] On its new evening, the "Texaco Star Theatre" replaced the "Ford Symphony Hour," a show that had been broadcast since 1937, mixing inspirational music with the Henry Ford-sanctioned anti–New Deal rhetoric of William J. Cameron. On his initial Sunday program Allen reminded the cast that they must present a "refined" and "reserved" show, just the touch that Ford listeners expected. The admonition failed to impress at least one rural listener, who wrote to Ford: "to think Fred Allen is taking that hour is nothing short of sacrilege."[25]

On October 4, 1942, Allen returned to a thirty-minute

format for the first time since March 1934. He was relieved about the reduced burden of script preparation, but it was actually the sponsor who decided on a shorter program. Although Allen in his memoirs attributed the move to the rising cost of talent, those costs must be considered in the context of Texaco's wartime marketing outlook. No consumer product came under more rigid government control through rationing than gasoline. The firm had little to sell but goodwill, which it could satisfactorily market on a half-hour program through public-service messages about conserving rubber tires and other automobile-related products.[26] The Texaco show's resource-conservation campaign earned recognition. An official of the federal Office of Facts and Figures stated in 1942: "I think Fred Allen has done the most magnificent job of rubber rationing of anybody on the air."[27]

Although he had spoken before of a vacation from radio's demands, it was not until the years with Texaco that Allen interrupted his annual routine. The desire to pursue other projects, weariness, and a potentially serious problem from high blood pressure, aggravated by his work, induced Allen to delay his return to the air in the fall of 1943, and to rest from all but guest appearances during the 1944–1945 season. Allen said he could do without what the doctors called "essential hypertension," but he understood that his work contributed to the condition.[28] During his year-long sabbatical the comedian terminated his association with Texaco, returning to radio in October 1945 with a new sponsor and on a different network.[29] His receipt of a Peabody Radio Award during his absence from radio was a source of pride and amusement to Allen. The comedian found it confusing, he told those attending the award ceremony, that the Peabody committee ignored him while he was on the air, but honored him after he had left radio. Was this an encouragement to remain out of broadcasting? Quipped Allen: "Next year, if I keep away from Hollywood, I will probably win the Academy Award."[30]

In the fall of 1945 Allen returned to radio, and to NBC, with the "Fred Allen Show," a thirty-minute broadcast, still performed live, at 8:30 on Sunday evenings. Beginning in January 1949, the starting time moved ahead to 8:00 P.M. Standard Brands paid the asking price of $20,000 per week for Allen and his cast, for the opportunity to promote sales of Tenderleaf Tea and Blue Bonnet Margarine to the listening audience.[31] Allen shared NBC on radio's most-listened-to night with Jack Benny and the ventriloquist Edgar Bergen and his dummy Charlie McCarthy during the 1945–1946 to 1947–1948 seasons. The Sunday time slot was a crucial factor in Allen's willingness to sign with Standard Brands, and the popular broadcasts of Benny and Bergen earlier in the evening no doubt helped to swell his listening audience.[32] Midway through the "Fred Allen Show"'s third season, in January 1948, the Ford Dealers of America replaced Standard Brands as Allen's sponsor. Although high production (talent) costs influenced Standard Brands' decision to drop Allen's program, the Ford Dealers agreed to pay $22,000 per week for Allen's services and his cast's salaries.[33]

During the four-year run of this last series of Allen's programs, the comedian experienced unprecedented professional triumph and then decline, as well as personal health problems. Allen's shows had always scored respectable but not impressive numbers in the audience measurement surveys. The most watched of these surveys during the 1940s was the Hooperating,[34] and in the 1946–1947 and 1947–1948 seasons, Allen was surprised to find himself at the top of its rankings of program popularity on several occasions. While the response to Allen's programs had always focused on the quality of his comedy—Jack Gould hailed the return of the comedian's "gentle yet incisive, dry yet intelligent" wit in the fall of 1945, for example—now their success could be measured.[35] But this popularity was short-lived. Responding to the current enthusiasm for giveaway programs that offered studio and home audience members the chance to win prizes, ABC inaugurated "Stop the Music" with Bert Parks in the winter of 1948. The new Sunday evening program was slotted to compete with the Allen and Bergen–McCarthy programs. The effect was swift and merciless. Allen's number-one ranking and 28.7 Hooperating of February 1, 1948, skidded to thirteenth ranking and a 16.4 rating by May 7. In March of 1949, Allen's show had its lowest "Hooper" ever, a rating of 7.9.[36] Of course, Allen's sponsor closely watched "Stop the Music"'s rise— "perhaps the most spectacular climb in rating history"— and its production costs.[37] By November 1948 the half-hour Allen program costs (not including air time) were $25,000 per week, whereas an hour of "Stop the Music," with its top-ten Hooper ranking, cost $12,000.[38] The next month, Allen announced that he would not return to radio in the fall. The Ford Dealers probably would not have renewed his contract in any event. His plans uncertain, his health still a concern, Allen signed a deal with NBC committing him to perform exclusively in its radio and television features; the network had recently lost Jack Benny and other leading talent to rival William Paley's "raids" for CBS.[39] Although Allen would appear on both media in the following years, he had come to the end of regularly scheduled comedy series when he performed in his final program on June 26, 1949.

Conforming to their creator's image of them as revues, Allen's programs presented a variety of comedy features, each usually lasting eight to twelve minutes, surrounded by musical interludes, commercials, and, at the half hour, a station break. Music remained an important auxiliary entertainment throughout the comedy–variety show's history on radio. Allen's succession of orchestras featured the big-band sound, singing ensembles, and soloists. Their leaders included Ferdie Grofe and Al Goodman, and among the regular vocalists were Kenny Baker, the DeMarco Sisters, and James Melton, who was later to sing at the Metropolitan Opera. Allen's musicians functioned in much the

From 1932 until 1949, Fred Allen broadcast weekly; show titles, times, networks, and sponsors changed periodically. Here is a complete rundown:

Series Title	Period on the air	Evening and Time	Network	Sponsor	Advertising Agency
Linit Bath Club Revue	10/23/32– 4/16/33	Sunday, 9:00–9:30	CBS	Corn Products Co.: Linit	Hellwig
Salad Bowl Revue	8/4/33– 12/1/33	Friday, 9:00–9:30	NBC Red	Best Foods: Hellmann's Mayonnaise	Benton and Bowles
Sal Hepatica Revue	1/3/34– 3/14/34	Wednesday, 9:30–10:00	NBC Red	Bristol-Myers: Sal Hepatica	Benton and Bowles
Hour of Smiles	3/21/34– 7/4/34	Wednesday, 9:00–10:00	NBC Red	Bristol-Myers: Sal Hepatica	Benton and Bowles
Town Hall Tonight	7/11/34– 6/28/39 (summer breaks)	Wednesday, 9:00–10:00	NBC Red	Bristol-Myers: Sal Hepatica and Ipana	Benton and Bowles to 11/1/35, Young and Rubicam thereafter
Fred Allen Show	10/4/39– 6/26/40	Wednesday, 9:00–10:00	NBC Red	Bristol-Myers: Sal Hepatica and Ipana	Young and Rubicam
Texaco Star Theatre	10/2/40– 6/25/44 (summer breaks)	Wednesday, 9:00–10:00, to 2/25/42; Sunday, 9:00–10:00, to 6/28/42; Sunday, 9:30–10:00, thereafter	CBS	Texaco	Buchanan and Co.
Fred Allen Show	10/7/45– 6/26/49 (summer breaks)	Sunday, 8:30–9:00, to 12/19/48; 8:00–8:30, thereafter	NBC	Standard Brands: Tenderleaf Tea and Blue Bonnet Margarine through 1947; Ford Dealers of America 1/4/48–6/26/49	Buchanan and Co.

same way as musical groups in other comedy–variety programs. They defined the start and finish of program segments and supplied entertainment of a different sort from the comedian's.[40]

Another convention of radio comedy programs, the skit, was also essential to Allen's personal concept of what a comedy show should include.[41] For this veteran of the smalltime circuits and the revue stage, the radio skit was a natural heir to the one-act play or blackout sketch.[42] So important were skits as comedy vehicles that they survived the winnowing process necessary when Allen's hour show was halved in 1942. They remained a centerpiece of his programs until the end, being performed by Allen's stock company, which was variously named "The Mighty Allen Strolling Players," "The Allen Art Group," "The Texaco Workshop Players," and, most memorably, "The Mighty Allen Art Players." Allen impishly chose the names with Eugene O'Neill's Provincetown Players and CBS's experimental "Columbia Workshop" in mind.[43]

Despite a diversity of program features, many comedy series achieved a necessary cohesion by focusing on the personality of the star or the relationships among the "family" of cast members. Such was true of the Jack Benny, Edgar Bergen–Charlie McCarthy, and Bob Hope programs, among others. Fred Allen built continuity into his shows with other devices. Determined not to focus the comedy on his own manufactured personality traits, Allen relied on comic situation or current news events treated in a satirical manner. Similarly, he did not emphasize individual cast members; although he promoted the name recognition of such cast members as band leader Peter Van Steeden and announcer Harry Von Zell, his most effective comedy support came from anonymous actors of the Art Players troupe. In his three brief series of 1933–1934, for example, and into the first year of "Town Hall Tonight," many of Allen's skits were located in Bedlam, a term that signified an irreverent, free-wheeling style of humor as well as a chaotic, insane place, with a host of eccentric characters. One week Allen was the dean of Bedlam University, another week the mayor of Bedlamville, and on a third program head of the Bedlam Matrimonial Bureau. By the summer hiatus of 1935, little mention was made of Bedlam this or that, but for a time it represented a thread of continuity in many programs.

During the first several seasons of "Town Hall Tonight," Allen featured the proprietor of a general store. Inspired by Allen's real-life friend Hodge White, from the Dorchester section of Boston, the storekeeper became part of the mythical village scene that served as the opening on "Town Hall" programs beginning on March 20, 1935.[44] To the folks gathered in the Town Hall, Allen passed announcements and bits of sage advice from the storekeeper in minute-long monologues. In one bulletin Hodge warned the members of the town band, which was scheduled to rehearse "at the G.A.R. Hall" on Friday evening, not to mistake his French horn for a cuspidor when they had to "bail out." "Last year the horn gave off a fine spray during band rehearsals and along about May the ceiling turned mahogany. So much for symphonic precautions," Allen concluded.[45] On another occasion, Allen notified the store's customers that the water pipes in the store's basement had broken, causing his stock of yeast to rise. His store, White announced, now was located "one flight up . . . and rising."[46]

The most successful program features were those that drew on the day's events. In March 1934, as he inaugurated the "Hour of Smiles" series, Allen introduced a segment that used Hollywood's newsreels and radio's "man in the street" interview programs as models. Over an approximately eight-year period, Allen's news feature assumed several names, including the "Town Hall News" (1935–1939) and the "March of Trivia" (early 1940s). Whatever its title, the news, which announced that it "sees nothing . . . shows all," drew comedy from human-interest stories, many resurrected from obscure bits in the newspapers Allen read faithfully. On December 6, 1942, Allen broadcast the first installment of "Allen's Alley," the comedy feature for which he is best remembered. The Alley is considered in detail in a later chapter; here we simply note that the Allen's Alley residents with whom the comedian visited each week and discussed a question of current interest were the successors to the citizens quizzed on earlier news segments. Allen simply had found a new way to exploit his interest in milking the news for humor, one that included the important addition of continuing characters.

The comedy segments heard on Allen's programs make an important point about his concept of radio humor and its proper origins. Until the Texaco programs, when larger production budgets made possible and radio's compulsion to imitate made "necessary" the featuring of guest stars, Allen made sparing use of one-shot celebrity appearances. Instead, he developed comedy from the lives of average people, the "little men" and women from the world beyond the RCA Building who were "average" only in their noncelebrity status. Their odd occupations or unique abilities brought a panorama of interesting human diversity to Allen's microphone; there was nothing like it on any other comedy–variety show.

In the early 1920s, radio had been crowded with amateur talent, as practically any singer or piano player could walk into a studio and broadcast. When Allen introduced a weekly talent contest on his program of January 2, 1935, he joined an "amateur craze" begun in 1934 by the Major Bowes radio talent show.[47] No doubt recalling that his own comedy career had taken root on vaudeville's amateur nights, Allen continued to present the Town Hall amateurs until December 9, 1936—during a period in which, *Variety* estimated, as many as eight hundred national and local radio programs found some role for amateur talent.[48] Long before the 1930s, many young Americans dreamed of being discovered for show business. While Harry Leon Wilson's fictional *Merton of the Movies* represented the Hollywood hopefuls, other young people, some still in the grasp of stage mothers, set out for the broadcast studios. The radio personality Mary Margaret McBride told one career success story in her novel *Tune in for Elizabeth* (1946).[49] Not surprisingly, few real-life amateurs got far enough to win a cash prize, much less start a career. Of the one hundred people who auditioned for an appearance on "Town Hall Tonight" in October 1935, for example, none revealed sufficient "entertainment value" to earn a place on the show.[50] Disappointed by the lack of quality amateur talent, Allen dropped the feature short of its second anniversary, substituting the "Town Hall Varieties," a showcase for unknown professional entertainers.[51]

The historian J. Fred MacDonald calls "amateurism . . . a democratic form of radio amusement. It was the average citizen entertaining his colleagues. It was as close as an audience came to controlling the content of its own programming."[52] Some contemporary observers of Fred Allen's experience with amateurs offered less lofty evaluations of its meaning. One journalist who watched an amateur segment in Allen's NBC studio found the amateurs boring, and a *Variety* reviewer who listened to Allen's "Town Hall Tonight" broadcasts noted that the comic's off-the-cuff badinage overwhelmed them. Aaron Stein, the perceptive radio critic of the *New York Evening Post*, wrote that the amateur segment of each show contrasted starkly with the quality of entertainment achieved during the program's first forty-five minutes, that it was a mechanical imitation of a current national fad rather than a natural expression of what Allen did best as an entertainer. For Stein, Allen's novices produced "radio's dullest amateur night . . . a sad waste" of the comedian's abilities.[53]

Allen's reaction to such criticism is not known. But he did value the popular participation in his show that the amateurs represented, and he enjoyed the freedom that their segment of the show gave him. Allen did not meet the amateurs before his live, on-air encounter with them during the broadcast. Liberated from script and rehearsals, Allen the master ad-libber unleashed his imagination in the informal chatter that preceded each performance. The

censors' blue pencils could not mark his unwritten interaction with the amateurs or his guests on similar program
segments.

In the fall of 1937, Allen created "People You Didn't
Expect to Meet," a weekly visit with someone with an odd
occupation. Prepared dialogue guided his way through interviews with these New Yorkers, who included a female
cab driver, the head of a bartenders' school, a singing tele-
graph operator, and a smokestack checker at power plants
of New York's huge utility company, Consolidated Edison.
In the 1939–1940 season Allen's listeners heard an unre-
hearsed "Mr. and Mrs. Average Man's Round Table." Seeking opinions on a matter of, say, etiquette from three members of the studio audience, Allen utilized this "midget
quiz" as a vehicle for his natural wit in interaction with
strangers. In 1941–1942, on the last hour-long Texaco programs, Allen introduced the weekly winners of talent com-
petitions held on various college campuses.[54] Allen regretted the passing of these features from his broadcasts in the
1940s. "He was at his best then, he thinks," wrote John K.
Hutchens in 1942, "and he would still like one serious sequence during which the 'little people' could talk." But
even star comedians did not fully control their programs in
broadcasting's bureaucratic complexity. "Networks do not
approve of that [average people] on a comedy program."[55]

Networks, together with sponsors and ad agencies,
heartily endorsed the use of guest stars on comedy shows.
Celebrities, by the late 1930s, enhanced the variety of
shows that offered varied entertainment; they supple-
mented the talents of the regular cast. And, or so the theory cherished by sponsors held, they added the celebrity's
fans to the comedian's regular listening audience. If guests
benefited the host program, they were willing participants
in the system. After all, a network radio show was a useful
means of promoting one's new book, one's new film, and,
thus, one's self. Over time, the fees paid to guests rose also.
In early 1943, nineteen New York-originated network
shows used guest stars. A year later, thirty-four weekly

programs featured guests.[56] By the early 1940s, "the average asking price" of a guest celebrity was $2,000, according to *Variety*.[57] Some shows paid only a token sum by Hollywood standards; "Information Please," a program on which few movie stars could survive thirty minutes of matching wits and accumulated information with the likes of Franklin P. Adams, paid guest panelists $300 to $500. But Eddie Cantor paid visiting personalities as much as $3,500.[58] Apart from the money, guests who made the rounds of the leading evening programs benefited from the good exposure. Vowing to make a career of guest apperances, Al Jolson pointed out that his hosts "have to make you look good; when you have your own show, you gotta make them [guests] look good."[59]

Although radio drew its guest stars from numerous arenas of national life, Hollywood and radio itself supplied the numerical majority, those with the most familiar names, and many of those who bore the highest price tags. The excessive use of these media personalities caused a swelling volume of critical comment that began in the late 1930s, a commentary to which Allen was a ready contributor. One listener called the "senseless back scratching" of radio hosts and their guests "an intolerable and insufferable nuisance to the radio public," and the *New York Times* columnist Orrin E. Dunlap, Jr. agreed. As radio personalities exchanged visits to each other's programs, the entertainment value dropped; listeners tired of jokes about Bing Crosby's family, Bob Hope's failures with women, and Jack Benny's age on program after program. These guest appearances also disrupted the basic element of a comedy show's success: an established format for blending such ingredients as comic situation and cast interaction.[60] During World War II, just as Fred Allen implemented a guest-star policy, some observers worried that an overdependence on guest stars threatened the future of comedy shows. Could the star comedians retain listeners when the supply of interesting guests dried up? With established stars, many from outside radio, monopolizing airtime, how could the industry develop the fresh talent that would ensure its future?[61] Implicit in this criticism is the charge that by relying on celebrities, particularly those from motion pictures, the creators of radio comedy shows failed to develop radio's unique aural humor. In effect, they borrowed visual images of movie stars and established a reliance on competing media of entertainment.

Fred Allen echoed these concerns by making fun of the celebrities. In 1947 he and his friend H. Allen Smith devised a guest appearance for Smith that satirized "the hordes of guest stars" who "beat their gums together briskly even though they . . . have nothing to say." Given a lavish buildup when he appeared on Allen's program, Smith stepped to the microphone and spoke a single sentence: "I have nothing whatever to say."[62] A dull sameness inflicted radio, Allen thought, since the same Hollywood personalities "appear on all the shows, doing the same type of condensed plays and bits plus a little talk about 'the grand fun' had making 'mr. moto gets a hotfoot,' or some other masterpiece."[63] On another occasion, he stereotyped the guest star as a

> temperamental Hollywood glamour girl. When the script is finished she insists that most of the jokes be rewritten. Her agent demands that the guest star's last three pictures, "Zombie in the Oven," "Chuck Wagon Clarisse," and "She Couldn't Say Maybe," be mentioned in the dialogue. When the program is over the comedian hears one laugh. It is the guest star as she takes her check.

The appearance on one program of Dorothy Lamour, famous for her "sarong" costumes in a series of movies, probably inspired this general description of "glamour girl" calamity.[64]

Although he experienced some unpleasantness, as when Bing Crosby canceled an appearance on short notice after Allen had appeared on the crooner's program,[65] Allen also enjoyed making creative use of his guests' talents. On May 14, 1944, for example, CBS writer–producer Norman Corwin appeared in a skit that retold the story of "Jack and Jill" as Corwin might have presented it on the "Columbia Workshop": a psychological drama.[66] When he began using guest stars in the 1940s, Allen avoided hiring them on the basis of name recognition alone. Believing that "it's the script that counts" in a radio program, Allen's method was to fit the guest to the program, rather than shape a script to conform to a personality.[67] In his memoirs, Allen expressed pride in his creative use of guest stars, especially when their incongruous roles produced humor: the operatic tenor Lauritz Melchior as a hillbilly singer, for example, and then Brooklyn Dodgers' baseball manager Leo Durocher "singing" his way through a Gilbert and Sullivan parody.[68]

During his first seven years on the air (1932–1933 to 1938–1939), Fred Allen's only celebrity guests were fellow comedians Jack Benny and George Jessel. Benny's appearances were a by-product of a "feud" with Allen that began during the 1936–1937 season, and Jessel's was part of a campaign to promote his show for Bristol-Myers. But during the decade bracketed by the 1939–1940 and 1948–1949 seasons, Allen participated fully in the guest-star business. He hosted 151 different guests during these years, all but 18 of them in 1941 and later, and thus mostly on thirty-minute programs. Because of repeat appearances, more than 151 of Allen's broadcasts featured guest stars: 57 guests, or 38 percent of the total, appeared at least twice. As did all comedians, Allen had his favorite guests, and interestingly, they were neither radio nor first-magnitude Hollywood stars. Allen wrote Doc Rockwell into seventeen scripts and Jack Haley into ten between 1939 and 1949. Both were personal friends, fellow New Englanders, and former vaudevillians. Allen booked the actress Shirley Booth ten times and Leo Durocher and George Jessel nine each. From other radio series Allen hosted Jack Benny on six occasions, Edgar Bergen and Charlie McCarthy four times, and Henry Morgan, seven. Overall, only 39 of the

151 guests, or 26 percent, had careers primarily in radio. By contrast, 55, or 36 percent of the total, came from the movies, more than one might expect on a program that originated across the continent from Hollywood. That Allen's guests represented varied backgrounds and accomplishments is suggested by this list: Buddy Baer and Joe Louis, boxers; Robert Benchley and Franklin P. Adams, writers and critics; Louella Parsons, gossip columnist; Orson Welles, Renaissance man; James Melton and Albert Spaulding, virtuosos; and Carmen Miranda, Beatrice Lillie, and Maurice Chevalier, foreign-born performers. Other guest stars featured on Allen's shows were an Arctic explorer, Admiral Richard E. Byrd; a Democratic party leader, James Farley; and the guru of self-improvement, Dale Carnegie.[69]

Allen also guest-starred on other radio shows. Beginning with a much-publicized "fight" with Jack Benny on the latter's program of March 14, 1937, through a visit to "The Big Show" on November 26, 1950, Allen appeared on sixty-five broadcasts as a guest performer. Many of these were courtesy calls, payment in kind to a performer Allen had hosted—including Jessel, Ed Gardner of "Duffy's Tavern," the Quiz Kids, Milton Berle, Frank Sinatra, and, in an exchange unique enough to attract trade comment, newscasters Lowell Thomas and H. V. Kaltenborn.[70] Other Allen guests appearances were multiple visits to a show on which Allen simply enjoyed working, "Information Please."[71] During the war, Texaco's radio comic added special public-interest programs to his list of guest stops, including "Command Performance, U.S.A.," broadcast to American troops stationed abroad, and "The Battle of Main Street," aimed at civilians and featuring Chester Bowles, William Benton's partner in the advertising agency that once employed Allen and now a top government bureaucrat. Allen, often with Portland Hoffa, made a large number of guest appearances during his leave of absence in 1944–1945. In Variety's idiom, Allen's "multiplicity of guestar shots [has] been netting him coin comparable to that of stars holding down their own weekly shows."[72] Finally, on some of his guest appearances, Allen stepped out of his normal role to perform in radio plays both comic and dramatic. In April 1941, for example, he played in Norman Corwin's "My Client Curley" on the "Campbell Playhouse." Later performances of this sort occurred in an adaptation of George Kelly's *The Show-Off* and a production of George S. Kaufman and Moss Hart's *The Man Who Came to Dinner*, among others.[73]

Allen played the celebrity game and at the same time pioneered a similar audience-building, publicity-generating gimmick: the radio feud. Both devices featured the show business community feeding on itself to generate comedy, by focusing on stars' personality traits, their private lives, their enviable style of living. The intimate lives of royalty and stage performers, and the public squabbles of politicians and society families, had provided public amusement long before radio's advent. Private lives and concocted feuds became central to radio comedy because they served the advertising goal of assembling a target audience for commercials, and for institutional reasons as well. Radio consumed such immense volumes of material that writers turned to any available source of humor, and the threat of censorship placed much of what occurred in the larger world off-limits to comedy. Still, in view of his critique of these devices as weak entertainment, Allen's use of the guest star and the radio feud represented a surrender to the laziest ways of generating comedy. Fred Allen may have creatively exploited the news of the day for comic purposes, but he took some of the easy paths as well.

The grand champion of all radio feuds was the ongoing verbal duel between Fred Allen and Jack Benny. Beginning in the 1936–1937 season, the feud remained vigorous enough in June 1949 to help inspire Allen's last radio skit; it survived, through his guest appearances, until Allen's death in 1956 and still echoes in the dialogue captured on records and tapes.[74] The contestants agreed that their feud had begun spontaneously, without any consultation or planning, on Allen's show of December 30, 1936. In the "Town Hall Varieties" segment, which had recently replaced the amateur performers, Allen met a ten-year-old violinist named Stuart Canin, who expertly played Schubert's "The Bee." Allen did not prepare a script for the Varieties feature, and during his informal conversation with Stuart ad-libbed a remark about Benny's inability to play "The Bee." On his next show, Benny responded by saying that he could play the piece, threw some insulting remarks Allen's way, and the fight had begun. If it attracted listener interest and swelled audiences, the benefits were mostly Allen's. "Town Hall Tonight" lagged somewhere back in the pack, behind Benny's number-one rated program. Allen, as he phrased it later, "would be hitching my gaggin' to a star" if the feud developed.[75] The first round in their verbal battle culminated on Benny's show of March 14, 1937, when the insult hurlers staged a showdown. Though normally dubious of program ratings, Allen was pleased that this single broadcast produced a huge audience and that, over time, "the association with Jack increased our listening audience greatly."[76] Although the feud continued for years as a basic comic device in Allen's repertoire, it intensified periodically. In the fall of 1940, for example, on the release of the Benny–Allen film *Love Thy Neighbor*, and in the 1941–1942 radio season when Allen moved his show to Sunday, following Benny's broadcast earlier in the evening, the level of invective increased notably.[77]

In addition to performers who were amateurs and everyday citizens, and the guest stars, a third support group was essential to the performance of Allen's comedy—the skilled professionals of the regular cast, the "stooges" in the argot of the trade. Although definitions of a stooge fall short of describing his or her important and varied functions, they accurately denote a comic foil for the lead comedian, a secondary figure who feeds lines to the star.[78] In 1943 Jerome Beatty defined a stooge as "a character of almost any eccentric type, who works with a comedian to build laughs."[79] While singer Kenny Baker and band leader

Peter Van Steeden received billing and played themselves when given comedy roles, Allen's anonymous support actors assumed a multitude of roles in such comedy features as Allen's Alley, the newsreel segments, and the weekly skit.

Those who understood the radio comedy business, and its vaudeville antecedents, recognized the importance of a strong supporting cast. "A good stooge is a great prize in the radio marts," Jack Gould remarked in 1946, a truth brought home to Allen a few years earlier when his stooges were unavailable.[80] Because of Allen's delayed return to the airwaves in the fall of 1943, several of his key cast members joined the Jack Benny and "Duffy's Tavern" programs. When Allen unexpectedly found himself free of a movie commitment and decided to resume his program in December, his former stooges found an immediate return impossible. Until Minerva Pious, John Brown, and Charles Cantor reappeared, Allen's abbreviated season suffered through a weak start.[81] Allen compared his Art Players to the theatrical stock companies that had once performed in repertory in many localities. Like these troupes of players, Allen's "actors were extremely versatile. Each of them was an accomplished dialectician."[82] These were voice actors, of course, though some also had careers in visual performance media. They were skilled at conveying varied roles to an unseen audience solely through the manipulation of their voices. Arnold Auerbach "marveled" at the skills of Allen's five cast members when he first observed their work in 1936: "between them they had an endless repertoire of voices. All were vocal quick-change artists; each played eight or ten roles during the show."[83] John K. Hutchens, six years later, credited Allen's players with "thirty or forty dialects."[84]

An unhealthy rivalry sometimes poisoned relations between radio comedians and their stooges. Allen joked about this problem in 1947: "The stooge is the unhappiest character in radio. He knows that he is funnier than the comedian. His wife is forever reminding him. The stooge is always stalking the comedian demanding bigger billing, more money or funnier lines."[85]

Yet few ego conflicts disturbed Allen's excellent relationship with his stooges. Often, when the script ran long at rehearsal, Allen cut his own lines to preserve those of his cast.[86] In the early 1940s, Allen created the poet Fallstaff Openshaw, a character described as "The Bard of the Bowery" or "The Ogden Nash of Trash."[87] In 1942, in what the industry would later call a spinoff, actor Alan Reed, who played the poet, got his own program. In a testimonial to Allen's unselfishness with his creative property, Reed thanked his boss "for doing what no other star in our profession has ever done": grant Reed the rights to Fallstaff, no strings attached.[88] Relationships such as this created a strong loyalty and camaraderie among Allen's stooges, and made the group, even as personnel changed, a smoothly functioning unit admired by industry observers. As John K. Hutchens wrote of Allen's stooges in 1942: "Their personalities and special talents are now merged as in a good repertory company, the writers writing with an exact knowledge of individual capabilities, the actors acting with an easy assurance of one another's mannerisms and tempo."[89]

A brief sketch of several members of Allen's stock company suggests the diversity of their talents and experience. Roy Atwell came to Allen's several series of 1932–1934 from a career in the theater that began around the turn of the century. In 1907 he played leading men in the productions of Marie Cahill's stock company, and by 1911 he headed his own touring troupe, the Roy Atwell Associated Players. A veteran of musical comedy, light opera, motion pictures, radio, and the legitimate theater, Atwell was still on the stage in the late 1940s.[90] Jack Smart (1902–1960) also gained stage experience in a stock company before joining Allen's cast from 1932 to 1936. After a year with Universal Studios, Smart rejoined Allen twice in the late 1930s and early 1940s, when he contributed an early characterization to Allen's Alley. Smart's 275 pounds and his capacity for numerous voice roles—"We wondered how

From 1932 until 1949, Fred Allen's cast performed important and varied functions on his radio shows. Major members of Allen's cast included the following:

Series	Supporting Cast	Announcer	Orchestra	Vocalists
Linit Bath Club Revue	Roy Atwell, Jack Smart	Kenneth Roberts	Lou Katzman	Charles Carlile
Salad Bowl Revue	Roy Atwell, Jack Smart, Eileen Douglas	Tiny Ruffner	Ferde Grofe	Phil Duey
Sal Hepatica Revue	Roy Atwell, Jack Smart, Minerva Pious, Irwin Delmore	Tiny Ruffner	Ferde Grofe	Songsmiths
Hour of Smiles	Roy Atwell, Jack Smart, Eileen Douglas, Minerva Pious, Walter Tetley, Irwin Delmore, Lionel Stander	Tiny Ruffner	Lenny Hayton	Songsmiths, Theodore Webb, Sal Hepatica Singers
Town Hall Tonight and Fred Allen Show of 1939–1940	Jack Smart (1934–1938), Eileen Douglas (d. 1939), Minerva Pious, John Brown, Charles Cantor (1936–1940), Alan Reed (1937–1938), Walter Tetley (1935–1937, 1939–1940), Lionel Stander (1934–1935)	Tiny Ruffner (through 10/35), Harry Von Zell (11/6/35–6/26/40)	Lenny Hayton (through 9/35), Peter Van Steeden (10/2/35–6/26/40)	Town Hall Quartet (1934–1939), Sal Hepatica Singers (1934–1935), Wynn Murray (1939–1940), Merry Macs (1937–1940), Lyn Murray and Town Hall Singers (1938–1939)
Texaco Star Theatre	Minerva Pious, Alan Reed, Charles Cantor, John Brown (1940–1943)	Jimmy Wallington, Arthur Godfrey (10/42–11/42)	Al Goodman	Wynn Murray (1940–1941), Kenny Baker (1940–1942), Hi Lo Jack and the Dame (1942–1944)
Fred Allen Show	Minerva Pious, Alan Reed (1945–1946), Kenny Delmar, Parker Fennelly, Peter Donald (1946–1949)	Kenny Delmar	Al Goodman	DeMarco Sisters

Note: Portland Hoffa appeared on all the programs. If no dates follow a name, the actor performed throughout the entire series.

he can manage to keep them straight in his mind," one observer commented—led to a busy career in radio, including the title role in the "Fat Man" series of the late 1940s.[91] John Brown (1904–1957) earned greater fame as "Digby O'Dell," the undertaker on "The Life of Riley" program, than he did for his many roles on Allen's shows between 1934 and 1943. Born in Great Britain and raised in Australia, Brown's favorite dialects were English, Irish, Cockney, and Lancashire, and few in radio could reproduce their subtle differences better than he. Typical of busy character actors, Brown appeared in seven radio shows weekly in 1941. According to a publicity release, he once "stooged for the same joke for four comedians in one week . . . each time with a different accent."[92] Radio had its child actors just as Hollywood did, and Walter Tetley (1921–1975) performed many "child stooge" roles on Allen broadcasts between 1934 and 1940. At the age of sixteen in 1937, Tetley had already acted in more than 2,800 separate broadcasts. Beginning in 1941, he played nephew Leroy on the radio comedy show "The Great Gildersleeve," a role that his vocal talents allowed him to keep well into his adult life.[93]

With the exception of John Brown, none of the actors highlighted here appeared as a character on Allen's Alley. I return to Allen's supporting cast in Chapter 8 and discuss the Alley actors in detail there.

The cast was an important part of the evolution of Allen's comedy, and enabled him to explore a wide range of comic possibilities. The next two chapters center on Allen's creative work and the frequently hostile context in which it occurred.

Creating Radio Comedy

Cherchez la writer.

FRED ALLEN
Variety, 1945

By 1930, the electronic media had revolutionized popular writing in America. The motion picture and broadcasting industries had introduced new narrative forms—silent film scenarios, sound film dialogue, and live radio
drama—and had altered such older kinds of mass communication as advertising copy and news reporting. Radio's
use of writers from the mid-1920s to the late 1940s illustrates important aspects of the larger change. The demand
was great, given radio's staggering appetite for words.
American radio stations broadcast 17,000 different programs daily by 1938; in the same year, radio voices on the
four major networks spoke a total of over a million words
every twenty-four hours.[1] Various institutions, including
high schools, university colleges of journalism, and mail-
order technical institutes, soon trained students to write
for broadcasting. Publishers offered a large selection of
writing manuals to students, as well as to those who
would teach themselves to write radio scripts.

But though it offered opportunity to many authors, radio writing was a troubled profession from the start, unable

to assure all but its top practitioners the satisfactions and rewards that writers enjoyed elsewhere. Whether the radio industry would have solved the difficulties plaguing its writers cannot be known. All too quickly, sponsors and networks abandoned radio in favor of television, and the question is left for historians to ponder.[2] Yet there is good reason to consider radio writing, even though its era is past. For thirty-five years, it presented authors with unique challenges and frustrations: challenges deriving from the medium's sensory limits, and frustrations growing out of the industry's stringent limitations on free expression. Fred Allen experienced both the achievements and restrictions peculiar to radio. To discuss his case is to illuminate the medium for which he wrote as well as acted.

The many critics who expressed dissatisfaction with radio programming attacked the quality of radio writing by implication. A virtual journalistic subgenre and academic specialty by the mid-1940s, the critique of radio's cultural contribution was devastating. As expressed by John Crosby in 1948: "Radio's social position remains low—lower even than the movies, which is about as far down as the social ladder goes."[3] Or, by Robert Ruark: "Nearly everything [in radio] is either corny, strident, boresome, florid, inane, repetitive, irritating, offensive, moronic, adolescent, or nauseating."[4]

Commentators from outside broadcasting found little to praise in radio writing. When columnist Harriet Van Horne suggested that radio "stood with reluctant feet where art and commerce meet," she meant that commercial values and pressures made a real broadcast art impossible.[5] The novelist James T. Farrell despaired of a genuine democratic cultural expression in radio and other commercial media, which produced instead a "counterfeit" mass culture. A professor of creative writing at New York University believed that broadcasting precluded "self-expression in any real sense."[6] Largely unwilling to judge radio on its own terms, critics who did no writing for radio made unsubstantiated and unrealistic evaluations of radio's role in the nation's cultural life. Farrell, for example, asserted that the mass media had lured "a large proportion of the literary talent of America" to manufacture its inferior product. In addition to his overstatement, Farrell failed to note that the media trained as well as consumed authors. Among the writers who abandoned radio for "real" literature were novelists Irwin Shaw and Herman Wouk and playwright Arthur Miller.[7]

The work of established writers did appear on the air, and not for the reason suggested by Farrell. The broadcast of Archibald MacLeish's radio play "The Fall of the City" in 1937, along with similar special presentations, gave hope to those who believed that radio could serve elite tastes, rather than the masses.[8] Radio's sustaining (unsponsored) network series, such as the "Columbia Workshop," did attract artists eager to experiment in a new medium with a huge potential audience. But such programs were rare, and they carried a hidden and not very constructive indictment of radio writing; they said, in fact, that only when radio drew writers from the serious arts and abandoned its customary audience and programming did it achieve anything of value. If experimental and socially conscious drama persuaded well-educated, sophisticated listeners to turn on their radio sets, who would write what interested the audience whose daily support sustained broadcasting? Presumably not Archibald MacLeish. For, as a *Variety* columnist speculated, MacLeish's work had a limited appeal. "The Fall of the City" was "interesting to a few, exciting to a smaller few, a hopeless jumble probably to the masses."[9]

Free of the delusion that radio could measure its success only against criteria appropriate in the fine arts, those close to the daily travail of radio writing perceived different issues. For them, writing for broadcasting was more a profession than an art, but as a profession, radio writing lacked the recognition, standards for judging excellence, and protection accorded authors in other media. "'When will radio take official cognizance of the fact that the real talent lies just as much in the man behind the typewriter as in the personality before the mike?'" The industry never seriously addressed *Variety*'s question, although many in radio asked it.[10] Undoubtedly, one part of the problem was money. While featured stars and guest celebrities earned thousands of dollars for a brief performance, those who created dialogue for the headliners could expect only low salaries, compared to the prevailing rates being paid to writers in the motion picture, theater, or magazine industry.[11]

But for most radio writers, a desire for recognition extended far beyond financial considerations. Advertising agencies, which produced most radio programs, were less willing than movie studios and magazine publishers to lift the shroud of anonymity surrounding their writers; few script authors were given air credit, for example. Broadcasting's consumption of material was another of "the factors which stand between radio writing and really good writing," according to Arch Oboler, a highly regarded radio dramatist. Oboler called his medium "a quicksand into which millions of words disappear without a trace," a characterization that was hardly an encouragement to either aspiring or established writers.[12] Another problem was that the standards of excellence that programmers applied to radio drama were borrowed from other popular arts. As John Crosby noted, "A great radio play was simply the dramatization of a good movie, a good book or a good play." Decision makers were more apt to subsidize the adaptation to radio of works first presented in other media than the creation of original productions.[13] The *New York Times* critic Jack Gould identified another "lack of incentive" to potential radio authors in "the rather antiquated contractual relationship" that was then standard in the industry. Most writers, by accepting a salary or fee, surrendered "all rights whatever to their own works." With no residual rights to their ideas, many writers of ability found radio to be an uncongenial environment. Gould confirmed that this situation still existed in 1946, nearly a decade after the Radio Writers Guild (founded in 1937) was organized to defend the professional rights and enhance the earnings of script-writers. Although in many ways a dynamic industry, radio resisted change in some important areas.[14]

Finally, radio writers lived each day with a degree of interference in their creative freedom known nowhere else in American writing.[15] Although comedians probably experienced censorship more frequently than other categories of broadcasters, the scrutiny of material was pervasive in radio. Imaginative radio writing was difficult, at best. Even Hollywood screenwriters, Bob Landry wrote in 1935, did not experience "the butcheries habitually performed on radio scripts by anybody and everybody in [the] advertising agency. . . . Radio authors, like Rover, get kicked around all the time."[16] One radio writer, Paul R. Milton, suggested that radio writers were constrained "by more taboos than a pomegranate has seeds"; radio drama excluded or distorted everyday questions of sex, race, and religion for fear of offending minority segments of the vast listening audience.[17] The writer's subordination to the sponsor or the ad agency angered some. "Radio writing as it is now developed is simply an adjunct of advertising," Norman Rosten protested. "The word is fitted to the product. The product is god."[18] Others, like author True Boardman, accepted the reality that the sponsor paid the bills and "has certain basic rights in what the program says and how it says it."[19] Few in the industry, however, defined or defended the rights of authors.

Comedy writers were subject to all the occupational abuse and pressure experienced by other broadcast writers—and then some. An elite group of twenty-five to thirty writers, who averaged considerably more than the $500 per week base pay that was the industry standard by the mid-1940s, produced most of radio's comedy scripts.[20] Several factors explain the high status and compensation of these comedy writers. Comedy programs were " 'the' staple article of network programming," in *Variety*'s words. Moreover, a comedian, according to the show business adage, was no better than his or her material, and although many comedians were skilled at editing the work of their writers, few were capable of creating their own dialogue.[21] The indispensable role of the radio comedy writer was highlighted during World War II when the armed forces commandeered young comedy writers, along with just about everybody else. Hollywood was quick to offer lucrative screenwriting jobs to older radio comedy writers, to fill the studio positions vacated by its draftees.[22] Enjoying a seller's market, comedy writers occasionally even enjoyed the praise of critics whose scrutiny of American writing extended beyond broadcasting. In 1943, for example, "The Listener" surveyed contemporary humorous writing for readers of the *Atlantic*, and implied a positive answer to the question "Can it be that the best humorous writing, which is to say the most popular current echo of true American humor, is being written for the RADIO?"[23]

Perhaps it was fortunate that radio comedy writers rarely encountered such praise. They would have been hard-pressed to explain it, given the volume of negative commentary directed at their work. Much of the dissatisfaction, especially late in radio's pretelevision life, was with comedy's lack of originality. By the postwar years, major comedians like Jack Benny, Fred Allen, and Eddie Cantor had been on the air for more than a decade. Listeners were thoroughly familiar with their program formats and personal comedy styles. The *New York Herald-Tribune* columnist John Crosby found that repetition and imitation pervaded radio comedy shows. With the exception of Allen and Edgar Bergen, he wrote in 1947, "all these comedians rely heavily on a formula invented almost fifteen years ago by Jack Benny."[24] Elsewhere, Crosby accused some writers of blatantly stealing material.[25] Radio's critics frequently demanded that the agencies and networks find ways to develop new talent, original to radio rather than the stage.[26] But corporate conservatism led to artistic inertia, as the industry avoided any drastic tampering with profitable programming concepts and schedules.

Although he exaggerated for effect, Crosby was not

alone in deploring the sameness of comedy programs. He and other critics found several explanations for the problem. Not only did authors frequently change jobs, rewriting old scripts for new employers, but they also "meet, eat, talk together, and are thrown together too much," according to Ernest M. Walker, a CBS comedy analyst. "Basic material is bound to be similar when writers live . . . in each other's company."[27] And given the fact that "no medium of enlightenment, information, or entertainment had ever gobbled up material so speedily," writers and comics were not always able to sustain a fresh, original verbal comedy.[28] In 1946, Edgar Bergen suggested that alternating two comedy series in the same time period would multiply the creative time available to writers, and he offered to share a thirty-minute slot on Sunday evening with Fred Allen. But his and other proposals to alleviate the sameness of comedy on a medium that, unlike vaudeville, used up material at a killing pace, died without any real discussion. The problem has remained to plague television.[29]

Known to the public as an actor, Fred Allen was also one of radio's most talented and honored comedy writers. Several colleagues considered him a literary humorist who worked primarily in radio. As Arnold Auerbach said, his one-time boss "wasn't an actor who happened to do some writing; it was the other way around."[30] "He never moved funny," vaudevillian Bert Wheeler recalled of Allen, and the remark reflects the fact that Allen was one radio comedian whose forte lay in verbal comedy and imaginative fantasy—that is, in written humor—and not in visual, physical slapstick.[31] In a revealing comment, Allen once called himself "the poor man's petroleum nasby," a reminder that, as a student of the classic American and British literary humorists, he thought "seriously" about humor.[32] This reflective, self-educated man had as much in common with Robert Benchley and James Thurber as he did with Jack Benny and Bob Hope. The many honors given his program, including the Peabody Award in 1945, attested to Allen's achievement in translating a sophisticated understanding of humor into a successful commercial radio show.[33] Consistent with this public recognition, knowledgeable contemporaries judged Allen as "the one comedian who really knows his material," "the greatest natural comedy genius in radio," and "the comedian's comedian."[34]

Allen employed a number of assistant writers (he preferred the word "author") during his years in radio, some of whom graduated from their apprenticeship to distinguish themselves in the theater, motion pictures, television, and the novel. Most notable were Harry Tugend during the first several years; Arnold Auerbach and Herman Wouk from 1936 until America entered World War II; and, among others, Nat Hiken, Vick Knight, Roland Kibbee, Sidney Fields, Bob Weiskopf, Elizabeth Todd, Al Lewis, Larry Marks, and Aaron Ruben for varying stints during the 1940s.[35] Allen's relationship with his writers was unusual, for the comedian essentially wrote his own material. His preference for a detailed personal control of the creative process, developed during the vaudeville years, allowed a limited role for assistant writers. Allen often complained about being chained to the typewriter, but in fact he would have it no other way. "we have a writing budget of $2600 weekly and i am still in the house doing most of the work," he wrote to a friend in his typical no-capital-letters style sometime after inaugurating the thirty-minute programs in 1942. "i write the whole opening, alley and fallstaff poem myself and most weeks the guest spot has to be done over." His instinct for survival as a comic and his commitment to quality argued for minimal reliance on others: "if a comedian expects to . . . avoid the trite he had better be prepared to do either most of the writing or the selection of subject matter himself."[36]

Those who observed Allen at work agreed that he was

responsible not only for the program's structure and comic style but also for much of its specific weekly content. In 1942, John K. Hutchens compared him to a "city editor, copy-reader, and rewrite man."[37] Assigning "stories" to his assistants, such as interviewing the upcoming program's person "you didn't expect to meet," Allen reworked their material to achieve a "unity of tone" across the entire script. In 1940, the comedian described his working relationship with the "young college lads with a flair for humor" he employed. After they had submitted ideas, outlines, and drafts for several portions of the hour-long show, Allen revised their work to give the writing consistency and polish. "Every word that's written by the others must be rewritten and adapted to my style and dialogue."[38] One of his "lads," Auerbach, recalled that Allen had allowed him and Herman Wouk ample time and freedom to grow as comedy writers. Using little of their contribution at first, eventually he relied on their material with "only minor tinkering."[39] Involved in the creation of each weekly program as few other radio comedians were, Allen, in Auerbach's opinion, "was the most gifted and prolific of Radio comedy writers."[40]

As well as anyone in the industry, Fred Allen recognized the difficulties radio comedy writers faced. And he nurtured no illusions about the importance of his work; indeed, he often devalued what he did, and in a business crowded with swelled egos, he was genuinely apologetic about not developing into a "real" writer. On his bookshelves, late in life, Allen stored bound copies of his hundreds of radio scripts beside a one-volume edition of Shakespeare's complete works—"In case I start thinking a ton of cobblestones is worth as much as a few diamonds."[41] Of the whimsical poems he wrote for the program's character Fallstaff Openshaw, Allen commented: "held up to the light fallstaff's rhymes cannot hold a candle to an early exray of percy bysshe shelly's chest."[42] "i am not a quality writer but if you want quantity," he told a friend in 1945, "i am your man."[43]

Allen's rather bleak obituary of his radio show might suggest that, except for the steady employment and large income it conferred, he regretted having left the stage for broadcasting.

> a radio program is not unlike a man. it is conceived. it is born. it lives through the experiences that fate allots to it. finally, the program dies and like man, is forgotten except for a few people who depended on it for sustenance or others whose lives had been made brighter because the program had existed.[44]

Yet, Allen derived creative satisfaction from his work. In a 1954 interview, the retired comedian rejected Gilbert Seldes's suggestion that because he had criticized radio and chafed under its restrictions, his years in the medium had been "wasted."[45] To Allen, the program was important. He experienced the fulfillment that comes to all who have communicated an intellectual concept, an aesthetic vision, or a dramatic rendition to a receptive audience. He shared a sense of completion and achievement with creative individuals in other media, in the arts both "high" and "low." On broadcast nights he shared his perception of life with a listening audience of millions. "For all his careful modesty," Arnold Auerbach writes, "he was a man of consuming pride. The radio show was . . . a personal creation, an expression of himself."[46]

Some critics of mass culture deny that genuine creativity is possible in the modern entertainment media. Producers of popular art, according to Dwight MacDonald, "are as alienated from their brainwork as the industrial worker is from his handiwork."[47] Bernard Rosenberg agrees: "The artist is basically an anarchist who should have as much solitude and tranquility and as much withdrawal from commercial or political clamor as society can provide."[48] The work environment this critic describes is the antithesis of Allen's, of course. Even Russel Nye, in his supportive history of the popular arts in America, admits that the mass media "depersonalize" the popular artist and "remove him from close involvement with his art."[49]

Allen's experience as a creator of broadcast humor points to a different interpretation of the popular artist's achievement. Minimizing the interference of others in his work, Allen imposed his individual comedic vision on his programs, and this in a large industry where collaboration and collective effort were the norm. He had to make compromises, to be sure. Still, on a weekly basis, he defended his independence and integrity as a writer against the often foolish assaults of sponsor, advertising agency, and network representative. Herbert Gans has affirmed that "many popular culture creators want to express their personal values and tastes in much the same way as the high culture creator and want to be free from control by the audience and media executives."[50] And David Marc has demonstrated that certain television *auteurs* have placed the huge, bureaucratic broadcasting networks "in the service of personal expression."[51] Surely this model contributes more to our understanding of Fred Allen's radio career.

Years before he wrote his autobiography, *Treadmill to Oblivion*, Fred Allen applied the word "treadmill" to his radio experience.[52] The word expressed the daily toil and petty frustrations, as well as the deeply rooted institutional obstacles to free creative expression, he confronted during a seventeen-year career in radio writing. Many of these obstacles were inherent in the complex effort to reach a massive, dispersed, unseen audience over an electronic medium, and with comic styles and material first devised for other forms of amusement, such as vaudeville. As Allen's efforts to cope with these problems were by no means unique, this aspect of his career reveals much about the professional lives of other radio comedy writers and performers.

In his radio memoirs, Allen recalled the "drudgery" of preparing a fifty- to sixty-page script for each hour-long broadcast; his weekly schedule was "a recipe for a nervous breakdown."[53] Clothing a serious message in humor, he often used the radio comedian's harried, even desperate search for jokes as a subject of comedy. When his sponsor, the pharmaceutical manufacturer Lee Bristol, was a guest on a program in 1939, Allen described a day in the life of a comedian.

> Well 9 o'clock I start to work on the script. 9 to 1, I think of a joke. 1 to 2, lunch carraway [sic] seeds and hot water. 2 to 6 I tell the joke to myself to see if it's funny. 6 to 7, dinner. I chew the paper pants from a lamb chop. 7 to midnight. Decide the joke isn't funny, midnight to dawn, talk myself back into using the joke anyway. 8 a.m. go to bed so that I can be up at nine to start worrying again. This goes on seven days weekly.

His days, Allen admitted, were often bad jokes.[54]

Allen's demanding real-life work schedule resulted from his conscientious efforts to minimize the standardization inevitable in a medium that devoured material rapidly and exposed a performer to the same audience too frequently. "After two hundred broadcasts," Arnold Auerbach observed of his and Herman Wouk's writing for Allen, "freshness and enthusiasm inevitably wane; formulas recur; set patterns emerge."[55] Acutely aware that he performed in an era of mechanized, assembly-line, mass-produced humor, Allen often regretted the passing of more relaxed styles and forms. "In one season of radio," he observed, "we would tell more jokes than Weber and Fields probably told in ten years."[56] The Remington Rand Corporation, famous in the 1950s for its Univac computer, was working on a device called "funivac," Allen joked: "this will be an electronic brain that will write comedy scripts." Only a writing machine could keep pace with the broadcasting machine. The comedy he had fed into micro-phones, Allen feared, had simply disappeared, "caught in the crotches of pigeons, sparrows and flamingoes who had dared too far north."[57] In a sense, Allen was correct. His vast output of script material is all but inaccessible to interested readers or listeners, while libraries and bookstores offer the published works of his contemporaries.

One reason Allen's comedy has not made a more permanent contribution to American humor is its topicality. Although he was not consistently successful in avoiding the gag style prevailing in radio comedy, Allen shaped his commentary on the passing scene as an alternative to joke-telling. A popular prewar analysis of humor accurately described much of radio comedy in a chapter entitled "The Gag Industry."[58] By "switching" or "twisting," this word industry manufactured new jokes from old.[59] For example, the raw material for a gag switcher was the story about the tomato that had cut a man when it hit him in the head. It was packed in a can. Slightly altered, the tomato became flowers and the can a flower pot; or the tomato a shoe with a foot in it. The sexist classic—"Who was that lady I saw you with?" "That was no lady, that was my wife"—became "That was no street, that was an alley" or "That was no ladle, that was a spoon," and so on.[60] Gag files, such as the legendary collection of comedy writer David Freedman, together with assistants who functioned more as file clerks than writers, brought order and system to the mass production of gags. A heavily committed writer found this an efficient method for producing scripts, but the gag-file approach to comedy also had its drawbacks. Writers who wished to grow in their craft, as well as to prosper economically, had little opportunity to create, occupied as they were with recycling tested material and clichés. Arnold Auerbach, for one, became "fed up" with Freedman's joke factory, its "rehashed routines . . . laughter by automation."[61]

Allen disdained the Freedman approach to comedy as much as he regretted the circumstance that made it necessary: radio's amazing appetite for material. In 1936, Allen predicted that "Town Hall Tonight" would soon be "the only comedy program not written by dave freedman," and that distinction would be its strength.[62] As early as 1933, he complained about radio comics who relied on joke-books. Their "rancid gags have been told and told until loud-speakers are vomiting in the middle West [sic]."[63] A year later, he said of the radio gag-man: "Every joke he hears can be switched. . . . His life is a rosary of twists."[64] Among the writers Allen admired were Freeman Gosden and Charles Correll, whose comedy success on "Amos 'n' Andy" derived from situation and character development rather than gag humor. These writer–performers

> are really the cleverst [sic] team in radio today. their dialogue holds up better than any of the other shows which is really something when you realize that for ten years they have been grinding out five shows each week. their voice changes, and the fading in and out of the characters as they come and go, are uncanny. most people cannot appreciate the skill involved.[65]

Allen's method of avoiding "straight gag" humor was to "keep a little note of satire" in his writing.[66] He did that when Bing Crosby was a guest on his show in 1947. To "escape a routine joke session," the comic and the crooner collaborated on a parody skit, "Hollywood Mikado," a bur-lesque of studio stupidities done to the music of Gilbert and Sullivan.[67]

As a practicing writer, Fred Allen surely realized that he often fell short of his comedic goals. Along with the familiar old vaudeville gags and repetitious microphone routines cited earlier, he routinely used some subjects as the butt of jokes. An early "Sal Hepatica Revue" initiated a series of jokes about New Jersey on Allen's programs. Port-land was puzzled by tourists who came to New York only to pay for a ride to the top of the Empire State Building to look at New Jersey. Thirteen years later, Allen's Alley resident Titus Moody found that more people traveled across the George Washington Bridge from New Jersey to New York than went in the other direction. "People will pay anything to get out of Jersey."[68] For years, Allen shared with a national radio audience the old vaudeville convention, most commonly used in New York City theaters, of ridiculing New Jersey.

Numerous petty aggravations and unforeseen complications plagued Allen's efforts to create an acceptable script thirty-nine times each radio season. His correspondence bristled with complaints about the treadmill he trod: "i have been attempting to get out the programs, truck with the mail, appease panhandlers and look for some gentleman on variety who said that i was verbose and made the information please broadcast dull entertainment."[69] While these words seem to validate Allen's reputation as a "sourpuss," we must discount much of his grumbling. Allen found the three afternoons each week he devoted to answering the mail therapeutic, and he derived deep satisfaction from slipping folded one- and five-dollar bills into the hands of down-and-out actors, many of them vaudeville acquaintances, who waited for him on Manhattan sidewalks.[70] But other problems were real enough. For example, the military draft during World War II robbed Allen of young assistant writers and caused other abrupt staff changes.[71] And the precise timing essential in radio forced weekly cuts and script revisions.

> You should be around some night just before the broadcast when we are trying to take out forty-five seconds. . . . By the time you get to the mike you're afraid to unbend or change a word lest the thing run over. You know at 29 minutes and 30 seconds you're cut off the air no matter where you are in a sentence.[72]

Allen began one program with this announcement: "Since our first four jokes have been taken out to save time, we turn abruptly to the latest News of the Week."[73] On his

copy of scripts Allen often penciled in the final rehearsal
length of each segment. On the show of April 20, 1938, for
example, musical bridges, featured vocalists, and commercials surrounded a news-of-the-week segment of 9 minutes,
10 seconds; a featured guest was on for 9 minutes and 50
seconds; Portland's appearance took 8 minutes, 55 seconds; and there was a 12-minute, 15-second skit.[74]

Allen's protests against the price of celebrity—of
spending "his waking hours in cellophane"—certainly
were genuine.[75] As part of its preparation for a cover story
on Allen in 1947, *Time* magazine sent researchers to interview many of the comic's intimates, which made him suspect an exposé: "you'd think i was wanted for goosing a
nun the way they tore up the country looking for data."[76]

The studio audience was another target of Allen's ire;
in fact, it was one of the primary sources of his frustration
as a radio writer. Others were the listener surveys that generated program ratings and the giveaway shows whose startling popularity during the 1940s the surveys charted. As
Allen saw them, all these factors intruded on the relationship he tried to establish between his comic vision and his
listeners. Each of them posed a dilemma for Allen as a
writer and as a performer. Each diminished his ability, as a
show business professional, to create and deliver what he
considered genuine entertainment to the radio audience. In
practice, of course, Allen often failed to apply his own prin-
ciples fully. As he denounced these broadcasting institutions, he also compromised with them, playing to the immediate audience at the expense of those at home, for
example, just as other comics did. But these failures under
pressure signal the power of commercial radio's support ap-
paratus to shape programming more than Allen's ambiva-
lence.

Allen did believe that radio comedy was meant for the
listening audience. Thus it had to be an aural comedy that
utilized broadcasting's unique characteristics to best advantage, even if that meant ignoring or eliminating the studio observers. "Radio is meant for people at home," Arnold
Auerbach heard his boss say.

Give 'em the right sound effects and music, and their imaginations will work for you. A man in his armchair can picture all kinds of fantastic scenes: a fly crawling up the Empire State Building, scenes in outer space or under the sea. . . . Radio's one great advantage is that it can't be seen.[77]

Although the point seems obvious, few in radio worked to develop entertainment that depended on sound, and of those who did, more worked in drama than comedy.

Why did most comedy writers and performers work for the audible response of studio audiences rather than appeal to the minds of listeners? Their stage training was one explanation; a second was that radio sponsors were "impressed by the laughter" of the crowd in the studio. Seeking easy ways to measure the effectiveness of the comics they employed to plug their products, sponsors tended to equate an uproarious studio response with success.[78] In 1935, NBC, whose program guidelines guarded against sponsor manipulation of the studio audience, rejected a request by Allen's advertising agency to illustrate a Sal Hepatica commercial with lantern slides. Hearing "the audience in the studio . . . laugh or clap," an agency account executive explained, would cue the folks at home "that they'd be smart to send in for the photographs." The network's program director, John Royal, a former manager of Keith-Albee vaudeville theaters, quickly squelched the idea: "NBC is sending programs to an air audience," he reminded a subordinate.[79]

During his first years on the air, Allen voiced few objections to the studio audience. Sounding like a sponsor, he once even praised a live audience as a useful gauge of his scripts' effectiveness, assuming that what provoked laughter in Radio City did so as well in the nation's living rooms.[80] But as quiz and stunt shows found new and controversial uses for in-studio audiences, and as Allen's own experience with them grew, he became more critical.[81]

In January 1938, a "Town Hall Tonight" segment satirized the dilemma that a dual audience posed for radio comedians. Allen had finished poorly in a newspaper's radio popularity poll, a result caused, Portland suggested, by his neglect of the studio audience. "Most of the other comedians wear funny clothes and hit each other over the head," she observed. When announcer Harry Von Zell agreed that the studio audience's audible response to comedy determined the reaction of listeners, Allen's cast ran an experiment. Sure enough, only when Allen and Von Zell wore comic hats and hit each other with folded newspapers did the audience respond to terrible old jokes—cuing a similar response, supposedly, at home.[82]

It mystified Allen that otherwise normal citizens would join a studio audience, since all they saw was "half a dozen people in business suits and tortoise-shell glasses standing around reading into microphones off pieces of paper."[83] Allen used words like "bums," "morons," and "yucks" to characterize those who wandered into the studios, seeking, he suspected, a warm room and a comfortable chair more often than amusement or getting some idea of the technical side of broadcasting.[84] Allen was especially amazed at the "class of people" that came to observe the live rebroadcast of "Town Hall Tonight" for West Coast listeners, which began at midnight, New York time. To him, "most of them look as though somebody had turned over a pool table and they crept out of the pockets. they will only react to the stupidist material."[85] Aware that many tourists visited NBC while in New York City, Allen decided that "a slow leak in Iowa" helped to inflate the crowd that filled his studio.[86]

In spite of his disdain for it, and it should be said that this was usually expressed in moments of weariness and frustration, Allen often played to the immediate audience, a sign that his escape from the stage was never complete. He frequently ad-libbed a reaction to the studio audience's silence during dialogue that was supposed to have elicited a laugh. By doing so, of course, he ignored the possibility that those at home might have found humor in what he said. His microphone behavior occasionally gave support to those who assumed that listeners depended on studio laughs to cue their own response to material. On the program of February 24, 1946, for example, Allen told the story of the grateful housefly. It seems that when sugar had been in plentiful supply, a fly had taken some from Allen's breakfast table daily, and he had not interfered. Now, with sugar scarce, the thoughtful insect returned a few grains of sweetener for Allen's coffee each morning. "That, Portland," Allen drawled, "is a grateful fly." (No laugh.) "Also a dead fly," he ad-libbed.[87]

On some shows, Allen presented entertainment more appropriate for a stage than a home listening audience. On the premier broadcast of the 1936–1937 season, for example, he featured amateur talent auditioned in Boston by his right-hand man, "Uncle Jim" Harkins. Among the performers were a tap dancer and a trick violinist, neither of whom could "show" the radio audience his specialty. And so radio listeners heard what sounded like shoe taps on a stage, and Allen described the contortions of the musician as he played between his legs and behind his neck, against the background laughter and applause of the studio audience.[88] Neither act belonged on the radio. On a few occasions, Allen resorted to the sure-fire laugh-getter that burlesque comedians like Milton Berle, Abbott and Costello, and others had bequeathed to broadcasting: he dropped his pants. With actor Monty Woolley as his guest in 1942, and again when hosting Jack Haley in 1944 and Don McNeill in 1948, Allen revealed his gaudy stage underwear to those in the studio, and he deprived Jack Benny of his trousers in a 1946 skit.[89] The home audience, of course, was not fully aware of what was transpiring on the stage in New York. Sight jokes of this sort drew criticism. After Allen had punctuated a guest interview with ad-libs on the final show of the 1938–1939 season, *Variety* charged that he "overplayed to the studio audience," a "fault . . . noticeable on many" of his programs.[90]

Allen's dislike of the quiz/giveaway/stunt programs was legendary in the industry. He began satirizing such shows in 1939, and for a decade, until "Stop the Music" helped drive him from radio, Allen formulated a devastating, often hilarious, critique of the genre. Some observers of radio believed that the rise of the quizzes signaled the decline of radio entertainment. That one such program could nullify "all the work and wit that go to make up the Fred Allen program," Hal Block wrote, simply by promising "a refrigerator . . . and a Persian lamb jacket," symbolized a general malaise.[91] "Radio actually died," Frank Buxton and Bill Owen have written, "when 'Stop the Music' got higher ratings than Fred Allen."[92] Although he was thoroughly identified with the opposition, however, Fred Allen shared complicity in the rise of the giveaway shows —a fact that he undoubtedly never recognized and would have found difficult to accept. As a pioneer in exploring the uses of amateur performers and average citizens on a network comedy–variety program, Allen helped to invent, and his success sanctioned, the audience-participation device as a source of radio entertainment. As the authors of a *Fortune* magazine article perceptively noted early in the quiz-show cycle: "One direct and important consequence of the amateur program . . . is the so-called 'audience participation' program," which involved studio and/or home observers.[93] Allen himself helped father the monster he later battled.

Sponsors loved audience-participation programs because they were inexpensive to produce. Studio audiences, and listeners sitting by their telephones at home, apparently found satisfaction in the post-Depression get-rich-quick fantasies that the giveaway shows created.[94] But radio's professional critics voiced serious reservations about this form of entertainment, unique to radio, and Allen, serving as a critic within the industry, joined them. The radio columnist Jane Cobb compared quiz contestants to lemmings. Only some fatal instinct would make people "display [their] ignorance" to the nation.[95] To Gilbert Seldes, the quiz programs demonstrated "how far in the creation of mass man radio can go."[96]

Through satiric skits lampooning the quiz shows, and in off-mike commentary, Allen said that the quiz craze raised serious issues. The phenomenon was a testament to ignorance, selfishness, and false entertainment values. Contestants were a "herd of morons."[97] "Many winners are so dumb they can't find their way out of the building," he wrote in 1948. "Months later their bodies are found slumped over their prizes."[98] Earlier, he had advised a young correspondent how to begin her career in radio. Get on a quiz program, he suggested darkly, and shoot the master of ceremonies: "a lot of listeners will be grateful to you for killing the m.c. and good will is important if you hope to survive in radio."[99] More realistically, and prophetically, Allen warned that, for all their immediate financial benefits, giveaways could destroy radio. Creative programming and good writing would be irrelevant in a medium devoted to simple-minded greed.

> Radio started as a medium of entertainment. . . . The networks that once vied with each other to present the nation's outstanding acting and musical talent are now infested with swarms of hustlers who are only concerned with the gimmick and a fast buck. . . . The millions of listeners who seek entertainment will eventually flee the give-away programs and radio and turn to television, the theater and leapfrog. Radio City . . . will become a Monte Carlo for morons.[100]

Although the tactic could be perceived as one that lent support to the quiz-show idea, Allen's most publicized mockery of the quiz craze occurred from October 3 to November 28, 1948, when he offered to insure his listeners against the loss of prizes. If any listener could prove that he or she had missed the chance to answer a telephone quiz-show question during Allen's Sunday half hour on NBC, he would pay the cost of the lost merchandise or cash up to a total of $5,000. No valid claims materialized, and Allen canceled the offer after exhausting its publicity value.[101]

Useless prizes for useless information or demeaning stunts—in Allen's view, this was the bankrupt amusement offered by the giveaway shows. But his arguments and efforts had no effect in stemming the tide of a formula that is still successful.

That the quiz shows could rise to prominence was, for Allen, an indictment of radio's excessive reliance on program ratings. Originally intended to give sponsors and ad agencies an estimate of the size of a program's home audience, by the late 1930s the numbers generated by the Crossley, Hooper, and other commercial survey firms had led to the ranking of the most popular programs. The executives of sponsoring firms, who made the decisions about advertising expenditures, rendered life-and-death judgments about programs based on these telephone survey data, rather than on the type and quality of the entertainment that was being offered to sell their products. The numbers game made possible by the Hooperatings and similar measurements encouraged the entire industry to court popularity rather than quality and to sacrifice good writing to gimmickry, despite the opposition of show business professionals like Allen.

Allen's frustration with audience surveys grew partly from the absence of the single, visible theatrical audience whose approval or rejection alone had determined success in vaudeville. But his reaction was more than the response of an old trouper overwhelmed by the sociology of public opinion measurement. Allen also perceived some of the statisticians' methodological shortcomings and the broadcasting industry's abuse of survey data.[102] He believed that radio's decision makers attached "entirely too much weight" to numbers that did in fact have a limited utility. And he recognized that such random factors as a program's competition on another network, rather than the quality of its entertainment, often determined its fate in the ratings.[103]

Often protesting that he was not interested in his show's ratings, Allen had to recognize that a declining Hooper caused consternation "in the agency and sponsor's

office."[104] Yet he lampooned the audience measurement figures, especially the Hooperatings, the industry's standard
in the 1940s. In a skit set in "heck" (there was no "hell" in
radio's theology), Edgar Bergen had dummy Charlie McCarthy ask Allen how he had gotten "down so low." "Well,"
the comic replied, "I was going along minding my own
business, and the new Hooperating came out."[105] Express-
ing doubt about the reliability of survey figures, he once
wondered if interviewers counted Siamese twins as one or
two listeners.[106] Allen told of a comedian whose Hooperating was a minus ten. "This meant that not only nobody was listening to the program but ten people who were
going to buy radios didn't because the comedian was on
the air."[107] Adept, as always, at turning a phrase, Allen referred to Hooperatings as a "great statistical figment," a
"mythical decimal record," "synthetic figures fraught with
decimals," and "mythical pulse feelers."[108]

Allen's response to such features of the radio "treadmill" as Hooperatings, quiz programs, studio audiences,
broadcasting's relentless consumption of material, and the
pressures of tight scheduling emerged from the individu-
alistic self-sufficiency of a popular artist schooled in entertainment's premachine age. His conviction that, even in a
mass medium, the writer and performer must enjoy the
freedom to create also produced Allen's restiveness under
the constraints imposed by the powerful men who inhab-
ited the executive offices of the sponsor, the advertising
agency, and the network. His experience with these powerful figures in the broadcasting industry is the subject of the
next chapter.

Along Allen's Alley

Fred Allen was one of the most urban of radio comedians, but his Alley (and his Town Hall) had a smalltown aura, too. That Alley became radio's most important byway. In Boston (*above*), this program and a native son are commemorated. The illustrations following point up some of the major themes in Allen's performing life and times: vaudeville traces, corporate network hassle, guest stars, "feuds," sponsors, the use of visual props in a sound-only medium, ethnic humor, and publicity stunts and stills. Out of this mix came a new kind of mass American humor, with Allen the artist of the language medium.

The pictures marked *AS* were provided through the courtesy of Anthony Slide, and those marked *NYPL* are used with the kind permission of the Billy Rose Theatre Collection, The New York Public Library at Lincoln Center, Astor, Lenox and Tilden Foundations. The 1975 photo above is from the author's collection.

Fred Allen in his early vaudeville days, ca. 1920. *AS*

On the Linit Bath Club Revue, 1932–33, Fred Allen does his executive turn, with lots of props, including secretary Mary Lou Dix. *NYPL*

When Dorothy Lamour, movie-star siren of the sarong and of the Bob Hope–Bing Crosby "Road" pictures, guest-starred on the Texaco Star Theatre in 1942, Allen had to tolerate publicity shots like this one. *NYPL*

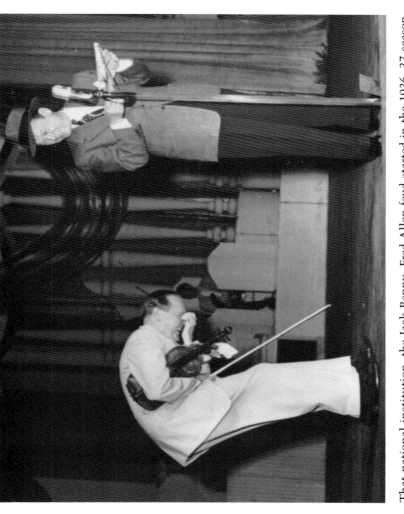

That national institution, the Jack Benny–Fred Allen feud started in the 1936–37 season over the lack of virtuosity in Benny's violin playing. It persisted through guest appearances, movies, television, and, as here, in theater appearances. Allen was a master of insult comedy, and Benny "broke up" easily. *AS*

Married in 1927, Portland Hoffa and Fred Allen were a real team professionally and personally, despite Portland's "little girl"/"dumb Dora" persona on the programs. *AS*

Long-time denizens of Allen's Alley. *Left to right:* Allen, Senator Claghorn (Kenny Delmar), Mrs. Nussbaum (Minerva Pious), Ajax Cassidy (Peter Donald), and Titus Moody (Parker Fennley). *NYPL*

Long summers spent at Old Orchard Beach, Maine, got Fred and Portland off the "treadmill" of writing, rehearsing, and broadcasting—and posing for publicity shots. Here, in the 1940s, Allen prepares for a seaweed clambake. *NYPL*

Fred Allen and
Radio Censorship

He was an independent man.

GILBERT SELDES,
Saturday Review, 1956

Mark Twain had his Mysterious Stranger say that "against the assault of laughter nothing can stand."[1] Whether or not that rhetorical claim applied in Twain's day and to his own writing, its relevance to radio comedy is most doubtful—if for no other reason than that radio censored its comedians. If Twain had worked in radio, and it flourished within two decades of his death in 1910, he would have observed a timid bureaucracy carefully filtering the programming that reached audiences and thus blunting much of its satiric content. At the time of Fred Allen's death in 1956, Herman Wouk described his comedy program as a "weekly satiric invention," and its contemporary observations "knife-like comment on the passing show of the thirties and the forties."[2] Although Allen was no Mark Twain, he did direct his laughter at some of the most powerful institutions of his day, including the radio networks themselves, the advertising agencies that created programs, and the sponsoring firms that underwrote them. If his was a typical "assault of laughter" during the age of

mass electronic entertainment, the powerful not only survived the attack but barely noticed it.

Fred Allen's goals were modest: he did not want to
change society through satire but to entertain a massive
audience with humorous material that included social
commentary. His seventeen years of mild fun-poking, in-
nocuous enough by most standards, often provoked bitter
hostility and heated controversy. A wide array of would-be
censors, ranging from heads of corporations to individual
listeners, attempted to limit his freedom to create (see the
appendix at the end of this chapter). Yet, on balance, comedians like Fred Allen, who properly protested against such
interference, enjoyed greater freedom than they were willing to admit.

Entertainment programs generated some of the *causes
célèbres* of radio censorship; Mae West's "Adam and Eve"
skit on Edgar Bergen's show in December 1937, in which
she vamped the serpent in her very suggestive style, is a
foremost example. Her voice and delivery, more than the
lines, occasioned listener charges of "pornography" and
"sacrilege." Still, it was the broadcast of controversial political, social, religious, and even medical views that most
often forced officials and the public to measure the limits
of free speech in this new medium of communication.
Strong and colorful personalities found radio to be an effective tool. The "radio priest" Father Charles Coughlin, the
Kansas goat-gland surgeon "Doctor" John Brinkley, the
Southern California evangelist Aimee Semple McPherson,
and the isolationist leader and one-time American hero—
aviator Charles Lindbergh were among those who tested
broadcasting's ability to accommodate minority view-
points.[3]

The monitoring of "mere" entertainment shows may
seem trivial compared to the critical public issues on
which such people spoke. But the ongoing contest for control of comedy material was a significant part of wider de-
bates about broadcast censorship. Affecting jokes rather
than the nation's health or foreign policy, the censors' ulti-

mate target was artistic freedom of expression. Was radio, indeed, primarily a medium of mass amusement? Or was the comedy incidental to the commercial pitch, in the interest of whose marketing effectiveness business executives had every right to shape and control program material? If so, were news programs to be subject to commercial interests to the same extent as comedy shows? In practice, neither radio's creative people nor its business managers exercised absolute control over program content. The parties to weekly disputes over script concepts and language usually settled their differences through informal, if often raucous, negotiations. The resulting compromises fell short of guaranteeing radio's performers and writers the freedom enjoyed by those in the fine arts, but the creators of radio programs were hardly passive, accepting the interference of puritans and profiteers as the necessary price of employment in the industry. The situation was more complex, and more interesting, than that.

As Fred Allen fought to preserve his freedom to write and perform comedy that reflected the concerns of his times, he became known as radio's most frequently censored comedian, but many radio entertainers faced similar difficulties during the 1930s and 1940s. Yet no individual experience can stand apart from the context in which it unfolded. By the early 1930s, a complex corporate structure produced and delivered network programming to national audiences. Since that structure consisted of independent but interrelated elements whose interests often diverged, "radio censors" were not a single entity, nor was the industry arrayed in all of its imposing might against the lone comedian. On occasion, a star might face a phalanx of sponsor, ad agency, and network, but he generally found both allies and adversaries within the broadcast system.

An early Herman Wouk novel centers on the shortcomings of commercial broadcasting and the network structure through which radio personalities had to guide their scripts. After wartime military service, his apprenticeship on the Allen program now only a happy memory,

Wouk launched his career as a novelist with the publication of *Aurora Dawn* (1947).[4] The plot of the novel ran like this: Convinced that the seductive power and deceptive claims of product promotion violate ethical tenets, Father Calvin Stanfield plans to denounce advertising on his regular program of radio sermons. But his sponsor, the Aurora Dawn soap baron Talmadge Marquis, enraged that a mere employee would undermine public confidence in the source of Aurora Dawn's marketing success, tries to remove Stanfield from the air. Although Marquis fails to do so, Wouk presents a frightening portrait of sponsor attitudes and authority. Learning that Marquis plans to deny him the microphone, the minister appeals to the network president, Chester Legrand. Surely the head of a national broadcasting corporation can overrule the sponsor of a single program and permit him to speak. Marquis cannot "own" the time his program fills each week, Stanfield objects. Time belongs only to the God who created it. But a legal contract, not a sermon, embodies business's theology, as Legrand explains: "The use of our microphones and sending stations belongs to Mr. Marquis on a certain hour each Sunday night. What is broadcast then, within the limits of decency, of course, is in his power, and nobody else's, to decide."[5] The network, Marquis reminds Legrand, merely rents equipment and time to sponsors. That time, says Marquis, "is mine to do with as I will."[6] Few portraits of sponsor-controlled radio are so stark as this one.

An incident from Fred Allen's experience is no less dramatic. In April 1947, Fred Allen was nearing the end of his second season on NBC for Standard Brands. Since his return to radio a year and a half earlier, the comedian had chafed under what seemed to be—no records were actually kept—more frequent and more unreasonable demands for script alterations than ever before. NBC had a deserved reputation as a more severe editor of comedy scripts than its major rival, CBS, primarily because of the policies of the NBC vice-president for programming, Clarence L. Menser. Allen later called the man a "petty tyrant." A journalist described Menser as "a conservative old-timer who holds fast to the policy . . . that gags about NBC on NBC are strictly taboo."[7] Allen, who loved to burlesque radio, was surely one of the network's stable of comics Menser had in mind when he vowed, in the spring of 1947, to "clean up the air." Well aware that the owners of some NBC affiliates had objected to the comedy material that they had to carry on network broadcasts, Menser announced that he would restrain funny men "who think they have the right to say what they want."[8]

Allen's show of April 13, 1947, went over its allotted time because studio laughter of greater duration than anticipated delayed completion of the carefully timed thirty-minute script. The network, employing standard policy, cut the program short. But on his next show, on April 20, Allen offered a different explanation of what happened to the severed ends of NBC programs. His story, which was aimed at Menser and was included in Allen's opening dialogue with Portland, alleged that a network official accumulated all the seconds and minutes cut from comedy shows for his own vacations. Menser had rejected the routine prior to airtime; Allen read the lines anyway. Menser cut the program from the air during the approximately twenty-five seconds that Allen took to relate what he later admitted was a weak attempt at humor.[9]

The response to "l'affaire Allen" revealed widespread dissatisfaction with Menser's brand of trivial, humorless, but nonetheless unjustified censorship. The American Civil Liberties Union (ACLU) registered its concern over freedom of speech. Other comedians rallied to Allen's cause by ridiculing the network. Compounding his error, Menser cut offending portions of Bob Hope's and Red Skelton's shows from the air during the week following Allen's blackout. But he could not pull the plug on the adverse mail and press comment that soon prompted network officialdom, in growing embarrassment, to offer Allen an honorary vice-presidency (he angrily refused) and welcome comedy scripts that satirized NBC.[10]

The president of NBC, Niles Trammell, admitted to company stockholders that the network had handled the incident badly; the admission was less of a concession to public and press criticism than to Allen's sponsor and advertising agency, who supported their comedian.[11] Four days after Allen's broadcast, Standard Brands defended his "right to free speech."[12] Within forty-eight hours of the "dead air" affair, the J. Walter Thompson agency announced that it would bill NBC for that portion of Allen's half hour that had been paid for but not broadcast. On the Sunday night time spot, that amounted to "a nice little chunk of dough."[13] For a while, industry rumors had CBS, whose executives no doubt enjoyed NBC's discomfort, preparing an offer that would lure Allen back to its microphones.[14] Allen gained relief from the censor's harassment without leaving NBC, however. In August the network replaced Menser with a new program chief, Ken Dyke. By employing a form of ongoing consultation with the company's comedians over program standards, Dyke liberalized the code under which they worked.[15] Allen later told columnist Ben Gross that Dyke understood the needs of comedy writers and performers. "For the first time since I've been at NBC, my relations with the script censors are pleasant."[16]

The relationship among radio's triumvirate of sponsor, advertising agency, and network was neither equal nor harmonious. Through their ability to censor scripts, the networks that seemed all-powerful to performers like Allen in fact used their authority in an almost desperate attempt to reclaim the control over programming that they had abdicated to sponsors and the agencies that served them. Many authorities confirm the sponsor supremacy that Wouk portrayed in *Aurora Dawn*.[17] During the 1930s and 1940s, advertisers, unlike those who sell via fifteen- or thirty-second television spot announcements today, owned entire programs, and some of them frequently meddled in entertainment matters. Not all of them, however, among the men who personified corporations, were like Allen's

"Town Hall Tonight" sponsor, Lee Bristol, who had no desire to intervene in the work of writers and actors. But others, like George Washington Hill of the American Tobacco Company, or the fictional Evan Llewelyn Evans of Beautee Soap in Frederic Wakeman's novel *The Hucksters* (1946), used their nearly absolute power to toy with performers and humiliate account executives.[18] Any radio sponsor, eccentric or not, individual or corporate, "was king," writes the historian Erik Barnouw. "He decided on programming. If he decided to change programs, network consent was considered 'pro forma.' The sponsor was assumed to hold a 'franchise' on his time period or periods. Many programs were advertising agency creations, designed to fulfill specific sponsor objectives."[19] John Royal, a retired NBC vice-president, recalled the arrogance of some sponsors: "In the old days they thought if they sponsored a show they owned us."[20]

In the Alice-in-Wonderland world of radio during Allen's era, the networks assumed public-service and legal responsibilities for a product, commercial programs, as opposed to sustaining or unsponsored ones, that they did not produce or own and that they only imperfectly controlled. Although some columnists drew attention to the advertising agency's key role in determining what programs sponsors would fund and networks would broadcast, most Americans would have considered it surprising news that "broadcasters have only the most remote connection with the programs they broadcast."[21] Some of those outside broadcasting recognized the system's shortcomings and were angry. Frederic Wakeman told "radio people" to "take back your programs from the hucksters. Take back your networks. Take back your stations and do your own programming without benefit of what any sponsor thinks any program should be."[22]

Many broadcasters recognized the dilemma they faced, but responded with nothing more than industry pieties. Although "many of our shows are built outside the organization—we are responsible for what goes out to the public," a network executive wrote in 1935. "NBC must maintain close supervision over all its broadcasts, whether agency built shows or NBC programs."[23] But as Bernard B. Smith observed during the war, the networks could not "exercise real control over the programs" they carried. Censorship of scripts was their only instrument of supervision and containment. Not only was it an imperfect tool for ensuring that "content is neither politically partisan nor offensive to the general public," but censorship also virtually guaranteed disputes with sponsoring firms, ad agencies, comedians and their agents, and others.[24]

The networks needed to control the content of programs that others created because they were uniquely vulnerable to listener dissatisfaction. Because ad agencies, writers, talent agencies such as the Music Corporation of America (MCA), and even sponsors easily escaped public notice, the networks were the logical (i.e., most visible) targets of alienated individuals and interest groups. And when disgruntled listeners voiced their objections about programming to the management of local network outlets in Fresno, California, or Memphis, Tennessee, the affiliates joined a chorus of complaint too loud for network officials to ignore.[25] That they not only took notice of public criticism but also overreacted to it by becoming excessively cautious arose in large part from the networks' sense that they had created a new kind of entertainment audience and had the responsibility of serving it. "The broadcasters have been warned since the beginning that they cannot in good taste do everything that the theatre does":[26] network executives read and remembered such reminders. Their radio programs reached a live, massive, national, undifferentiated home audience. The contrast with theater—legitimate, vaudeville, or movie—could not have been greater. Theatrical audiences were local rather than national, and actors or directors could and often did shape a performance to suit local conditions. To join a theater audience, individuals had to make an effort not required by radio: dress for a public event, leave their homes and travel some distance to a theater, and purchase a ticket. To a significant degree, theatrical fare segmented the audience by class, age, and gender; and law or custom segregated it by race in most American towns and cities.

By contrast, network radio's audience, if it did not include literally everyone, included representatives of nearly every group and interest. All received the same programs, with no local variation possible. Inevitably, some segments of the broadcast audience could be counted on to take offense at some part of almost every program, and many of them were eager to share their objections. The networks realized that their prosperity derived from the marketing of a sponsor's product and not from selling tickets to a show, and alienated listeners made poor customers. Thereby, censorship of program content was essential to corporate well-being, and consequently to a comedian's continued employment and large salary. The imperatives of the marketplace for goods, not ideas, governed radio's application of censorship. When one recalls that vaudeville and the movies, which did not invade the home, employed rigid censorship at the time to retain their audiences and protect profits, perhaps it is understandable that radio did the same. The cultural historian Russell Lynes writes that the Motion Picture Production Code of 1930, which Hollywood's trade association began to enforce four years later, "danced to the Catholic tune, a surrender by the industry to a parochial system of morality."[27] Although radio responded to the "public" outcry orchestrated by the Catholic Legion of Decency and other religious groups after the Mae West-as-Eve incident of 1937, it never capitulated on so massive a scale as the Hollywood studios did to pressures for change.[28]

While it was vulnerable to pressure groups, radio also had to worry about government regulators. The technology of radio required that the federal government allocate frequencies among stations and issue licenses to them. Although the radio legislation of 1927 and 1934 forbade government control of program content, the potential of such interference was a factor in radio's exercises in self-censorship. Public criticism of programming often came first to the Federal Communications Commission (FCC), which had the authority to renew or withhold station licenses. Broadcasters acted out of fear, Earl Sparling noted in 1939, "fear of a club held over their heads by a handful of political appointees in Washington . . . who, in turn, are at the whim of any Nice Nellie in the country."[29] Sparling's journalistic style overstates the case, but a part of the unique context in which radio self-regulation occurred was a governmental presence that was conspicuously missing from other industries of mass entertainment.[30]

For their own good reasons, in short, network broadcasters felt compelled to control program content. But they refused to interpret script censorship as merely an act of self-preservation, declaring instead that censorship was not an adversarial but a cooperative process, benefiting all who enjoyed radio's growth. NBC may have admitted its error in the Menser–Allen affair, but that kind of admission was rare. Ordinarily, as network officials saw things, it was the unreasonable agency copywriters or radio comedians who upset the coveted stability and predictability that were the aim of published, impartially applied program guidelines.

The 1938 guidelines offered by NBC can serve as an example. Executives worked hard to create a detailed set of Program Standards, incorporated in a document that was a booklet of do's and dont's, for "those who use . . . our facilities," especially sponsors and agency people employed to write commercials and prepare entertainment.[31] In theory, employees of NBC's Continuity Acceptance Department, "who are on the firing line daily," measured scripts against the Program Standards and eliminated conflicts by editing the scripts. The (theoretical) result: improved program quality, satisfied listeners, and therefore a network fully able to "help a client sell his goods."[32]

At least some NBC executives knew that attempts to define prevailing standards of good taste for a national community would be vague or too restrictive. One of the commandments in an early draft of the 1938 document, for example, was "avoidance of unpleasant or gruesome statements."[33] In a meeting of the Program Standards Committee, William S. Hedges informed his colleagues: "To observe this regulation would leave little in the field of drama, literature or the opera for broadcast material."[34] Similarly, the standards required "reverent" references to the "Deity," proscribed remarks offensive to religious or racial groups, outlawed obscene material, and advised an attitude of respect for public officials in all programming. Whatever their merit, such general guidelines left enormous room for honest differences of opinion and interpretation, as did guidelines that prohibited the exploitation of "insobriety" and references to "criminal or morbidly sensational news stories."[35] Intended as much for sponsors as for performers, the NBC document banned the distribution of product samples to studio audiences and protected listeners from "tiresome repetition" in commercial copy.[36] Advertisers were not to compare their products with the competition's products or make false or exaggerated claims. To avoid any suggestion of the discredited medicine shows, NBC threatened to investigate claims made for health products.[37] The Program Standards regulated the use of testimonials from such fictitious "experts" as alleged doctors, regulated dramatic scenes in ads, and carefully laid out guidelines for children's programming.[38] As for procedure, NBC required that its editors see "all continuities"—any words to be spoken on the air—at least forty-eight hours in advance of broadcast. The decision of the network in cases of disputed dialogue was final.[39]

On paper, it was a tidy system, motivated by the finest intentions, and designed to control overzealous capitalists as much as comedians. But NBC's standards failed, in the application, to prevent arbitrary script changes derived from silly personal prejudice, ignorance of show business conventions, or inflexible blanket prohibitions. Top company executives, who did not have to apply the guidelines, privately admitted that failure was inherent in the very concept of standards. To exclude from radio drama such devices as terror and suspense, Niles Trammell recognized, deprived even children's programs of their audiences—and thus their sponsors. Much would depend, he told fellow executives, on "how this regulation is administered." Along with Trammell, William Hedges objected to prohibiting the use of slang in dialogue. "What is 'slang,' and when does a slang phrase by common acceptance become a part of the American language?"[40] If the company's leadership harbored misgivings about the application of standards, outside critics had no doubts about the failure of radio censorship.

John Crosby, the astute radio critic of the *New York Herald-Tribune*, called broadcast censorship "the misuse of an originally sound purpose." Obviously networks wished to avoid offending listeners, but "this desire to please . . . is pursued to such lengths that radio programs are robbed of much of their vitality. The intentions are good but the administration is ridiculous."[41] The fear of pressure-group or government retribution discouraged experimentation with program concepts and development of new talent that radio so badly needed, just as it shackled established performers like Allen. Crosby described broadcasting as

> the most timid medium of them all. Radio was afraid to offend the Negroes, the Irish, the Jews, or the Women's Bowling League of East Orange, N.J. . . . The only group radio ever stood up to was the atheists. Atheists were never allowed time on the air because the broadcaster was afraid God couldn't stand criticism. . . . Sheer inoffensiveness is so small a virtue as to be no virtue at all.[42]

Many others shared Crosby's concerns. Peter Artzt was a copywriter employed by an ad agency, and an advocate of sensible script monitoring by stations and networks. But his experience with censors exposed a "unilateral approach" that was not always open to the sponsor's interests. "They set the regulations—they prosecute—and they render judgment."[43] Others found fault with the censors' stupidity. Don Quinn, who wrote the "Fibber McGee and Molly" scripts, offered to put out a book on radio censorship entitled "Idiots Delete."[44]

Fred Allen's particular censorship problems deserve some explanation. To begin with, it was in the nature of his work as a comedian to poke fun at people and subjects that others regarded quite seriously. Yet, to make some people laugh is to offend others; this was a reality ever on the minds of radio censors. In addition, radio comedians regularly attracted audiences that were among the medium's largest. Potentially controversial material thus received wide exposure. Allen was a stage comedian transformed into a broadcast performer, and this fact also increased the chances that he and the censors would clash. Allen performed a carefully prepared routine in vaudeville, but he could and did depart from the script. This spontaneity, recalled by such observers as Douglas Gilbert and S. J. Perelman, would inevitably challenge radio's obsession with control. On the Broadway revue stage during the 1920s, Allen had breathed in an atmosphere of creative freedom that would be totally foreign to radio's business leadership during the following decade. "There are so many things that enter radio that the theatre is lucky to miss," he observed after several years on the air. The noisy complaint of "a druggist in Texas" could alter an entire network series. In the theater, entertainment professionals made the decisions. In radio, listeners, censors, sponsors, and others "who know nothing about show business" could destroy a good program.[45]

Disputes over ad-libbing, a common stage device, troubled the networks' relations with their comedians. One censor, Dorothy Kemble, wrote: "Ad libbing on the part of comedians is probably the most difficult problem that NBC encounters."[46] Impromptu remarks contradicted the network's drive to control program quality, the concept on which its Program Standards rested. Don E. Gilman, the chief of NBC's Hollywood studios, reported "considerable difficulty" with ad-libbing West Coast comics in August 1938.

> As an example, only last week, after considerable argument, the continuity on Burns and Allen was changed so that reference to their new sponsor [to-be] was not included. Despite this, they put it in by ad libbing it into the program. Eddie Cantor simply cannot be trusted at any time not to mention his own sponsor when appearing as a guest star somewhere else. The same is true of Jack Benny, Bing Crosby and others.[47]

Fred Allen, back in New York, loved to ad-lib, and he was good at it. He sprinkled his conversation with off-the-cuff remarks that helped spread his reputation as a natural wit, and ad-libbed almost as frequently when he spoke to millions over the air. As NBC's only major comedy performer to broadcast from its Radio City headquarters in New York, by the late 1930s his spontaneous remarks attracted close network scrutiny. "Mr. Allen ad libs continually," Kemble reported to a superior in 1938, and on occasion his remarks gave new meaning to approved dialogue. "Some portions of the Master Copy bore little or no resemblance to what actually went over the air. . . . There have been cases where particularly dirty jokes were made out of seemingly innocent ones."[48] She gave no examples.

If Cantor and Benny ad-libbed their sponsors' products when making guest appearances, Allen often, and in violation of network policy, mentioned brand-name products on his program. In 1938, General Mills asked NBC to verify a report that Allen had mentioned the breakfast cereal Wheaties. A web of correspondence that connected Denver, San Francisco, Chicago, New York, and Minneapolis eventually relayed the network's finding that the reference "was an ad lib proposition and thus impossible to trace."[49]

Allen's ad-libs produced more than superfluous paperwork. His "plug" for RCA Victor records in February 1938 brought an angry response from the network. "Will you please impress upon the agency," one NBC official wrote to another, "that their funny man is not to mention any recording company on the air under pain of mayhem."[50] Although Allen understood the needs and joys of the ad-libber, the remarks of a wisecracking cast member could cause him to share the network censor's anxiety. Roy Atwell, in a 1933 repeat broadcast "for the Coast" at an early morning hour, departed from the script to say: "I can lick my weight in wild-pratts." Sometimes NBC itself caused an ad-lib. When a clerical error transposed PWA (the New Deal's Public Works Administration) to WPA (its Works Progress Administration), Allen observed on-air that the network was "taking liberties" with government agencies.[51]

Both on the stage and in radio, Fred Allen drew much of his material from contemporary American life. The sources of his humor—politics, business life, manners and morals—were matters that the networks considered sensitive and likely to generate a flood of angry letters. Allen's contemporaneity, his satire of the current scene, caused particular problems with Janet MacRorie, the head of NBC's Continuity Acceptance Department during the second half of the 1930s, and members of her staff. Allen's ad agency, Young and Rubicam, complained about Tom Robinson, a MacRorie assistant. "Mr. Robinson is devoid of humor in the broader sense and is . . . completely out of sympathy with practically everything that Fred does. . . . He has expressed complete bewilderment at some of Fred's most characteristic techniques."[52] MacRorie was similarly unsympathetic to Allen's brand of humor. Recognizing that his "course of program building includes a barrage of names of real persons" from the news, she fretted over the legal responsibility, should such individuals sue.[53] As early as February 1938, Allen referred to a possible third term for President Franklin D. Roosevelt, a sensitive topic and one certain to upset some Democrats as well as Republicans. If MacRorie suspected that her proposal regarding such incidents was futile, she made it anyway: "Do you think it would do any good if we had a meeting with Young and Rubicam and Mr. Allen and discuss Mr. Allen's sources of humor?"[54] Throughout his lengthy career, Allen never changed his "sources of humor"; they pleased him, and they worked with audiences.

The traits of Allen's comedy style and substance mentioned thus far applied to many of his colleagues as well. But one cause of his continuing censorship problem was the unique Allen personality. Just as the network felt that it needed to control the programs it broadcast, Allen insisted on controlling his life, including his regular weekly routine of creating a radio script. A part of Allen's larger quest for security, we may speculate, was establishing and guarding the integrity of a predictable, and therefore comfortable, work routine. "Mr. Allen's entire professional life is directed toward next Sunday night's broadcast," John K. Hutchens wrote of the Texaco programs during World War II, "and his schedule is relentless."[55] One NBC executive, I. E. Showerman, wrote in 1938: "Please bear in mind that Fred is a rather unique sort of fellow. We speak of creatures of habit—Fred is in a rigid mold of habit."[56] Recalling the years during which he worked as an assistant to Allen, Arnold Auerbach commented that his boss's "life was ritualistic in its regularity. . . . His week, immutable, symmetrical as the solar system, revolved around a single sixty minutes—the hour on Wednesday when 'Town Hall Tonight' was on the air."[57] Allen resented and fought against tampering with his patterned weekly existence, at the heart of which was the creation of his programs. And among those who most frequently intruded on his routine, with blue-penciled objections to his work, were the censors.

Many who had only a passing acquaintance with Fred Allen and Portland Hoffa considered them eccentric. Allen never learned to drive an automobile, for example, and the couple preferred walking or taking the subway to hailing a taxi. They studiously avoided New York's nightclub society. For years, Portland and Fred lived in a theatrical hotel, and when he finally acceeded to her desire for an apartment, they settled into an undistinguished building on West 58th Street. Allen worked on his scripts alone, at a wobbly card table in his littered study. Portland or her sister Lastone (the name reflects the fact that she was supposed to have been the last Hoffa child) typed the scripts from Allen's pinched handwriting; no one else could decipher it. A simple and predictable life—a workout at the neighborhood YMCA gym several times a week, dinner at an Italian restaurant on the same evening each week, letter writing on three afternoons, small gatherings with a few close friends like the H. Allen Smiths and Alton Cooks. Such was Allen's routine. He lived for Portland and for the program. And in New York's show business community, her devotion to him was legendary.[58]

Allen's privacy and work style did not mesh well with NBC's bureaucratic imperatives. His weekly routine varied over time, of course, as the scheduling of his program changed. But in the late 1930s it formed around the broadcasts of "Town Hall Tonight" from 9:00 to 10:00 P.M. Wednesdays, with a repeat broadcast for the West Coast from midnight until 1:00 A.M. Thursday. While he thought about his next program during the remainder of the week—he was an inveterate pocket-stuffer, filling his jackets with ideas for routines jotted on scraps of paper—Allen waited until Sunday to write the new script. He wrote through the night, and at 8:30 Monday morning NBC, without variation, received the fifty- to sixty-page manuscript. By 11:00 A.M., after mimeographing, the Continuity Acceptance staff began checking it. The censors worked under pressure and without lunch, for Allen's cast gathered at 1:00 P.M. for the first rehearsal, and the agency called by 3:00 to receive the network's objections. The censors complained that, frequently, material that they wanted revised or omitted remained in Allen's first revision, prepared for Tuesday, and the second, for broadcast day, Wednesday. Allen rewrote parts of the script that were too long, other portions that simply had not worked in rehearsal, and in the rush of rehearsals and revisions it is probable that many of the censors' comments did not gain his attention, especially since the agency had to relay them to him. It was also, of course, relatively easy to ignore network objections in all the confusion. The censors believed that, willfully or accidentally, Allen and the agency disregarded their requests for script changes. Allen often felt wronged too. In December 1946, for example, as he returned to the studio from dinner on the night of his broadcast, NBC ordered that some previously approved lines be cut. It is surprising that the all-too-real atmosphere of prebroadcast tension and frenetic activity did not undermine the comedy fantasy that was the program.[59]

These tensions are evident in the controlled sarcasm of Janet MacRorie's description of her weekly experience with Allen and his agency's people. From about

> one o'clock on Monday . . . until Wednesday at nine, post meridian, Continuity Acceptance presents politely, begs and cajoles Agency representatives to persuade their talent, namely Fred Allen, to refrain from such examples of libel, derogatory reference, vulgarity, cross-reference, and other irregularities as may have been encountered in the script before us. No representative of Continuity Acceptance has approached said Fred Allen on the matter of producing the script earlier. Our heart-felt sympathy is extended to the unfortunate person who did.[60]

Although Allen, in fact, did accept most suggested script changes, "when goaded too far, he rebelled." Arnold Auerbach supports this conclusion with a rendition of Allen's response to a "must" deletion delivered by a young agency employee.

Here's a "must" order from me to you. Since reading probably wasn't on your college curriculum, I'll deliver it verbally. I want you to paddle into the slime of your censor's subconscious, lower your head into its fetid depths, and tell him I am *not* cutting that joke. It's what we call a blackout, and an entire bit has been built around it. . . . Tell him there's only one other sound that resembles the squealing of bagpipes, and that's the noise the censor will emit when I commit intimate personal mayhem on him with his own shears.[61]

It is not recorded whether the junior executive pursued a career in radio.

Radio's fear-driven censorship affected Allen's scripts in two basic ways, and a few examples of disputed dialogue illustrate how censors complicated comedy writing. Censors, of course, attempted to identify objectionable material before airtime, excising, or attempting to excise, words, phrases, or entire routines. But, despite such vigilance, the comedian, his agency, and the network were the targets of angry protests when material that survived the editing process managed to offend some listeners.

Until his retirement in June 1949, Allen often drew on the Cold War for comedy, but the network disallowed some references to the international situation. A case in point is this one: "Why is Thanksgiving postponed in Moscow?" "Because Russia can't get that piece of Turkey."[62] Afraid that they would offend New York City's Mayor Fiorello La Guardia, the Commonwealth Edison Company of Illinois, and large corporate advertisers, NBC axed a prison skit with implications for a recent city scandal, a joke about the indicted utility magnate Samuel Insull, and mention of the word "huckster" on separate Allen broadcasts.[63] Allen wanted to write a sketch on the new social security idea then being debated, but he gave it up because it would have attracted the unfavorable notice of radio's

New Deal regulators.[64] John Crosby called NBC's removal
of the statement "Motion pictures are your best entertainment" from an Allen radio script "the funniest battle Allen
ever lost."[65] Radio found it embarrassing to admit that
Americans found amusement while separated from their
radio sets. Yet, on another occasion, censors deleted Allen's humorous commentary on a radio broadcast that
had unintentionally gone beyond entertainment: Orson
Welles's Halloween 1938 version of "The Invasion from
Mars." What Washington investigated, comedians could
not kid.[66] And although both sponsor and agency approved
the following joke in a 1939 Allen script, the network re-
moved it: "What causes your dog to bark so much?" "It's
the guy upstairs. He's a Pole." Dorothy Kemble explained:
"There is no doubt in our minds that this joke will be particularly offensive to persons of Polish extraction or nationality," and the resulting "illwill" would tarnish both
the sponsor's program and product.[67] While the censors
were sensitive to ethnic-group alienation, they were not
open to, or willing to learn from, Allen's use of words that
were not a part of the average American's vocabulary. At
various times, he was challenged on "Rabelaisian," "titil-
late," "saffron," and "pizzicating." All sounded "suggestive," as in "pizzicating a woman's lavaliere."[68]

Prebroadcast deletions illustrate the industry's men-
tality; postbroadcast complaints reveal something about
public sensitivity and, in some instances, avarice. If protests over content cannot justify radio's nervousness, perhaps they help explain it. On occasion, Allen wounded
local community pride. In the late 1930s he publicly apolo-
gized to Pottsville, Pennsylvania, after a "broken down
gag" riled the local chamber of commerce.[69] On his program of December 6, 1939, Allen and guest Jack Haley, recalling the theatrical hotels of their vaudeville experience,
joked about the tiny rooms they had occupied in Philadelphia back in 1914. Two days later, a Philadelphia newspaper, the *Evening Public Ledger*, objected editorially to
Allen's implication that the city's hostelries offered visi-

tors cramped quarters. The newspaper's sensitivity to something Allen had not said reflected Philadelphia's efforts to attract the 1940 national political conventions. On the December 13 broadcast, Allen, enjoying the opportunity to have the last word, shaped his apology into another humorous observation. Were the city's modern hotel rooms large? asked Harry Von Zell. "Large, Harry?" Allen replied.

> Why the Benjamin Franklin Hotel is so named because you can fly a kite in any room. The Walton Hotel rooms are so big the [New York] World's Fair is stopping there when it goes on the road next Fall. . . . The Warwick has rooms so big Billy Rose is rehearsing his new edition of the Aquacade in a sink there.[70]

Just as inadvertently, Allen ruffled professional pride in January 1940. Chatting with the Hotel Astor's veteran doorman about the large tips that Wall Street brokers had given while the bull market raged in the 1920s, Allen mentioned that some of "those boys still chuckle about their financial pranks as they're sitting around up in Sing Sing [prison] today." Against the barrage of protest from the financial district, which included complaints to the FCC, Allen wrote a humorous apology.[71] Well before his Senator Claghorn character bothered some southern patriots after World War II, white regional and racial pride, easily offended by the Yankee media, caused Allen minor annoyance. On the program of May 8, 1935, both Allen and guest Beatrice Lillie ad-libbed comments about Robert E. Lee that "drew a hefty backfire from listeners" in the former Confederacy, according to *Variety*. Lillie, a British musical comedy star, called the late general "the old guy with the whiskers," while Allen recalled Appomattox in the words of a song hit: "I Surrender, Dear."[72] The respect that some southern listeners demanded for a deceased hero they also demanded from an athelete who, to many black Americans, was a modern hero. As Allen wrote to a friend in

1940: "many southerners complained about joe louis calling me fred on the program."[73]

Persons who claimed violation of their rights threatened Allen with legal action. Quite by chance, Allen occasionally duplicated the names of real people in his quest
for humorous-sounding names for fictional characters. An
actual Sergei Strogonoff and Sadie Moskowitz claimed
compensation from NBC, but, as the network wrote to the
latter's legal representative: "There was . . . no adequate
basis for the inference that your client was being imper-
sonated or that her name was being used."[74] In 1938, a
Georgia firm claimed that Allen had infringed its copyright
for a game called "Kwiznite" when he drew members of
the studio audience to the microphone for conversation
and a "midget quiz."[75] On separate occasions, listeners
handicapped by anemia, unemployment, and stammering
protested that Allen's routines had exploited them. "I have
the privilege to turn his Radio Program off," a WPA (the
New Deal work-relief program) worker, Sid Haster, reminded Allen's sponsor. "Fred Allen owes the stammers
[sic] an apology," wrote George L. Reimer of Indianapolis.[76]

One of Allen's favorite lines was " 'heck' is an NBC
word. They don't believe in heaven or hell or the Columbia
Broadcasting System."[77] He played with the words "darn"
and "damn" in a similar attempt to joke about radio censorship. Jack Benny, appearing on Allen's show in December 1937, spoke of "water over the darn." Allen questioned
the phrase. "Yes," Benny answered, "you know how careful we have to be in radio." A female caller, minutes later,
told a staff person at NBC's New York outlet: "We caught
the full implications of those 'over the darn' remarks." The
network "will hear from our organization [the League of
Decency] tomorrow. You may count on it."[78] Other listeners maintained that Allen's use of the fictional name
Jillaber Q. Muckenfuss referred to an obscene story, and
that Allen, who was a devout Catholic, had disparaged organized religion.[79] Allen offended both capitalists and communists, along with colleagues in radio. In 1934, "the
Communist colony around Union Square" denounced Al-

len as "a tool of the capitalists" for unspecified comments made on his shows; earlier in the year, a transit firm in New York had denounced Allen for making light of a taxicab strike whose "leaders were allied to a communist group."[80] Allen's burlesques of husband-and-wife breakfast programs, and of daytime serials, also brought injured protests from affronted broadcasters.[81]

Fred Allen often complained about the limited subject matter that radio's apprehensions forced on comedians, as he did in a letter to H. Allen Smith in 1940: "each week fifty percent of what i write ends up in the toilet. . . . if there were only more things in radio to have fun with the writing would be a cinch. as it is practically everything is taboo and we end up with ersatz subject matter and ditto humor."[82] Allen's point about radio comedy is well taken, but he exaggerated. Although written Program Standards seemed rigid, and their interpreters strict constructionists, Allen in fact managed to broadcast a considerable amount of material that challenged, when it did not violate, his networks' criteria for acceptable script copy. This generalization applies to written and approved, rather than to ad-libbed, dialogue. An indication of what Allen "got away with" balances our catalogue of censors' cuts. Although his was a limited freedom, Allen enjoyed more of it than he admitted.

For example, although he consciously avoided the social security program as a skit subject, Allen joked about other New Deal programs. In 1940, to give one illustration, he sang: "O bury me not on the Lone Prairie. Or I'll be plowed under by the C.C.C." So much for the New Deal's Civilian Conservation Corps. The networks announced their intention to monitor political humor carefully during the 1940 presidential campaign. But during that year, and again in the 1948 Truman upset election and indeed throughout the decade, Allen made light of such natural targets of laughter as the Republicans' political exile. The party chose Philadelphia as its 1940 convention city, he quipped, to "be closer to Washington."[83]

On a number of occasions, Allen playfully stepped on,

and even over, the network-imposed and watchdog-monitored line that separated mild profanity and sexual innuendo from sanctioned subject matter. His scripts place in doubt an early reviewer's conclusion that Allen would need little script supervision "because he is too clever ever to have to be off-color."[84] Ruth Brindze cited a sermon title used on an Allen program in the mid-1930s: "Skiing on the Sabbath," or "Are Our Young Women Backsliding on Their Week Ends?" Allen's delivery stressed the word "ends."[85] A seemingly obvious target of criticism, the line nevertheless received NBC approval. Allen often made fun of marriage, domesticity, and divorce, which subjects obviously also evoked some rather racy exchanges. In a 1935 program, Portland announced that she was going to the pet shop. Allen responded: "Don't tell me they've opened shops for petting . . . with automobile dealers still making closed cars."[86] In a 1938 skit, with Allen portraying a bank president, one of his vice-presidents develops a hangnail, prompting the double-entendre observation: "You know how important the finger is in the banking business."[87] On more than one occasion, Allen's scripts employed, without actually saying them, words that common usage categorized as profanity. A real town in Maryland outlawed swearing in places of business, and Allen tore out the newspaper item for a 1936 sketch. In it, a constable leaps out of hiding to make an arrest when Mrs. Green asks the hardware man for lye. Grease is "dammin" her drain.[88] In other Allen comedy features, a college band gets into trouble for forming all but the *o* in its "Hello" on a football field; a presidential candidate, who promises a government dam for any area that gives him their support, will not "give a _____" if he loses; a contortionist makes "an *S* of himself"; and daily injections by a doctor make a sickly child "all shot to health."[89] An early "Town Hall Tonight" script contains the phrase "you silly ass," but there is no notation that the censors cut the line.[90]

The network censored. Allen groused and complained. Yet he managed to twit the purity leaguers with naughty references, and, more significantly, to cast his satiric eye on sacred beliefs and powerful American institutions. Allen's long experience in radio's bureaucratic maze produced not only frustrating incidents and angry comments but also some of his finest, most distinctive comedy. His delightful yet devastating burlesques of ad agency executives, sponsors, and network vice-presidents remain among his most memorable contributions to radio humor. It is worth remarking that, given the context in which radio writers and performers worked, institutional restrictions and interference stimulated comedy almost as well as they suppressed it.

Appendix: The Complex World of Network Radio

Between the radio artist and the audience stood a network of powerful business and governmental organizations. It is no wonder that veteran performers fondly recalled the simpler world of vaudeville, where performers presented tested material to live audiences. On network radio, the often conflicting goals of each of the following had to be considered.

The comedian and writer. Their goal (in Allen's case, he combined both roles) was to entertain a huge, unseen, dispersed, and undifferentiated national audience with aural comedy. Fred Allen was a show business veteran who believed that sponsors and network executives were ignorant of mass entertainment and should confine themselves to manufacturing toothpaste or improving the technical quality of broadcast signals. He would be responsible for the writing and performance.

The sponsor. The sponsor bankrolled the program package: network time, talent, and so on. Sponsors were clients of advertising agencies; agencies defended the interests of sponsors in conflicts with networks over such matters as the propriety of advertising appeals. Sponsoring firms naturally feared alienating potential customers with program content, a fear strong enough to sanction censorship.

The retailer of the sponsor's product. Retailers played a part in the broadcasting equation when they depended on the product for all or a large portion of their business— Rexall Drug Stores, for example, or, in Allen's case, the independent retailers of Texaco products or Ford automobiles and trucks. These networks of small businesses were involved in the shows because they formed a major part of the firms' promotion.

The advertising agency. The ad agency was the locus of activity in the broadcasting industry, the initiating and coordinating organization that made the system work. The agency acted as the broker and brought other elements of the system together. It acquired a sponsor for an existing program or a new program concept. The agency bought the network time and facilities on behalf of the sponsor. The agency was a major source of program ideas, and it employed the talent. For its services, the agency received a 15 percent commission. The agency could, and often did, defend the comedian against sponsor discontent with the program; it defended the comedian and script against the network's desire to alter it. Part of the agency's job was to defend the client (sponsor) against restrictive program standards at the network.

The talent agency. Large talent agencies, such as the William Morris Agency, represented performers in a number of show business fields, including radio. Originating in vaudeville and the earlier days of Broadway, the agencies adapted nicely to motion pictures, radio, and television. In the 1940s, talent agencies themselves entered the business of producing program packages for sale to networks, thus short-circuiting the ad agency.

The network. The radio networks owned the equipment and studios, and organized the linkage of affiliated stations around the nation, leased by those who owned the programs. The networks themselves owned some programs, primarily sustaining shows that satisfied the vague and rarely enforced expectation that radio should provide education, serious cultural events, and other public service to listeners. Networks stood in the midst of conflicting interests. They received the criticisms and complaints of listeners, affiliated stations, sponsors, ad agencies, and talent. The government's regulatory power, especially the power to grant and withhold licenses from affiliated stations, could not be ignored by network officials. With actual pressures and potential consequences in mind, networks established public guidelines for program content and advertising copy. The networks' difficult position grew out of their imperfect control of the material for which they were legally and morally responsible.

The network censor. Each network invented a euphemism for its censorship office—Continuity Acceptance at NBC. The overburdened staff of these offices filtered scripts in an effort to enforce a network's program standards. In disputes with agency representatives and talent, the lower-order bureaucrats in censorship often called on the support of more powerful network executives, such as the vice-president for programming.

The affiliate. With few exceptions, affiliated stations were owned independently of the network. On occasion, owners of affiliates objected on regional (e.g., southern sensitivity on racial matters), moral, political, or other grounds that program content was tasteless, insulting, partisan, or otherwise objectionable. The affiliates' complaints might reflect their listeners' opinions or merely their owners' sensibilities. Local station owners played a role somewhat similar to that of theater managers in vaudeville: both could register negative reviews of entertainment with the national office, which might force a change in the "act" or bring about its early demise.

The ratings. For fees paid by subscribers (networks, agencies, sponsors, and others), audience-measurement firms generated quantitative data on listeners, which became the measure of a program's and performer's success and the show's life span. Decision makers easily translated quantitative shortcomings into qualitative failure.

The Federal Communications Commission (FCC). With the power to grant and renew station licenses, the FCC held a powerful instrument of retaliation over the heads of broadcasters. Networks were not licensed, but their ability to function depended on the licenses of affiliates. The FCC, in theory, also could recommend that Congress consider censorship legislation if private broadcasters allowed content to get out of hand in any one of a number of areas. Network officials tended to exaggerate the potential of government censorship.

The audience. Very few listeners ever expressed objections to programming or performers in letters. But those few, simply because they spoke out in anger, had influence, and timid radio executives feared that the alienated were legion and that they were massing to institute a boycott of the sponsors' product.

Fred Allen's Comedy
of Language

In Radio . . . nobody sees you.
"TEXAS STAR THEATRE,"
April 2, 1944

The 1930s and 1940s were years of mighty as well as mighty interesting events in the United States and abroad. For Fred Allen, the Great Depression, the world war—especially on the home front—and postwar tensions with the Soviet Union all found a place in his skeptical observance of current events, as did "human interest" stories from the newspapers' back pages. Allen's scripts were especially sensitive to goings-on in his own town, New York City. More than on any other network radio program, the metropolis of Mayor Fiorello La Guardia, Coney Island, immigrant neighborhoods, the subway, and the Brooklyn Dodgers played a continuing role on Allen's shows.

The medium in which he labored also influenced Allen's comedy each week. This chapter details, as Chapter 1 tried to suggest, ways in which the sound medium estabished unique comedic possibilities, which Allen used effectively. At the same time, broadcasting's technological and organizational imperatives confronted entertainers with a vast audience that demanded an unending supply of fresh material, and material that would not offend anyone. Radio also imposed routine but significant temporal restraints on its comedy writers and performers. Although magazine and newspaper humorists obviously worked within editor-determined spatial limits, they avoided the anxieties of live radio broadcasting: more material than time would allow, for example, or extra minutes to fill. Allen had twelve minutes of airtime in which to develop an idea through dialogue. While humorists in the print media were able to employ descriptive passages or linger over a character's thoughts or feelings, and stage humorists could utilize visual comedy, over the airwaves comedians had to convey their material through lean fragments of thrust-and-response conversation. Understanding Allen's comedy means keeping this and other features of broadcasting in mind.

Influences less immediate also gave contour and nuance to Allen's comedy. His comedic vision, his particular view of the world, grew out of biography and personality. Allen emerged from a turn-of-the-century urban, ethnic, Catholic milieu. Moreover, his style of communicating with an audience—the comic devices, presentational forms, personae and archetypes that appeared in or inspired his scripts—emerged with substantial maturity from his stage experience. And since the popular theater of vaudeville and revue had their own history, Allen unconsciously represented decades of Anglo-American theatrical tradition every time he sat before his typewriter to create a broadcast.

The historian Lawrence W. Levine, impressed with the achievement of American humorists in several popular arts during the 1930s, interprets their triumph as a unique response to particular historical circumstances. "The distrust of institutions, the sense that the world no longer worked as it was supposed to, that the old verities and certainties no longer held sway, was expressed in one of the decade's most ubiquitous forms of humor: the humor of irrationality."[1] Students of culture require more than a his-

torical context to explain the shared comic style of Goodman and Jane Ace, Bud Abbott and Lou Costello, the Marx
Brothers, Ogden Nash, James Thurber, and W. C. Fields, to
mention those whom Levine cites—and Fred Allen. We require more if for no other reason than that these humorists
developed their style before the stock market crashed in
late 1929. They learned their trade during years of journalistic apprenticeship and stage or motion picture experience. Many of them settled on a zany, nonsensical form of
humor because it satisfied their personal artistic requirements, while it pleased the urban reading and theatergoing
public. That Fred Allen in the 1930s was the same "nut
comic" who delighted S. J. Perelman in 1921 cautions us to
be as cognizant of long-standing traditions as we are of the
spirit of the times. A "humor of irrationality" may have
offered an especially appropriate response to the mind-
numbing impact of the Great Depression, but it evolved in
happier times.[2]

Without question, Allen worked in a formulaic mass
medium, and much of what he did was conventional and,
after a while, predictable. But he shared much with nine-
teenth- and early-twentieth century literary (or "high culture") humorists.[3] All creative people work with assumptions shared by others, usually many others, and with set
character types, plots, and themes. The famed *New Yorker*
style of comic expression settled into a rather formulaic
pattern between the late 1920s and World War II.[4] Some of
the conventions Allen used were trite and trivial even in
his day, and some, like ethnic and racial stereotyping, measure the cultural distance that separates our time from his.
But devices such as satire remain vital weapons in the humorist's arsenal as writers and performers continue to observe, with a smile, the world around them. Fred Allen's
substantial contribution to his generation's satiric commentary will stand as his most important legacy.

Allen's style of comic expression, one that was especially effective on radio, might be called verbal slapstick. It relied on the mainstays of traditional American oral humor—language, talk, pronunciation, and dialect (although it did not take the form of rambling stories shared 'round the wood stove).[5] The best of radio's comic language, including Fred Allen's, was not restrained, subtle, or understated. Listeners, often engaged in domestic activities, could not easily ignore this broadly farcical comedy that encouraged, even commanded, people momentarily to abandon reality, to revel in the fantastic. *Variety* tried to convey its qualities in terms like "dementia" and "topsy-turvy thinking." Some of Allen's lines were "gems from the boobyhatch."[6]

The most effective language of radio comedy conveyed a sense of spontaneity, of delight-provoking surprise. It was a comedy of exaggeration reminiscent of the tall tale, of characters and situations improbable, often literally impossible. Allen practiced what Arlen J. Hansen terms "transformational humor," one that uses language to alter "reality through creative and inventive talk." The transformer's words create worlds of fantasy, dreams, "magnificent lies."[7] Of the many vaudeville comics who came to radio accomplished in the language of exaggeration and the surrealistic humor it conveyed, Allen, and other "nut comics" combined "outrageous distortion, noisy satire, and mad humor, adding up to an insanely imaginative entertainment," in Douglas Gilbert's words.[8]

To be sure, more subdued approaches also flourished. Characterization was the hallmark of such comedians as Jack Benny, the fallible, lovable butt of his cast's jokes;[9] George "Kingfish" Stevens of "Amos 'n' Andy," the con artist and henpecked husband; Henry Aldrich, the frantic teenager; "Our Miss Brooks," the underpaid schoolteacher frustrated in romance; and Fanny Brice's "Baby Snooks," the impish child. And the typical problems, settings, and characters found in radio's situation comedies of the 1940s and 1950s, such as "Father Knows Best" and "Ozzie and Harriet," assured listeners with familiar, true-to-life circumstances. But those who best exploited radio as a sound medium departed from reality, stretched the imagination, tested credulity. From so many examples, one can recall Ed, Jack Benny's long-time subterranean vault guard, who had known Paul Revere and responds to the password "the British are coming," or Fibber McGee the "handyman," whose rewired vacuum cleaner hid underneath the couch when Molly turned it on.[10]

Allen's comedy created a world of "bedlam," to use one of his favorite words, a world in which all things were possible. On one Allen show, a professor at Bedlam University missed a faculty meeting; he was "so slow he's probably been overtaken by the ivy again," the president (Allen) decided.[11] On another, an unemployed and hungry fire-eater from a disbanded circus caused a ski resort to close when he gorged himself on flames from its furnace.[12] The instances are many. Portland Hoffa described the Australian Fig-Bird: "It lives on the seeds in figs." "But there aren't any figs in Australia," Allen objected. That's all right, Portland assured him. "The Australian Fig-Bird dies at birth."[13] A hurricane hit the East Coast in 1933 with "wind so strong in one New Jersey town that it blew two prohibition workers into a speakeasy. Luckily, the wind blew the speakeasy into a church and the bartender was converted."[14] In a creative effort to save his plantation from the creditors, a southern gentleman decided to cross a cotton plant with a glassblower. "Ah'll sell Aspirin bottles with the cotton growin' right in the top, Suh."[15] In conversation with an upstate New York fishing guide, Allen revealed his method for catching eels. After emptying a box of starch into a river, he waited downstream at the first sharp bend. Unable to make the turn, the rigid eels beached themselves.[16] During a wartime campaign to conserve tires, New York City used a magnet to clear the

streets of nails. But the too-powerful magnet moved the
Flatiron Building two blocks off its foundation and "pulled
U.S. Steel down seven points" as it passed through Wall
Street.[17]

What follows in this chapter is a discussion of the
world of radio and show business as sources of Allen's
humor. I criticize Allen's reliance on several conventional
comedy devices, such as insult humor, but I praise his efforts, which went beyond those of most contemporary
broadcasters, to explore radio's unique qualities as a sound-
only medium of mass entertainment.

As we have noted, Fred Allen resorted at times to popular
comedy conventions because they were ready-made and
convenient—whether or not they fit the broadcast medium. Some, such as gender stereotypes, pervaded the national culture, assuring an instant response, especially to
jokes about female behavior or character. Some contemporary media critics complained that stereotypes—"the ab-
sent-minded professor, the sexually unattractive schoolteacher"—and other tired comedy devices not only bored
but also insulted the intelligence of listeners.[18] A convenient source of gags, these devices found their way into
even the best radio comics' work. Whether laziness or the
constant need for new material pushed comic writers toward the easy laugh, their use points to a failure of creativity.

In real life, a Roman Catholic ceremony joined the
Irishman Fred Allen and the Jewish woman Portland Hoffa
in what was to become a successful marriage. Yet, on his
radio broadcasts, Allen presented marriage as a farce. During the Linit series, his scripts made light of marital infi-
delity, a theme more common in "sophisticated" Broadway revues than on radio. "Judge Allen," in one courtroom

skit, advises a woman not to sue for divorce, even though she has caught her husband kissing other women. Why? "It may be your turn next," says the judge.[19] "We Want Divorces . . . Down with Allen" chant a group of disillusioned husbands outside his matrimonial agency in another skit. These domesticated males push baby carriages occupied by their "soiled samples of posterity," symbolizing man's loss of freedom in marriage.[20] And when husbands stagger home after an evening of drinking, their shrewish, neglected spouses beat them up and empty their pockets of loose change.[21]

In equally hackneyed views of women, wives shirk domestic responsibilities as readily as men. In a role-reversal skit entitled "Ten Nights in a Bridge Club," a wife-and-mother abandons her family to play cards every night. Her young son pleads in song:

> Oh mother, dear mother,
> come home with me now.
> The clock in the steeple strikes two. . . .

With familial as well as musical disharmony, the mother croons:

> Oh Junior, dear Junior,
> don't raise such a row.
> I'll wipe up the floor with you.[22]

A society woman's most recent divorce rests on grounds of "insufficient closet space." Her husband had appeared unexpectedly while she entertained guests: "There were four gigolos and three closets."[23] In some of his domestic burlesques, however, Allen seemed to voice the traditionalist's regret that unwelcome change threatened marriage and family life in America. The spread of easy divorce laws from Nevada to Florida in 1935 prompted him to imagine vending machines that dispensed marriage licenses and divorce decrees: "a marriage certificate and your correct weight for five cents."[24]

The "dumb Dora" stereotype, a legacy of vaudeville, "had become a national tradition off stage as well as on" by the 1920s.[25] Comics Gracie Allen and Jane Ace typified early radio's confused, delightfully innocent sources of malapropisms, non sequiturs, and other nonsensical talk. Marie Wilson, as "My Friend Irma," played a similar role in the 1940s and 1950s. Portland Hoffa's microphone persona drew on, but was not limited to, the dumb Dora or "dumb girl" stage tradition.[26] Portland appeared as a "little girl," perhaps in her early teens, who reported the absurd goings-on at her home, and who sometimes extracted gems of insight from the sludge of her confusion. But not often. When Allen asked for bookends, Portland handed him the last few pages of two novels.[27] Playing a coed at Bedlam University, she recited what she knew about the Middle Ages: "They raise the dickens with most women's figures."[28] The stereotype held that women talked too much. When Allen's fictitious news microphones visited an elderly woman who was growing her third set of teeth, her husband expressed only mild interest. "But," he added, "if she starts growin' a new tongue—I'm off to Reno."[29]

Many of Allen's comedy bits expressed the traditionalist's fear that the results could be serious, as well as comic, when women assumed male roles. Even during wartime, as Rosie the Riveter became a national heroine, Allen had a construction boss complain about the "headache" that women workers gave him: "Since the company started usin' women sandhogs, we had to put a powder room in the decompression chamber."[30] Allen's treatment of women in traditional comic forms predated the unaccustomed changes created by World War II. In a 1936 newspaper, he found a prediction that the American people would elect a female vice-president by 1940, and a woman chief executive a decade later. Speculating about what that could mean, Allen imagined a secretary of the interior who thinks her job is interior decoration. She orders yellow robes for judges and lavender paint for battleships. The many buttons on her telephone confuse the President.

"Why," she sighs, "can't the White House afford a zip-per?"[31]

Fred Allen joined numerous popular entertainers in the practice of gender stereotyping for comic effect, but he shared a second comedy convention, parody, with creators in both the fine and popular arts. The scholar Gilbert Highet comments that parody is one of the major vehicles of satire.[32] As a satirist of some of the dominant values and institutions of his time, Allen occasionally used parody to good effect, but he also used it simply because it was an ancient and effective convention of his profession.[33]

Parody had deep roots in entertainment. One need only recall Mark Twain's use of Shakespeare in *Huckleberry Finn* to know that Allen had skilled and honored predecessors in the use of parody. As Lawrence Levine notes: "Twain was employing one of the most popular forms of humor in nineteenth-century America."[34] Nathaniel Benchley, whose father, Robert, was a skilled parodist, has suggested that the goal of such writing is more than exaggeration to the point of ridicule. The author, work, or category of works parodied ought to represent real achievement because "there is no point jeering at third-rate material." Parody poses unique challenges for the writer, who must enlarge and distort while imitating, and must have an audience with some knowledge of the original.[35] Measured against such literary criteria, most radio parodies, Allen's included, failed.

Many of Allen's parodies were of contemporary works, a strategy that allowed him to exploit what he and his audience knew best. But his successful adaptations of Sir William S. Gilbert and Sir Arthur Sullivan's *H.M.S. Pinafore* and the *Mikado* proved that he could deal with other materials as well. Parodies of both works had appeared as early as the late 1870s, and Allen took advantage of a new wave of interest in them in the 1930s and 1940s.[36] Allen's "Brooklyn Pinafore," first broadcast on November 25, 1945, also drew on the media-generated zany reputations of New York's Borough of Brooklyn; its baseball team, the

Dodgers; and the team's manager, Leo "The Lip" Durocher.[37] It was the music of *H.M.S. Pinafore*, rather than its story or characters, that listeners recognized, a feat in itself when we consider the very limited vocal talents of Allen and Durocher. The story line of the parody ran as follows:

The arch rivals of the Dodgers, the New York Giants, have invaded Ebbets Field, the Dodgers' home park, to challenge the Brooklyn team.

> Brooklyn rooters are sitting around in their underwear. Ushers are running up and down the aisles with rocks looking for Giant fans. Peddlers are going through the stands selling raw meat sandwiches . . . for the kiddies.

Dodger captain Leo Durocher gathers his players around home plate, and sings his boast: "I am quiet and subdued. . . . I never call an umpire jerk!" The chorus of ball players knows better: "So give a cheer and give a shout/For the Dodger captain wit' the big loud mouth!" From the bleachers a "mystery girl" throws a rose to Leo. More accustomed to flying rocks than flowers in Ebbets Field, Durocher finds the young woman. "Go out and moider dem slobs," she shouts encouragement to the Dodgers, and then confesses her love for Leo.

> I'm called little Bobby-Socks
> Sweet Little Bobby-Socks
> My heart for you, Lippy, could boist.

But they cannot marry until her "old man" approves, "and dat's gonna be tough."

The climax occurs in the bottom of the ninth inning. With two men out, Leo drives the ball into the outfield. He rounds the bases and slides across home plate as the Giant defender's throw arrives. The home-plate umpire, "Cockeye Allen," screams the verdict: "You're *ouuuuuuttttttt*."

As the argument over the call rages on, Bobby-Socks introduces the umpire as her father. "Me marry an umpire's daughter?" Durocher exclaims. "They'll throw me outta 'Who's Who.'" But umpire and manager make peace, as Cockeye sighs: "At last an umpire hears a kind word in Brooklyn." The production ends with a gentle thrust at baseball, as Allen explains how he became a major league umpire.

> As the years went by I grew up a schnook
> My eyes were so bad I couldn't read a book
> The Army took me but they sent me back
> I tried to kiss the General 'cause I thought he was a
>   WAC
> I'm still half blind with no physique
> That's why I am an umpire in the National League.

As the "Brooklyn Pinafore" closes, Durocher pledges not to berate umpires any longer. A new day has dawned in Brooklyn.

Other Allen parodies drew upon a broad range of materials. During his initial series of programs for Linit, Allen parodied the drama of Eugene O'Neill (program of October 30, 1932), Sir Arthur Conan Doyle's Sherlock Holmes stories (November 27, 1932), the Greek drama *Lysistrata* (January 1, 1933), and the Tom Show based on popular dramatic versions of *Uncle Tom's Cabin* (February 12, 1933). In later series, he wrote parodies of the following: *Mutiny on the Bounty* (November 21, 1935); *Showboat* (June 21, 1939); *Dr. Jekyll and Mr. Hyde* (October 8, 1941); *Les Misérables* (October 18, 1942); *Jane Eyre* (February 20, 1944); the motion picture *The Lost Weekend*, with guest Ray Milland (March 24, 1940); *Western Union* (February 26, 1941); *Citizen Kane* (November 5, 1941); and *The Egg and I* (April 13, 1947). In the skit "Nicotine Alley" Allen had fun with the long-running Erskine Caldwell play *Tobacco Road*. Experienced at caricaturing hillbillies—Allen's character Teeter Fester (wordplay on *Tobacco Road*'s Jeeter

Lester) tells his son to "run yer arm down the Gopher Hole" to get dinner—Allen built the little drama around the idea that backwoods folks dislike cleanliness. When the government man says that Teeter will be in "hot water" if he refuses to sell his land to the army for its training camp, he sells—to avoid taking a bath.[38]

On three of his programs, Allen did versions of the Richard Rodgers and Oscar Hammerstein II musical *Oklahoma*, which had made its debut on the wartime Broadway stage in 1943. In one skit, the musical became "North Dakota," which Allen described as a "farmhand's Ballet. The stage is a wheatfield. 200 farmhands going against the grain." The opening number begins:

> Nunnnnnnnnnn-orth Dakota
> There's nothing there but sky and dirt
> Where the boundary lines
> Are Burma Shave signs
> And buzzards circle round alert.[39]

Whether irate North Dakotans wrote letters to CBS is not known. But on the following week's program, Allen scheduled Rodgers and Hammerstein, who appeared with a "lawsuit" charging plagiarism. All kidding aside, Allen found that parody could stimulate actual legal charges. Eleanor Biggers Cole, the widow of Charlie Chan's creator, sued Allen in 1942 for plagiarism in a parody of the Chinese detective.[40]

Allen kidded the "B" Western motion picture, Hollywood's reliable revenue producer during Allen's years on the air, with horse-opera heroes like Roy Rogers and Andy Devine or with some incongruous cast choices. Hollywood gossip columnist Louella Parsons, for example, played an Indian—"Sweet Souix."[41] Allen ran a divorce ranch in "Reno—Land of the Great Divide," a skit that confirmed that wordplay, rather than sagebrush, grew luxuriantly across Allen's western landscapes.[42] And dialogue like the following appeared, as "Sheriff" Allen orders a Mountain

Martini: "A tall glass of Buffalo Drool with a puma's eyeball floatin' in it." "A puma's eyeball?" the bartender asks. "Ayer. When ah say 'Hyar's lookin at ye,' ah like to have suthin looking back at me."[43]

Allen's clear favorite for parody was the detective story; it supplied his programs with their longest-running continuing character, and Allen's personal favorite, the ·Chinese detective One Long Pan, who debuted on May 1, 1935.[44] Spoofing the Sherlock Holmes tradition, hard-boiled American private eyes, and police investigators, Allen assumed many crime-solving roles: Inspector Allen of the Bedlam Detective Agency in the early 1930s; Inspector Bungle and his bloodhound Watson; Holmes imitators Hemlock Bones, Fetlock Bones, and Hemlock Drones; and Sam Shovel, Private Eye. In 1942, Allen and guest Maurice Evans presented *Macbeth* as a murder mystery, and he mocked Humphrey Bogart's popular film *The Maltese Falcon* in a skit entitled "The Maltese Parrot."[45]

Allen's detectives were incompetents who somehow stumbled their way through misinterpreted clues and past falsely accused suspects ultimately to a solution, all in twelve minutes of dialogue. The slapstick pace of Allen's murder-mystery skits, reminiscent of the Keystone Cops, helped reduce the detective formula to a shambles. The radio historian J. Fred MacDonald speculates that the detective story, as "a secular Passion Play," offers more to the public than entertainment. In radio's detective shows, the invariable triumph of justice reaffirmed society's moral values. The punishment of those who violated person or property sanctioned order over disorder, stability over chaos.[46] If so, then Fred Allen's detective parodies clearly came down on the side of comic chaos.

None of Allen's detectives commands respect. A police chief questions Inspector Allen's ability: "You couldn't find a Cohen in the Bronx."[47] In the skit "Who Killed Kirk Rubin?" One Long Pan announces: "I am the great Pan!" Mrs. Rubin responds: "Say, I could use you under my ice-box."[48] A woman tells Inspector Bungle: "By me

you couldn't inspect a gas meter."[49] Long Pan has trouble
with the language. For "ends abruptly," he says "bends cor-
ruptly"; he calls Ellery Queen "Celery Spleen." In each
case, he discovers a "lewolower" (revolver).[50] Trying the
wrong doors, Long Pan mistakenly enters closets in victims' homes, then tries to save face. It was a "clues
closet," he explains in one episode.[51] Inspector Bungle orders all present at the crime scene not to move. "I got yez
covered." Then he fires his gun: "It's the Bungle Test, Bud.
De party dat don't jump is the body."[52] When several ban-
quet guests confess to the murder of the after-dinner
speaker, Bungle turns to the "Eenie, Meenie, Meinie, Mo"
method, and fingers himself for the killing![53] "Fetlock
Bones," Sherlock Holmes's brother-in-law, appears to practice an amazing deductive ability, in imitation of his famous relative. Arriving at a country manor, he explains: "I
know you are Mr. Basketville's butler, Rancid. You were
born near Surry With The Fringe On Top. You have no
shin in your right leg. Your father raises aspidestras and
you have a cousin Cecil who has a punctured ear drum."
Astounded, the butler asks, " 'Ow did you know?" "I'm on
your draft board," Bones confesses.[54]

The bizarre solutions to Allen's murder mysteries, in
keeping with a comedy of exaggeration and fantasy, uncov-
ered crimes of shallow frivolity rather than greed or passion. A "Vegetarian Fanatic" named Quentin Scurvy murders wealthy businessman Barclay Rappaport, "the
Meatball King."[55] A mystery writer, S. S. VanBrine, fakes
his own death. He wants Long Pan to solve his "murder,"
which he then will incorporate into his latest novel.[56] A
sports reporter kills the football star because he cannot
spell his name, Koskicheckowitch.[57] Gaffney Grimes did
not die at the hands of a murderer, but rather passed away
while quietly listening to the Jack Benny program. "Gaffney Grimes was bored to death."[58]

Insult comedy was especially prevalent on Allen's
programs during the 1930s and early 1940s. Allen's "feud"
with Jack Benny was the most prominent, but it was

hardly an isolated application of the theory that verbal abuse is humorous.[59] To create and sustain listener interest, program planners created, among others, feuds pitting Bergen's dummy Charlie McCarthy against W. C. Fields, Bob Hope against Bing Crosby, Fibber McGee against Doctor Gamble, and the Bickersons, husband and wife, against each other.

Insult comedy was one expression of a broader category of humor that prospered on radio's comedy–variety programs. It could be termed insider or celebrity comedy, since it milked show business, particularly its stars' daily lives and their physical and personality traits, for laughs. As he featured weekly celebrity guests beginning in 1942, Allen increasingly resorted to insider humor, which did nothing to enhance the quality of his comedy or his reputation as a creative popular artist.[60] Insider and insult humor also largely ignored the listening audience, except when Allen's comic ridicule featured imagination-stretching language to create some vivid images. Celebrity humor was generally vapid—"the mechanical joke," as John Crosby called it—based on stars' traits (Sinatra's skinny frame; Benny's thinning hair; Durante's nose) or possessions (Jessel's big house in Beverly Hills; Crosby's racehorses).[61] Edwin O'Connor termed such sterile comedy "no laughing matter," a judgment validated by time.[62]

Nevertheless, insult humor was a mainstay of radio comedy, as Allen's announcer Harry Von Zell once acknowledged: "You know how all these programs start, Fred. If the announcer doesn't insult the comedian, people don't even know it's a comedy show."[63] If he received their barbs, Allen also insulted the men who read his commercials. Calling one of them, Jimmy Wallington, a "drip," he continued: "You are so wet . . . if you ever lie down the government will stock you with trout."[64] Other cast members joined the verbal warfare. Allen involved his orchestra leaders, for example, just as Jack Benny did Phil Harris and Edgar Bergen employed Ray Noble. A continuing comic pretext was that Peter Van Steeden on the "Town Hall Tonight" series believed himself to be a more able comedian than Allen, and therefore deserved a larger role. Allen disparaged these aspirations with such remarks as "You're as funny as a tack in a baby's rompers" and then dismissed Van Steeden's musical talents as well. "You wouldn't be on key if you sat on a Yale lock."[65] Vocalists, like tenor Kenny Baker in the early 1940s, were natural targets of gibes also. Allen said of him: "He not only doesn't know anything. He doesn't even suspect anything."[66] Characters in skits earned definition and dimension from the insults they attracted. "You little waste of skin" described the assistant to a radio network vice-president.[67] Entire quarter-hour segments of Allen's programs during the late 1930s and early 1940s featured carefully written, artfully contrived insult sessions that pitted the comedian against announcer, against band leader, against tenor—with Portland thrown in for good measure.

Portland appeared during her "spot" on these programs with friends who, if anything, were crazier and more obnoxious than she was. As they pestered Allen, the war of insults escalated.

Allen: The Allens are the cream of society, Mr. Shill, and we curdle in the presence of the riff as well as the raff.
Shill: Man your tonsils, tornado mouth. I'm studyin' to be a tree surgeon and I'm apt to do a little homework and tear you limb from limb.
Portland: Gosh, If I'd know it was going to be this kind of a fight I'd have brought a dictionary.[68]

On another occasion, a Mrs. Bisby and her "answer to Margaret Sanger," son Gansvort, invade Allen's program. "With a name like that," Allen tells the boy, "a lot of people are going to get a good laugh passing your tombstone." He reminds Mrs. Bisby, a stage mother, "that all of the nags aren't at the Racetracks."[69]

Allen's feud with Jack Benny, in which he was the more aggressive originator of acidic *bons mots*, offered listeners a verbal feast of deprecatory characterization. The feud was the centerpiece of one film, *Love Thy Neighbor* (1940), and it spiced others, such as Allen's *It's in the Bag* (1945). Over the years, the two comedians pursued their rivalry in face-to-face broadcast appearances, through commentary volleyed between their respective shows, and as their stooges, such as Benny's black valet "Rochester" (Eddie Anderson) and tenor (Dennis Day), appeared as guest celebrities on the enemy's program. Each comic parodied the other's program format, especially Benny, who presented "Clown Hall Tonight" and "Benny's Boulevard" (for Allen's Alley) on several occasions. For his part, Allen wrote reams of dialogue about Benny, including skits— such as "The House That Jack Built" in May 1938—and one entire hour-long program, on May 7, 1941, as a ten-year "panaversary" of Benny's radio career.[70] It was a "tribute" in which Allen managed to avoid speaking Benny's name even once, while praising Jack's cast members.

Samples of Allen's Benny insults deserve inclusion here, as further illustrations of insult comedy. One Benny trait that Allen highlighted was his supposed anemia and poor physical condition. Benny had no muscles. "His arm looks like a buggy-whip with fingers. I've got veins in my nose bigger than Benny's arm. Benny's as soft as a bag of wet mice."[71] And, on another occasion, "Benny looks as though he just got down to give his pallbearers' shoulders a rest."[72]

Each man belittled the other's professional success. During their big "showdown" in March 1937, Benny claimed that, unlike Allen's, his show had listeners. "Keep your family out of this" was Allen's retort. Benny bragged that while Allen's movie audiences left before the end of the picture, his stayed to the finish. Of course, Allen explained, "because the manager promised to run it backwards to see if it made any sense."[73] Benny had played Abraham Lincoln in a tableau in the 1930 edition of Earl Carroll's *Vanities*. "If Benny was Lincoln he'd have freed Rochester years ago," Allen observed.[74]

One of the major themes of self-deprecation on Benny's own show was his violin playing. Allen joined in the fun. "When Benny starts to saw on that melody coffin of his, it sounds like a she-wildcat defending her young. Benny a violin-player? He's been playing the violin 30 years and still has trouble getting it out of the case."[75] Benny's cheapness was another enduring theme. "That guy's so cheap," Allen said, "he'd put his finger down a moth's throat to get his cloth back."[76] The only time Jack ever left a tip "was the day he couldn't finish his asparagus."[77] And a final word on his rival's contribution: "If Benny goes down in history it will just be gravity."[78]

This remark, and others quoted here, signify Allen's interest in manipulating language to create aural comedy. Radio aficionados know his program of March 20, 1940, as the "eagle show," during which the feathered "Mr. Ramshaw" escaped from his trainer during the guest spot. But the show is as notable for the puns as for the bird, which flew about Studio 8-H in a typical evening of Allen's comedy of language. Words with similar sounds and words with double meanings were among the tactics of verbal confusion that the comedian and his cast employed throughout the hour-long show. The resort community of Old Orchard Beach, Maine, for example, recently had designated Allen an honorary constable. He brags to Harry Von Zell that he will "get the drip on criminals" with his water pistol. The annual flower show in Madison Square Garden brings forth a growth of word twisting. Portland and her mother admired the "rotodoldrums" at the show. Visitors could admire "every rose . . . but Billy," and "every bloom but Sol" (showman Billy Rose and congressman Sol Bloom). The Pussywillows brought their "Kittywillows." A sunflower, after receiving a dose of vitamin B-1, "went out looking for Alf Landon." On the Republican ticket in 1940, Allen muses, "it might come out dewey." Prior to the eagle's flight, Allen emptied his comedic vocabulary onto that "bloated sparrow," that "King Kong robin." Pretending to be afraid of his feathered guest, the comedian claimed he "hears no eagle, sees no eagle, and speaks no eagle." Inspecting the bird's weaponry, Allen remarks: "I'd like to have his clause in my contract."[79]

The language play in which Allen reveled suggests continuity with an older, word-dominated culture that some thought had died with the advent of the electronic media. And even though it is an elemental source of humor, verbal gaming ought not, for that reason alone, to attract derision. Not only was it an appropriate humor for radio; it also drew upon a timeless, cross-cultural well-spring of laughter. As children learn to speak, Joseph Boskin points out,

> they experiment and play with word sounds, meanings, and patter. The world of language becomes a marvelous playpen of the toys and fun of double meanings, twists, oddities, confusions and repeats. In the early years, the play of words enables fantasies and absurdities to abound undeterred by rational considerations.[80]

The commercial mass amusements that preceded radio recognized the appeal of language play to adult audiences. "On the whole," Albert F. McLean, Jr., writes, "vaudeville humor tended to be verbal, finding its most effective expression in words rather than gestures."[81] Earlier, the minstrel show popularized "a new verbal humor" that dealt with the problems of modern city life. Robert C. Toll observes: "In the rapid-fire exchanges between interlocutor and endmen lay the origin of modern urban humor, the humor of vaudeville and radio, the humor that depended on playing with the use and misuse of words."[82] Norris W. Yates points out that Robert Benchley, S. J. Perelman, and James Joyce were among the many modern writers who employed the pun frequently and effectively.[83] And nineteenth-century humorous essayists and lecturers, such as Artemus Ward, "Petroleum V. Nasby," and "Bill Arp," spread generous doses of wordplay throughout their work.[84]

"Language became a prank" in the movie comedies starring the Marx Brothers, Andrew Bergman writes; even in a visual medium, "the brothers made word play an art."[85]

Another variety of Fred Allen's language-based comedy was dialect, the forte of versatile voice actors who played a wide range of foreign ethnic and American regional character types. Appropriate on one of the last comedy shows to broadcast from New York, for example, was that city's version of English-language pronunciation. Allen often depicted confused out-of-towners grappling with the local dialect, as they received directions—"you gittabus at toidy-toid and toid"—to the "erstaba" (Oyster bar) or "moom pitcha" (moving pictures).[86] Although the use of ethnic humor diminished under increasing criticism during Allen's years on the air, it, together with American regionalism, remained an effective source of audible comedy, as Chapter 8 demonstrates.

Allen poked fun at those who would reform the vernacular and change specialized argots in the interests of "proper" English. In 1936, the city of Charleston, South Carolina, encouraged its law enforcers to improve English usage over the police radio. Exaggerating this real news story, Allen had his "Town Hall" news show college professors instructing cops in a before–after contrast. The old-style police radio message:

> Mob of finks in hot boiler casing First National. All heeled. Get drop and fan for rods before they crash the joint.

became this:

> Paging Police Vehicle Number 7. Group of unspeakable characters in purloined motor conveyance inspecting First National Bank. The ruffians have concealed weapons. Suggest you submit their wardrobe to severe scrutinization.[87]

At other times, Allen made light of politicians' and lawyers' stilted language. Again on the "Town Hall News," a windy senator protested to the chairman that he could not concentrate on the work at hand because of "a miniature roll of the plant genus nicotine which has been kindled through the application of a splint of wood so prepared with sulpher as to make it ignitible by tinder." In other words, someone in the balcony was smoking.[88] Allen exposed the deficiencies of the pompous and pretentious through exaggerated versions of their specialized argots.

Many radio comedy writers strained their imaginations to devise preposterous names for program characters as a part of their comedy of language. Allen was one of the best at inventing names that described skit characters or that simply sounded ridiculous. A few examples follow, with the program date in parentheses:

> Tungsten B. Timid (11/24/33)
> Lotta Spunk, chorus girl (4/10/35)
> Dr. Rampant Pelf (10/14/36)
> Dalrymple Offal (12/29/37)
> Folderol Retard (5/11/38)
> Holden Strap, subway commuter (5/10/39)
> Professor Latent Trend (5/17/39)
> Judge Nullen Void (12/6/39)
> Roquefort Fumes (5/1/40)
> Farfel Tard (1/8/41)
> Urquhardt Pollen (5/21/41)
> Dr. Rancid Squirm (12/3/41)
> Eustis Gwelf (4/12/42)
> Nanette Newt (5/3/42)
> Welby Tidball (5/30/48)

Outlandish names, a form of verbal slapstick, were ideally suited to the broadcast medium.

Verbally inventive also were Allen's comic definitions of words and concepts that appeared randomly in his skits;

while not comparable in quality to a work such as Ambrose Bierce's *Devil's Dictionary*, these playful definitions continue a tradition of humor. On the radio (rather than in print), this wordplay demanded the careful attention and momentary reflection of the audience. Allen characterized a gentleman farmer as "one who ignores crops and only raises his hat" (December 18, 1932); a hot dog is a "pork zeppelin" (April 18, 1934). He described as "parenthesis-legged" a cowboy whose legs conformed to a horse's sides (August 29, 1934). An evangelist who would prohibit other people's pleasures was a "Banishing American" (January 16, 1935). An old maid was "a woman who was engaged once too seldom" (June 5, 1935). "Insurance is a contract people sign agreeing to go through life poor so that they can die rich" (February 19, 1936). A red nose was a "smouldering proboscis" (June 15, 1938); a pretzel a "surrealist breadstick" (November 23, 1938); piano tuning "Steinway osteopathing" (February 15, 1939); a spitball a "saliva-spheroid" (December 6, 1939); a zephyr "a typhoon with no ambition" (March 27, 1940); a worm a "nudist caterpillar" (May 1, 1940). Minerva Pious, in the Brooklyn dialect that she did so well, defined a nymph: "It's like a pixie, only yer wet" (October 30, 1940). "Life," Allen said, "is a lull between the stork and the epitaph" (May 1, 1940). Not all these definitions were original with Allen, of course, but even when he appropriated material from entertainment's public domain, he had in mind radio's unique requirements as a listening medium.

In many scripts, either by reproducing sounds or by talking about reproducing them, Allen further explored the varieties of aural comedy for his listeners. During early "Town Hall Tonight" broadcasts, for example, he closed his news segment with "the outstanding sound of the week." A simple exercise in utilizing radio's unique properties, the feature would have made no sense in a visual medium. Since Allen did not continue the feature for long, he may have doubted its success. But while it lasted, listeners received audible "punch lines" like these: General

Hugh S. Johnson pans the Supreme Court's decision over-turning the National Recovery Act—sound of kitchen pans rattling (May 29, 1935). Vendors at Coney Island sell 3 million hot dogs in a single day—dogs barking (June 19, 1935). Republicans complain that New Deal spending for public works "will empty the nation's coffers"—cast members cough in unison (October 23, 1935).

Listeners to Allen's Linit series came to know one featured supporting actor, Roy Atwell, for his audible mangling of spoken English. Known on the stage as a "purveyor of 'spoonerisms,'" Atwell also called himself the "Doctor of English as it is broken."[89] In his weekly (and, for today's listener, weak) program appearance, Atwell transposed the first letters of words and in other ways provided listeners with audible comedy. "Good morning" became "Wood Gorning," "free speech" "free screech," and so on.[90] Audiences in the early 1930s seemed to appreciate Atwell's comic manipulations of language.

A more creative use of the aural medium were those instances in which program participants talked about sounds, perhaps in the context of a sound technician's assignment. Allen told guest Norman Corwin, who knew something about radio production, about one of his greatest challenges: "We had a caterpillar slide down a slippery elm tree, bump against a pussy willow and then land in a pile of chicken feathers." After several failed attempts to reproduce that sound, the engineer "tied some peach fuzz to the end of a tassel and started spanking a wet toupee."[91] Other scripts played with sound in different ways. One of his murder cases brought One Long Pan and Mr. Moto (played by his guest, the mystery film actor Peter Lorre) to a broadcast studio. For a time, the detectives puzzle over the contradiction between two bullet holes and reports by witnesses of a single gunshot. Suspecting that the murderer had fired from within the control room, and then had exited so quickly that the sound of one shot remained trapped in the soundproof room, they open the door. Listeners heard a shot.[92]

While some of Allen's dialogue lightheartedly played with sound, other script material created vivid images in listeners' minds. Appearing throughout Allen's long career, ridiculous and improbable fragments of comic exaggeration betrayed the tall-tale tradition and stretched beyond belief the listeners' sound-dependent imaginations. A carnival's tattooed man, for example, complains that added pounds have distorted his tattoos by stretching them: Whistler's Mother has moved from his chest to under his arm. The freak show's rubber man, wondering if he needs a shave, pulls his face into his lap to "have a look at it."[93] With "John Doe," an early resident of Allen's Alley, the comedian discussed the recent cold wave in 1942. Doe reported: "The mercury finally went down so far it got out of the thermometer and went down a mousehole." Since the mice ate the mercury, Allen asked, does that mean that they will rise when the mercury rises? Maybe so, Doe responds, and he has an answer to mice who scurry about his house several feet off the floor. "I'll jack up the cat."[94] In another Allen's Alley interview, "Socrates Mulligan" tells Allen about his experience with a loan shark. For years, Socrates had paid 6 percent interest on a loan. But when the loan shark died, his son raised the rate to 9 percent. "I says what will your father think when he looks down from Heaven and sees you chargin me nine?" The loan shark's heir has this response: "When my father looks down from Heaven and sees this nine—to him it will look like a six."[95] Portand's mother's skin was so tight after her face lift that when "she sits down her mouth flies open."[96] Allen knew of a farmer who discarded used razor blades in his fields. His crops grew in slices.[97]

From the first script in October 1933 to the last in June 1949, Allen indulged in puns as titles of skits—"The Story of the First Lighthouse, or How Pincus Quagmire Brought Home the Beacon (August 8, 1934) and "Pure As The Driven Snow, or As Ye Snow So Shall Ye Sweep (January 30, 1935). Other delightful twists of phrase appeared wherever there was an opening for them. Those that follow represent a random sampling: Professor Gulpo, the sword swallower in a freak show, "swallows anything from his pride to a lightnin rod" (November 20, 1932). The British Lord Bottom Bottom calls his wife "Eczema because the old girl has her rash moments" (October 27, 1933). The Mighty Allen Art Players were "that sterling troupe that may be part pewter . . . sterling to themselves, and pewter their audiences" (October 30, 1935). "Come up and saw me sometime" says the magician's assistant to One Long Pan (March 4, 1936). Allen is "easily upset," Portland claims. "His grandmother was frightened by a canoe" (April 29, 1936). A ship's passenger complains that there are no eggs "in the crow's nest." "Captain" Allen: "Tell her I'll have the ship lay to" (March 10, 1937). Allen says to a guest who runs an ice business: "I guess there are times when an ice-lady has to hold her tong" (March 23, 1938). Of the marble lions stationed at the steps of the New York Public Library: "New Yorkers like to read between the lions" (April 26, 1939). People who smuggled cigarettes into New York from New Jersey were "buttleggers" (December 6, 1939). Timken Slaw, quiz-show contestant, says he works as a "kite-retailer." Asks Allen: "You sell kites retail?" "No, if the tail comes off of your kite, I re-tail it" (January 8, 1941). A college talent winner from Pittsburgh praises his city. "It soots you," responds Allen (April 5, 1942). Resurrecting an old vaudeville joke, Allen asks "Ajax Cassidy" of Allen's Alley, "Have you got vertigo?" No, the Irishman replies. "Only two blocks" (November 24, 1946). And finally, a comment on Mayor Fiorello La Guardia. "The Mayor's a dynamo, Miss Reel," Allen says in a skit. "That's why City Hall has to be kept near the Battery" (January 22, 1941).

Like the bags under his eyes, Allen's nasal voice was the target of considerable kidding from magazine writers and his own program's guest stars. His voice was his trademark, and it was a fortuitous one for a comedian who was so attentive to the needs of a listening audience. Portland Hoffa's broadcast voice was also distinctive. In his memoirs, Allen recalled that his spouse's radio character, "a subnormal adolescent," grew out of her radio voice, which he described as sounding like "two slate pencils mating or a clarinet reed calling for help."[98] Both performers' voices validated columnist Orrin E. Dunlap, Jr.'s maxim of radio comedy: "By their voices ye shall know them."[99]

And that is the major point of this chapter: Allen made significant and successful efforts to shape his material to the medium on which he performed. His comedy of language, his verbal slapstick, stand out even today.

Fred Allen, Satirist

A great field for jesting.

AARON STEIN,
New York Evening Post, 1934

Among the most popular and durable American entertainers of the twentieth century, Bob Hope may also be its most typical comedian. His gags are purely "a vehicle for laughs," his biographers write. "His comedy was not meant to be social satire or to be used for didactic purposes."[1] In contrast to Hope's comedy style, which is representative of the mainstream of popular humor, Fred Allen's humorous social comment belongs to the tradition of satire.

The function of satire is to criticize, to expose, continually to reexamine and question contemporary values, institutions, and elites. Both the entertainer and the satirist draw on the topics of their day, but the satirist is the naysayer, the one whose negative voice performs a positive role in an open society. He represents the humorist's highest calling. Louis D. Rubin, Jr., writes:

The seventeenth-century English critic Dennis's remark, that "the design of Comedy is to amend the follies of Mankind, by exposing them," points to the value of humor in searching out the shortcomings and the liabilities of society. In a democracy, the capacity for self-criticism would seem to be an essential function of the body politic, and surely this has been one of the chief tasks of the American writer.[2]

Louis Kronenberger concurs: "Humor must largely constitute an appreciation, even an airing, of one's own and one's community's and one's country's faults, rather than a tribute to their virtues."[3]

Great humorists, the poet and critic Kenneth Rexroth writes, must ground their work in a reflective skepticism. They must recognize that "the accepted, official version of anything is most likely false and that all authority is based on fraud." The humorists' abandonment of the skeptic's role at midcentury prompted Rexroth to perceive the "decline" of American humor, one cause of which was the dominance of profit seeking in the broadcast media, which had become a major conduit for comedy.[4] As Fred Allen's career amply illustrates, popular entertainers lacked the freedom enjoyed by many writers to apply the rigorously skeptical stance that Rexroth and others prescribed. Engaged in a team effort, Allen experienced each day the limits inherent in radio's commercial purpose and bureaucratic operation. Yet he was, by the consensus of contemporaries and the evidence of his scripts, a satirist.[5] He used humor to pass judgment on facets of American life that concerned him, as well as to amuse his large audience, during the eventful years from the election of Franklin D. Roosevelt to the blockade of Berlin.

One of the twentieth-century's central dilemmas is how a society that values individual freedom and dignity can protect them from the trampling hooves of organizational behemoths, public and private, whose effect, if not conscious purpose, is to snuff out personal autonomy. Along with many "serious" cultural observers, some popular humorists have confronted the problem. That they have done so should not cause astonishment. Humorists draw their material from the life around them, and an important part of the experience of Allen's generation was the transition from amateur vaudeville, rooted in city neighborhoods, to the hierarchical, technically complex, nationwide industries of radio and motion pictures. If a satirist is one "who jokes about serious things"—who treats contemporary problems in the vernacular, using ludicrous distortions and exaggerations to shock the audience, and frequently a grotesque style to stimulate its laughter—then Allen belongs to the grand tradition of satire in Western culture. Gilbert Highet observes that if satire does not achieve its goal of altering an unacceptable condition, then "it is content to jeer at folly and to expose evil to bitter contempt."[6] Allen had no reasonable hope of changing the corporate giants he worked for; jeering was its own reward.

The film maker Mack Sennett once fondly recalled his celebration of anarchy in the Keystone comedies: "I especially liked the reduction of authority to absurdity, the notion that sex could be funny, and the bold insults hurled at Pretension."[7] Largely denied the opportunity to explore the fun of sex, Allen joined Sennett and other popular humorists, of his era and earlier ones, by mounting his own attacks on order, power, propriety, and respectability. In 1942, ten years after Allen's radio debut, John K. Hutchens observed that Allen's "principal victims continue to be the pompous and the foolish, from Wall Street to Hollywood."[8] He ridiculed business executives, the police as well as private detectives, the courts, politicians and public administrators, reformers and do-gooders of all sorts, and popular idols such as movie celebrities. The radio system of advertising agency, sponsoring firm, and broadcasting network that so vexed him during program preparation provided Allen with the raw material for his most biting and hilarious assaults. In 1934, fairly early in the networks' evolution, the columnist Aaron Stein proposed that comedians would find in "the foibles and vagaries" of radio itself "a great and relatively unexploited field for jesting."[9] Allen, more than any of his colleagues, accepted Stein's challenge, and placed the satire of radio and radio comedy at the core of his art.

As a critic of the media and other pillars of modern life, Allen was not a reactionary—a laughing Luddite set to smash radio's transmitters, yearning for a return to the simpler life of two-a-day vaudeville. Although he was, in some measure, a traditionalist disturbed by change, his wish to defend the freedom of the individual creator fueled his satire. He asserted the autonomy of the lone artist within the corporate structure that had emerged dominant in the world of popular entertainment during his lifetime.

Interestingly, Allen did not appeal to the mass audience for support of free creative expression, even during the "proletarian" 1930s. An implied element of any cry for artistic freedom is the elitist suspicion, born of experience, that the rank-and-file citizen prefers the familiar and noncontroversial to the critical, experimental, and disruptive. Acutely aware that network censors responded unthinkingly to public outcry at program content, Allen shared that suspicion of the mass audience, whose power of protest reached maximum effectiveness in a consumer economy fueled by radio advertising. For this reason, among others, one suspects, the "little people" of Allen's comic world were often more pathetic than heroic.

This outlook toward the "common man" rooted in circumstance coincided with a broad philosophic shift in attitude among American humorists, one that had transformed the autonomous republican citizen of the eighteenth and nineteenth centuries into the faceless mass man of the twentieth. That is to say, the outlook we term modernism had assumed an important role in American humor. Over a period of years prior to Allen's radio career, literary humorists had replaced comic personae earlier regarded as representative. Still present in the early years of the twentieth century, but diminished in importance, was, for example, the wise fool, one of whose earliest manifestations was Benjamin Franklin's Poor Richard. Will Rogers helped carry the tradition into the 1930s. Newly significant, beginning especially in the new century's second decade, was the bumbling, neurotic "little man" as developed by Robert Benchley, Clarence Day, Jr., and numerous others. In time, in a multitude of film, stage, and comic strip characters typified, perhaps, by Dagwood Bumstead, this pitiable character spread from sophisticated publications like the *New Yorker* into popular entertainment. Perhaps Charlie Brown of the "Peanuts" comic strip was the character-type's best mid-twentieth-century popular expression.[10]

The smalltimers of Allen's vaudeville fiction contributed to the genre of "little man" humor. And in skits written between 1938 and 1942, Allen adapted the by then conventional little soul to radio. Smalltimers in life's dull daily drama, his frustrated lower-middle-class figures were pathetically short of the intelligence or luck needed to succeed in the urban environment of New York City. Although these little people lived in the midst of a miraculous communication technology, they betrayed the human family's persistent failure meaningfully to communicate: person to person, or individual to organization. Allen's reminder that we neglect sympathetic listening and careful explanation at our peril was appropriate for a comedian who spent his life searching for effective ways to convey ideas and feelings to seen and unseen audiences. The people who populated his sketches, Allen suggested, made the 550-pound circus gorilla Gargantua happy to remain in his cage. Free of the "harassed, neurotic-looking" Mr. Average Man's problems, Gargantua silently laughed at those who came to gawk at him: "beaten biped[s] fraught with occupational ails acquired attempting to survive in this modern age."[11]

His audience could only visualize Allen's little people

imaginatively. But their names and circumstances announced that these characters lacked the ability "to survive in this modern age." For instance, little Hormone
Wobble wants to light one skyrocket on the Fourth of July.
But her father, Oliver, inexperienced at manipulating New
York City's politics of personal influence, fails to obtain a
permit from the fire department. He has to set his house
on fire to attract bureaucratic attention to his legitimate
request.[12] Another "loser," meek Gallahad Dubb, a whisk-
broom designer, lands in jail after he deposits his wad of
gum on a New York City sidewalk. At the end of a tor-
tured trail of circumstance, caused by the greed and insen-
sitivity of his defense counsel, Renegade Tort, Dubb earns
a date with the electric chair, all because he cannot convey
his victimization to the judicial system.[13] And it costs
Dunbar Squirm, a subway commuter, $61 to ride from
Times Square to his home on 110th Street. The push and
shove of a rush-hour mob tears his clothing, destroys his
hat, and shatters the $40 china umbrella stand that a sharp
auctioneer forced him to buy.[14] Or consider Bransom Snide,
loyal fan of Siwash U's football team and visitor to New
York, who cannot find Yankee Stadium, site of the big
game with Army. The directions he obtains from locals,
with their peculiar dialect and brusque manner, may as
well be in a foreign tongue. After days of wandering in the
urban wilderness, alone among millions, he ends up in the
East River, a tragic victim of indifference and misunderstanding.[15]

Even apparent winners find dark linings in white
clouds. Witness Timken Slaw, "a humble commuter from
Nutley, New Jersey," who wins two silver dollars on a
New York radio quiz show. Friends back home, prone to
favor unsubstantiated rumor over the truth that Timken
relates, exaggerate his good fortune. A local news broadcast
reports the prize at $500. Timken's wife, convinced that
the $1,000 he won is committed to another woman, leaves
the poor fellow. His boss expects Timken to quit his job,
since he has won $5,000. Government investigators, be-

lieving his prize to be $50,000, jail him for tax evasion. Unable to communicate the truth to those around him, and harassed by an interview program that will pay $2 for his opinion on a public issue, Timken commits suicide. Knowing a good program concept when they see one, broadcasters create the "Timken Slaw Murder Quiz," which welcomes listener theories about his death.[16] It is true that Timken, Bransom, and other losers were sometimes "dopes," as script voice directions often indicated, and could trace some of their failures to personal inadequacy. But that people have weaknesses is all the more reason for a society that has mastered macrocommunication to work harder at careful listening and sensitive sharing on an individual level.

A gruff, alienated, lower-middle-class version of the "little man" was John Doe, an early resident of Allen's Alley. If Doe was as typical as he claimed—"I'm married. I have one wife and two point six kids. . . . I'm the average man"—the country had slipped into a sullen wartime mood.[17] "Some night," Doe responds to Allen's knock at his door, "I'm gonna mistake you for the landlord and beat your brains out."[18] Mocking emergency rationing, Doe hoards canned goods in his cellar, where leaking water pipes foil his self-seeking by washing off the labels. He has to pay a doctor to x-ray his cans to reveal their contents.[19] Doe's repulsive personality and weak lines may help explain his short lease in the Alley.

Other pathetic souls appeared on Allen's news-of-the-week feature as people who "didn't." They were ticket holders who did not win the Irish Sweepstakes; nobodies in Hollywood who did not earn Oscars; dubious achievers who did not merit notice on radio's "year-in-review" programs. These loonies were slapstick characters at home in a world made humorous by slapstick language, dialect, and outrageous personal names. For example, two unsuccessful songwriters appeared on the "Town Hall News" to speak of their two hundred flop tunes of 1937. The tunesmiths, Rubin and Dugan, spent the year composing variations on

a theme: "Thanks for the Rendezvous" or "Thanks for the
Au Revoir." In December, while they enjoyed a two-week
vacation, someone else wrote the hit, "Thanks for the
Memory."[20] Other "stumbles in the march of time" included Ditmar Wink, who set the 1940 record for sending
in box tops. For 30,000 of them, he received a neon hall
tree—one that people would not stumble over in the dark.
And Allen interviewed "Professor Phoenix Trad," who accidentally split the atom. He was fooling around with an
atom one day, and it simply split.[21]

Allen created numerous portraits of little people, and
he seemed to enjoy doing them. But more central to his
satirical comedy over time was his depiction of those with
power, position, and wealth. These fictional characters
were not victims of a capricious world. Occupying places
of authority, wielding power that affected other people's
lives, their own foolish weaknesses brought disaster. The
comedian worked many variations on this theme, some
less important than others. From time to time, to mention
a minor application, Allen brought as guests to his program
real-life performers of eminent respectability and serious
achievement, whose art he leveled to the average's citizen's taste. Twice, the Metropolitan Opera tenor Lauritz
Melchior appeared, complaining of Frank Sinatra's financial success and begging Allen's help in obtaining his own
popular radio show. With that assistance, Melchior—and
concert violinist Albert Spaulding on another program—
landed a place with a hillbilly band.[22] And the British
Shakespearean actor Maurice Evans helped Allen demonstrate how the Bard would function as a radio writer.[23]
Much more important than these gentle satiric jabs at the
arts, however, was Allen's treatment of those who ran that
most American of institutions, the business enterprise.

There is no reason to believe that the ideological climate of the 1930s, which assigned responsibility for the
economic collapse to business leadership, prompted Allen's ridicule of the corporate world. In his case, at least,
the general climate was receptive to, but not responsible

for, the satiric treatment given capitalists and managers. Allen ridiculed business executives just as he did politicians and patricians: their socially defined prominence, augmented by an exaggerated egotism, made them obvious targets of the satirist's thrusts. Sinclair Lewis's *Babbitt* (1922) was only the most prominent of many works that demonstrated the businessman's vulnerability to humorous treatment prior to the Great Depression.

Allen's good-natured burlesques of business almost without exception ridiculed fictional companies on the verge of collapse, headed by an executive of grossly exaggerated incompetence, played by Allen himself. Only rarely did he allude to real firms or recognizable names. On one Linit program, broadcast during the Great Depression's worst winter, Allen's imagination cross-bred a Wall Street pundit named John Jacob Rockemorgan. After delivering a confidence-inspiring speech on the economy to a group of tourists, the financier draws Allen aside. "Could you spare a dime for a cup of coffee?" he asks meekly.[24] A tone of bitterness infused Allen's satire only in his treatment of NBC in the postwar years, and that appeared in random dialogue rather than in skits. Allen's business satires lacked the power to alienate listener groups. Publicists at CBS, in fact, must have believed that Allen's uncomplimentary portraits of the business world helped win, rather than repel, a following. When Allen returned to radio in the fall of 1943, the network promoted Allen's new season as one "on which radio is to get another going over, [and] the bigwigs of business will get their balloons busted."[25]

In many skits, Allen ran small businesses. Often bearing names that included the telling word "Bedlam," these insane enterprises generated greater confusion than profits. The Bedlam Gables resort hotel, the Bedlam Detective Agency, the Bedlam Drug or Department Store—these and others were shoddy operations, teetering on their financial last legs, suffering from Allen's mismanagement. Swampview, "a Summer Resort that makes the coming of Labor Day a pleasure," was a business suited to the nation's condition in 1933. It overlooked the ocean. In fact, "We overlook everything but an unpaid bill."[26] That Allen's small entrepreneurs are fools escapes no one, least of all his wisecracking secretaries. To a client of the Bedlam Detective Agency, she describes Allen as a gumshoe: he stepped in some. When he brags about "grilling" suspects, she responds: "You couldn't grill a whitefish if the [Battery Park] aquarium was on fire."[27] Allen instructs his receptionist not to disturb him. "I'm wrapped in thought." Her response recognizes his mental capacity: "You'd better slip on a coat, you'll catch cold."[28]

If the small business sector of Allen's economy inspired little confidence in the return of national prosperity, the state of his large corporations seemed to condemn the country to perpetual depression. Allen, of course, was no authority on business management. But his constant and merciless ribbing of executive leadership, that of corporate vice-presidents in particular, reflected his experience with such types in the radio and motion picture businesses. In Allen's dictionary, the phrase "little man" encompassed the triviality and incompetence of those in positions of responsibility and power, as well as harassed average people.

> Within the hierarchy of the little men there is no man who can outlittle the minor executive in a large corporation who treats his authority as he treats a tight suit. In a tight suit he is afraid to make a move. With his authority the minor executive takes the same precaution. . . . It was once rumored that fledgling executives walked around their offices backwards so they wouldn't have to face an issue. . . . We had men of this ilk in radio.[29]

Here, as in his correspondence, Allen lambasted the organization men who frustrated, often without reason, the smooth flow of program production. Long before NBC vice-president Clarence Menser cut a portion of Allen's show from the air to censor it, Allen referred to radio's "lead-assed, memo sending executive bastards."[30] He pondered the function of an NBC functionary, Ben Pratt: "he always seems to be roaming the halls. . . . he may be bait for the tours. as pratt's pratt disappears through various doors in the building the guides may shout 'there goes a friend of kate smith's' or 'quick! there goes singing sam.'"[31] Allen told the story of

> the head of an advertising agency who never looked up at a conference. when he was in college he played quarterback on the football team. every time he looked up he saw nothing but a lot of asses. that is why he never looked up during a conference. it made him think he was a quarterback again.[32]

One of "James Whitcomb" Allen's better poems, written in the fall of 1940 for his own amusement and sent to friend H. Allen Smith, described a corporate decision maker as "A busy man/Who sits around/On his frustrated can." He nourishes his sense of self-importance by manipulating telephones, intercoms, memos, and subordinates. Of clichés, he has an endless supply: "He runs with the ball/Hits the nail on the head." The executive's politics and his health are not laughing matters. Cruising on his yacht, he denounces the New Deal for impoverishing him. "His stomach's a composite/Duodenal ulcer."

> For Man must toil
> And Man must work
> And the Executive is
> A dynamic jerk
>
> Hail! Neurotic Napoleon
> Long may you live
> Amok on your buttocks
> Bold Executive![33]

Throughout his radio career, Allen shared his opinion of corporate leadership with a mass public. As early as his second radio broadcast, for example, he introduced "yes men," characters whose major, unproductive function was to boost the egos of company presidents.[34] Although programs aimed at millions of listeners may not have been the most appropriate forum for specialized, inside-business humor, Allen's continued use of it helped make business satire a part of radio comedy. It was a case of comedians leading, not just reflecting the concerns of their audience, most of whose members were, at best, only dimly aware of the raw material for business satire. Vaudeville, which drew much of its humor from the streets outside neighborhood theaters, was more likely than radio to kid those with whom the audience had had some contact—cops on the beat or lower-level political functionaries. Radio humor, broadcast from corporate skyscrapers, knowingly spoke of the vice-presidents down the hall or in the control booth. Business humor attests to the inappropriateness of the "lowest common denominator" principle as an exclusive key to understanding popular humor.

Allen's irreverent portrait of the once-mighty and revered business executive worked to erode the aura of confidence and competence on which that figure's authority rested. On occasion, though, Allen presented yes men who were useful. For example, whenever "ad man" Allen develops a headache, "my three hundred vice-presidents sense it and take aspirin immediately."[35] At Bedlam Studios in Hollywood, a man walks around the office all day repeating the word "maybe." The producer explains: "He's only a Yes man with an inferiority complex."[36] Another motion picture executive employs a "portable Yes Man. I have to carry Sneed wherever I go—doctor's orders. . . . I have a chronic Hollywood ailment, cirrhosis of the ego. My doctor prescribed ten yesses on the half hour. That's all that keeps me going."[37]

Although ego support was an essential function at the upper reaches of the business world, the job descriptions of most executives were trivia lists, and lists that excluded initiative. One of Allen's satires, in which "Caldwell Bemis" is tenth vice-president in charge of envelope lick-ing at a large advertising agency, is a case in point. Realizing that none of his colleagues has seen Bemis for several weeks, "President" Allen investigates. Bemis lies unconscious on the floor of his office washroom. Rinsing his hands three weeks earlier, Bemis could not open the door with his slippery fingers. But, Allen asks, why didn't you wipe the soap from your hands? The sign says "Use paper towels only," Bemis replies, and there were no paper towels. "The vice-president in charge of towels let me down."[38] Another of Allen's corporate functionaries loses his job to a hot-water bottle, which warms the chair as well as he had done and, as a bonus, "doesn't take time off to attend Dartmouth reunions."[39]

Allen's chief executives were as useless and ridiculous as his vice-presidents. His secretary answers the phone in Allen's office at Titanic Pictures in Hollywood: "He's in the waste basket," she explains. "He forgets and throws himself away every so often."[40] As the head of Colossal Pictures, Allen makes screen tests. "The scripts have been drawing flies. Mr. Allen's testing some new screens."[41] As an ambulance-chasing lawyer who has not had a case in six months, Allen "admit[s] I've lost a few cases." His secretary marvels, "A few! Woodlawn Cemetery voted you the man of the year."[42] A key part of a company president's job is to facilitate group decisions. But the conferences of Allen's executive teams seem unproductive:

V.P. #1: Yes, D.D.?
V.P. #2: Yes, D.D.?
Boss: Memo!
V.P. #1: Check!
Boss: Eye to eye
V.P. #2: Sold to hilt
Boss: Check
V.P. #1: Memo!
Boss: Contact!
V.P. #2: Confirmation!
V.P. #1: Close deal!

Boss: Cut expenses!
V.P. #1: Check!
All: Memo
Boss: Okay[43]

Executive-ese was babbling jibberish to normal people struggling to communicate meaningfully in an increasingly irrational world.

The executive talent on Allen's shows could produce only disappointing balance sheets and odd schemes to avoid bankruptcy. For example, business at the Bedlam Department Store falls from one week to the next. In neither week does Allen have a sale, but in the second week a customer returns an item purchased earlier. Struggling to improve sales, Allen hires an efficiency expert "to take stock"; he takes it out the back door.[44] And as head of the Mammoth Meatball Company, Allen brags about his product's freshness: "Don't ever say 'Here Bossy' to a plate of Mammoth Meatballs. They'll back up and leave a quart of milk in your lap." His secretary knows the truth: "All the bull around here isn't in your meatballs."[45]

Allen's most penetrating and riotous satire treated the mass communication and entertainment media—the industry in which he labored, the one he knew best. Advertising, radio broadcasting, motion pictures: these were familiar businesses to Allen. During his lifetime the American economy's service sector grew to rival its well-established industrial and agricultural bases, in an increasingly consumer-centered, leisure-available society. While the communication industries' accelerating sales and employment figures helped fuel the nation's economic growth, their influence on public thinking was real, and was more feared than understood. Media's role in our society remains controversial, whether the immediate question is advertising practices, the transformation of political campaigns or athletics, the alleged lowering of cultural standards, or the decline of the local press. Fred Allen's voice, heard early in this debate, spoke in comic tones as his programs, with frequent success, reduced these powerful institutions, together with the bureaucrats who ran them and the fare they generated, to a state of foolishness.

Allen spoke his mind, through radio fiction, on two related issues of importance. One was the protection of individual artistic freedom within the large business structures that came to dominate public entertainment during the first half of the twentieth century. Business people and business values obviously had an important place in the communication and entertainment media, but Allen argued that their place must remain separate from the domain of the popular artist. Corporations like the National Broadcasting Company, the J. Walter Thompson Advertising Agency, Best Foods, and Paramount Studios (companies that had worked with Allen) performed a proper role when they facilitated and profited from comedic or dramatic materials—but never when they wrote or attempted to shape or block them. Or to influence the news and documentary programs that the media created. In 1946, Allen imagined what would happen to a truly gifted writer in radio. Allen's William Shakespeare, of Stratford-on-the-Bronx, approaches a large ad agency with the manuscript of his play *Hamlet*. In need of a new soap opera, the agency head adapts the drama to broadcasting's daytime formula. First, he eliminates Denmark: "It's got to be a small town in the Middle West. Centreville." The royal castle is out too. "The family is living in a Quonset Hut," he dictates. The advertising genius also vetoes the play's violent deaths; on radio, people never die on daytime programs. Forced to change his play's title to "Ophelia Faces Life," Shakespeare at last shoots himself. "Radio," he concludes despairingly, "is much ado about nothing."[46]

Obstacles to meaningful communication constituted a second focus of Allen's media satire. As we have seen, his little people had difficulty communicating ideas, needs, and feelings to the others in their restricted habitats. American society as a whole shared this handicap, and the media were partly at fault. Although miracles of mass

communication occurred daily, Allen observed a remarkable paradox. Honest and clear communication was rare.

Professional communicators, in both advertising and
entertainment, had little or nothing genuinely important
to say to a public that, to them, consisted of statistical consumption units rather than living audience members. That
was the implicit message of Allen's media satire. The products that radio huckstered were shoddy and of questionable
utility, his comedy showed. Sales campaigns strove to de-
ceive potential customers who, fortunately, were often perceptive enough to see through the puffery of promotion.
The celebrities of movieland were hollow men and
women, devoid of talent, concealed behind false hair and
heavy makeup, the creation of public relations experts.
With few exceptions, the media industries produced in-
sipid motion pictures, tired radio comedy shows that imitated one another, audience-participation programs that
demeaned their contestants and masqueraded as entertainment, and false sentiments that were rhymed and set to
music in popular songs.[47]

Introducing a skit on the greeting-card business during his first season on CBS, Allen reflected on how it had
altered the expression of affection. For many years, "poetry
has been the language of love." But in the twentieth century, "Big Business took over the greeting industry and today girls receive synthetic love messages. . . . Sentiment,
today, has gone commercial."[48] Professionals in the communication industry not only retarded the exchange of
genuine feelings between little people; they also had difficulty talking with one another. For efficiency's sake, some
of Allen's fictional ad agency personnel speak in initials:
"G.B.," for good-bye, seals a telephone call; "G.M.," instead of good morning, initiates the office day.[49] The cliché-
filled argot of the ad game even leads to murder. Allen's
Eureka Advertising Agency hires an Englishman who is
unfamiliar with ad agency slang. Responding literally to
the request of three colleagues to "shoot me a memo," he
kills them.[50] If advertisers cannot speak to one another,
how can they talk to the public?

The problems facing radio comedy in Allen's day allow the first detailed elaboration of these generalizations. The causes of radio comedy's ills, as we saw in Chapters 4 and 6, were the subject of several of Allen's nonfiction pieces.[51] Our interest here is how his scripts treated his own profession. Allen assigned both the comedian and his writer with responsibility for the low state of radio comedy. In one skit, a tourist in New York City, looking for Grant's Tomb, comes upon Radio City instead. "Who's dead in here?" she asks. "Only the radio comedians, Lady. They're dead from the neck up."[52] Unable to originate humor and dependent on writers no more talented than they, comedians recited bewhiskered vaudeville jokes and foisted visual comedy on an unseeing home audience.[53] In a courtroom scene, Allen showed a trial in which a radio writer sues his comedian for breach of contract. "I made this guy a sensation, Judge," the author claims. "I wore out ten pairs of scissors writin' jokes for him." The testimony quickly proves, however, that it is the writer who is guilty of trafficking in stale humor, by supplying it to the comic. "Officer, take him away for life," rules the judge.[54]

But the comics and their writers were symptoms of more fundamental causes, victims themselves of institutional forces. Program ratings, generated by "the only guys in the numbers racket the police haven't caught up with yet," were a case in point.[55] In one of Allen's scenarios, radio comedian Bob O'Berle is not a top talent under the most favorable circumstances. But when Puma Cigarettes, his sponsor, contracts with Dr. Scallop's Institute of Private Opinion to survey listener feelings about him, the comedian experiences extreme pressure. Random telephone calls produce a unanimously favorable public response. "If these figures continue," Dr. Scallop exalts, "you'll pass the Fireside Chats any minute." But he and the sponsor catch O'Berle intercepting the pollsters' phone calls and supplying his own plaudits. The moral? "Many a radio comedian who's on top of a poll should really be hung at half-mast."[56]

If the need to achieve success in the numbers game drove some radio comedians to dishonesty, the competition of quiz shows, with their bogus entertainment, brought tragedy. At least this is true in Allen's case of Mort Tripe, the radio comedy writer. Hidden in the studio during the broadcast of the audience participation program "Truth or Subsequences," Tripe murders three contestants. Before going to jail, he explains his desperate act to Ralph Deadwood, master of ceremonies, and to listeners across the nation.

> These quiz programs are puttin' us gagmen outa business. . . . Who needs jokes on the radio nowadays? Get people outa the audience eatin' bananas, dressin' up like babies—the audience dies laughin'. Dese studio stunts get bigger laughs than my jokes kin ever get. That's why I shot em. I'll shoot em all, all![57]

More explicit interference in the comic writer's art than competing programs and ratings compromised the humorist's freedom, however.

Comedy writers were not Shakespeares. But the powerful decision makers of broadcasting, housed in executive offices of the ad agency, the network, and the sponsor, altered the writers' work with as little regard for its integrity as for that of classical authors. In 1941, Allen created "an average radio comedian," Kenny Dank. Like Bob O'Berle, Dank's listener popularity is weak; in fact, his rating is a minus 2.2. The head of his agency, Boliver Balaam Button, brushes aside Dank's explanation that his show "was on opposite two fireside chats [FDR's broadcasts to the nation] last month." Button replies, "You can't blame him for everything," as he plans some changes in the Dank "Funfest" to bolster ratings. A conference with vice-presidents Bumble, Fumble, and Jumble produces several "flashes," among them the elimination of the studio audience. But that would be cruel: "You can't cut out studio audiences and render thousands of people homeless." When Button learns that only sixteen writers create Dank's thirty-minute weekly script, he calls in reinforcements: "Second Platoon,

Company two of agency joke writers reporting, Sir." The "gagged up" script then must pass muster with the censors. They cut a mention of Florida in the interest of California sensibilities, and eliminate a reference to a ship hitting a rock because there is a rock in "Rock of Ages" and no one dares alienate the church crowd. By the time the agency has finished improving Dank's script, "even Fred Allen wouldn't use [it]. . . . And he'll use anything." A discouraged Kenny Dank sums up his ordeal: "By the time you agency guys and the broadcasting company get through cutting out a comedian's jokes, he isn't funny." Button reminds the comedian that "radio is a big business." Radio and its comics are "not to be laughed at."[58]

Sadder than Dank's fate is that of another of Allen's creations, little Gulliver Scribble, radio gag writer. He and wife Dahlia, who live in shabby quarters near Times Square, barely survive by supplying jokes to comedians. Desperate for a gag to sell to famed funnyman Bob Mope, Gulliver and Dahlia stumble on what they think is a gem of wordplay:

Comic: My sister married an Irishman.
Announcer: Oh, really?
Comic: No, O'Reilly.

Gulliver rushes his joke to those who must approve: the advertising agency, the comedian, the network censor, and the sponsor. By the time he enters the office of Thomas Jefferson Gristle, Jr., the sponsor, the original limpid joke is totally unintelligible. Each of the other authorities has changed it in anticipation of negative reactions from listener groups. "What does this mean?" Gristle asks. "Ask them," the frustrated little man answers. "The censor, the comedian, the agency man. All those nitwits who ruined my masterpiece." In an attempt to calm Gulliver, the sponsor tries to doctor the joke, and comes up with the original. Convinced that he can write Mope's material himself, and save money in the process, he then fires Gul-

liver. The devaluation of the art of comedy can go no further.[59]

If comedy programs fell short of their potential, at
least they offered promise as genuine radio entertainment.
Most other programming seemed to exemplify Allen's on-
air comment to a guest in 1938: "One constantly strives
for irrelevancy in radio."[60] Many expressions of what the
networks considered quality programming—including
even the pauses between program segments—attracted
heavy, and sometimes heavy-handed, satiric treatment
from Allen. He ridiculed the station breaks, which reminded listeners where their dials were set, as symbols of
radio's useless information.

> If they did that in theatres people would burn up.
> Imagine a man coming out every half hour during
> *Hamlet*, and saying to the audience, "This is the St.
> James Theatre on 44th Street. You are listening to
> Maurice Evans and Kathryn Locke. We return you
> now to the Gloomy Dane."[61]

Allen had fun with the "radio uncles," as he called the
men who hosted children's shows, the upbeat role models
who announced Johnny's and Jane's birthdays, and encouraged kids to clean up their plates at dinner. How could
anyone be so perpetually happy? What would these men
say if they spoke their minds? "Hello, you little punks. . . .
Boy! Have I got a hangover! My mouth tastes like the heel
of a jitterbug's stockin'. Listen, you little double-crossers. I
told you to buy Clancey's Caramels. You been buyin' Toot-
sie Rolls."[62] Or what juvenile clubs would children's programmers like to organize? "A word about our Stuperman
Bandit Club. Here's how you join, kids. Simply tear off the
top of Daddy's safety deposit box. Send us whatever you
find inside. Take an oath to Stuperman you won't talk."[63]

In similar fashion, Allen burlesqued amateur talent
programs, among them that of Major Bowes, the Quiz Kids,
radio crime and western dramas, and musical variety hours

like Rudy Vallee's. Many of his skits speculated, with tongue in cheek, about future program possibilities. What would it be like if surgeons operated or dentists extracted while speaking into live microphones? How would a program sound that broadcast citizens' tax returns? "Real businessmen tell their incomes to you. Hear their exemptions. Laugh at their surtaxes. Hiss their net incomes."[64]

Of all the categories of contemporary radio entertainment that deserved ridicule, however, Allen reserved his most unrestrained parodies for soap opera and quiz programs. Allen picked on the daytime serials for the same reasons that others did: they were well known, even by nonlisteners, and they were vulnerable. Parodists easily exaggerated what the serials themselves exaggerated: human emotion and weakness, personal entanglements, and tragic circumstance. In the early 1940s, when radio soaps reached the height of their commercial success, Allen wrote his most delicious renditions of the genre. On his first thirty-minute program, for example, the actor Charles Laughton was Allen's guest and joined the comedian to present an episode of "Poor Old Charlie."

> You remember as we left Charlie yesterday things looked mighty glum in Centervale. Charlie had just had a mysterious phone call from Midville telling him that the body he found in the dum-waiter [sic] was not his Uncle Norris. . . . Charlie's grandfather Henry, who got his beard caught in the assembly line at the big airplane factory, came home with a propeller riveted to his head and his landing gear retracted.

As we once again drop in on Charlie and Poor Old Mary, his wife, the couple receives more bad news. In separate mishaps, their two sons die under the wheels of a truck in the street, one when the driver arrives, the other when he backs up. The family has had enough. Charlie phones "the only man kin stop this misery." But before this mystery man can reach the house, the delivery truck runs over him too. This frees Charlie and Mary from additional sorrow because the deceased is "the author of Poor Old Charlie!"[65]

If the grief-saturated serials were unrealistic, the quiz shows were wholly synthetic products of advertisers' and broadcasters' hunger for profits at the lowest cost for program production. Long before "Stop the Music" threatened to end Allen's radio career, he parodied quiz shows, although his satire became more shrill as his ratings declined in 1948 and 1949.[66] Perhaps his ribbing of Ralph Edwards's new audience-participation program in 1941 best represented Allen's objections to these shows. On "Truth or Subsequences," stupid citizens miss simple questions—for example, name the first U.S. president—and then perform silly tricks to win the prize that a correct answer would have secured. For example, Allen has Mr. Barclay Krawl of Poison Pen, Iowa, dress up like a baby. Mrs. Krawl, pretending to be the child's father, smokes a cigar while reciting "The Village Blacksmith," as the obnoxious master of ceremonies *Ha! Ha! Ha!*s in unison with a howling studio audience.[67] It would be difficult to imagine, Allen seemed to say, a more wasteful use of broadcasting facilities—and of their potential to unite and communicate with millions of Americans.

Public dissatisfaction with broadcasting's all-pervasive hucksterism peaked after World War II, just before the onslaught of television transformed radio forever.[68] By that time, Fred Allen had made a comic issue of radio's commercial excesses for years. He believed that the philosophy of sacrificing the quality of entertainment to product advertising generated such perversions as the quiz and audience-participation shows. Allen certainly recognized that without sponsors, there would be no radio entertainment. What he objected to was their attitude, as voiced by the soap tycoon in Allen's "Radio Mikado": "I just want commercials—thirty minutes of commercials."[69] Sponsors seemed willing to resort to any claim or gimmick to sell their product in radio ads. Allen's skits frequently satirized the claims.

> Try Oato. Oato is the only mouth wash that contains
> . . . hydro-whappitate.
> Your druggist knows hydro-whappitate is purified
> nitro-gimmick.
> Your grocer knows purified nitro-gimmick as
> undiluted fildil-sulphate.
> Your tailor knows undiluted fildil-sulphate as genuine
> noxo-strombide.[70]

Then there were Mother Murphy's Meatballs, which provided entertainment as well as nourishment. Blended with the beef was "a small quantity of liquid rubber."

> If you drop a Mother Murphy's Meatball on the floor, don't be embarrassed. It will bounce back on your plate again. Have fun with your meatballs, folks. . . . Dribble them up and down the table. Tie a meatball on your spaghetti and make a yo-yo. But buy them. Buy—spelled B-U-Y.[71]

Some products tempted listeners with special offers. On one Allen show, Toothpep sent a trained specialist into the customer's home.

> For ten days he will live at your house—Absolutely Free! Every morning and every night our demonstrator will brush your teeth with Toothpep. If at the end of ten days you are not satisfied our demonstrator will beat your brains out.[72]

The motives for murder on Allen skits were many and varied, and they included the fear that radio listeners would learn the truth about the products they bought. According to Allen, Putney Pomroy had for years sold his firm's pens under the slogan "Pomroy Pens last a lifetime." But when one of them broke in the hand of Balsam Bemis, president of the Acme Broadcasting Company, the sponsor murdered the network executive to conceal from the public "that Bemis had outlived a Pomroy pen."[73] And then there was Crovney's Coffee, Allen's answer to Maxwell House; it came stale in the can—no waiting necessary. Advertised during World War II, promoters touted it as "the talk of black markets everywhere!" Customers could sit up at night "thinking of its rich tasty goodness," since it was "98 percent caffein." And the topper: "Crovney's Coffee— is good till you at last drop!"[74]

On Allen's shows, broadcasters spend more time creating commercial appeals and placing ads than they do on entertainment. But the results of their labors suggest wasted effort. "Gimmie my spinach or gimmie death," suggested the maturity of one radio advertising campaign. Mr. Spratt, the spinach baron, asks "President" Allen of the Bedlam Broadcasting Company if it is time for another ad. "You bet," Allen replies. "The listeners have enjoyed themselves for fifteen seconds."[75]

In Allen's parody of early-morning husband–wife programs, co-starring the husky-voiced and sultry actress Tallulah Bankhead, ads trip over each other in eager succession, triggered by the most casual of suggestions. "Tallu" compliments "Freddie dear" on his refreshed look this morning. "Yes," he begins an endorsement, "thanks to our wonderful Pasternak Factory-Tested Pussy-Willow Mattress. . . . Only the hearts of the tender pussy-willows are used." The couple's canary, little Jasha, twitters happily in the background. "He knows that the newspaper on the bottom of his bird-cage is New York's leading daily." Then Freddie and Tallu reverse the mood, showing what radio's married teams who feign happiness at sunrise really think of the products they peddle. There are no pussy-willow hearts in the mattress. "It's stuffed with cat-hair. Every time I lie down . . . my back arches." Grumpily, Allen asks: "Where do you find these sponsors? At a police line-up?"[76]

A contestant on one audience-participation show refuses to accept a free sample of the sponsor's product, Mysto hair tonic. The master of ceremonies chokes the guest to force him to take the sample. "You might start a trend. Free samples are the life blood of Radio," he screams. The sponsor rages: "If we can't give Mysto away, how can we sell it? "[77] That question was implicit in Allen's treatment of radio advertising, season after season.

Behind the broadcasters busily worked the Madison Avenue ad agencies, home to people like "Mopey," the subject of another Allen skit. After the removal of half his brain in a medical experiment at Quinceton College, Mopey escapes from his locked room. "Gad! " the college president (Allen) exclaims. "A man with half a brain loose on the campus. He's going to be difficult to find." But Mopey has spent the six months since his escape on Madison Avenue becoming Sylvester P. Weaver, a successful ad agency vice-president. The grateful half-wit endows his college with a fortune. Inspired, President Allen rushes to the laboratory to undergo total brain removal. "With no brain at all I'll make a million dollars in the movie industry and Quinceton will be saved."[78]

The world knew the half-wits of the advertising game by the distortions and excesses of their promotional campaigns. Says ad executive Allen, who has no intention of losing any money on his offer of $500 to anyone who can remain awake on a Wilson Mattress, "I soaked the mattress in ether."[79] To market Kumfee Kut, a new suit of long underwear, Allen arranges a surefire radio show. He begins by lining up an audience. No matter what the program contains, "Thousands of families are under contract to stay home and listen."[80] A twelve-year-old boy is on the staff of the Bedlam Advertising Agency as an expert analyst of Allen's sales pitches. He is "the age of the average person paying attention to our slogans." Bedlam's vice-presidents have ideas on how to promote sales of the Socko Fly Swatter, among them a model for left-handed persons and a combination fly swatter and ping-pong paddle, for those wishing to keep occupied between flies. In case their campaign is too successful and flies become scarce, the agency decides to breed them.[81] Hired to promote sales of grape-fruit, Allen's agency hires two hundred boys to squirt potential customers with water pistols. "It'll make them grapefruit conscious." The campaign's slogan: "The Eyes Have It."[82]

When Allen cast his satiric glance at Hollywood, he found men as vacuous and messages as inane as the ones that cluttered broadcasting and advertising. It is unfortunate that among the numerous journalistic and fictional renditions of America's movie industry during its "golden age," Fred Allen's is relatively inaccessible and thus virtually unknown. For his skeptical treatment of this powerful American medium for communicating collective dreams and reflecting shared nightmares was the work of a perceptive humorist.

Network radio programming and Hollywood films interacted in many ways during the 1930s and 1940s. Most obvious to the public, perhaps, was that each drew on the entertainment personalities developed by the other. While screen stars re-created film roles for such programs as the "Lux Radio Theater," studios produced movies featuring such radio names as Jack Benny and Amos 'n' Andy. Fred Allen was among the radio performers the studios lured to Hollywood. Between 1935 and 1952, he made five undistinguished films, and since he helped write the screenplays for several of them, the visits to Southern California broadened Allen's writing experience. But unlike many radio performers, including Benny and most comedians, who moved their programs from New York to Los Angeles broadcasting studios, Allen remained physically in New York City and emotionally distant from Hollywood.[83]

Unavoidably, Allen took part in promotional campaigns for his films and in other aspects of the hype and hoopla that was, and is, Hollywood. He plugged his movies on his radio programs, and wrote newspaper pieces, like the one entitled "Allen in Wonderland," to generate box-office interest.[84] Although he undoubtedly hoped for his films' success, Allen never took his screen efforts very seriously. On his radio shows he was as likely to belittle his mediocre film career as to market his movies.[85] And in his writing, Allen made clear his distaste for Southern California and its most conspicuous industry.[86] But it was in his many Hollywood-based skits, presented to a large radio audience for more than fifteen years, that Allen shaped his most vivid portrait of the dream factory as insane asylum.

On his shows Allen, invariably, was the studio head at Bedlam or Colossal or Titanic Pictures. (The receptionist at Titanic answers phone calls with the greeting "Happy Crossing.")[87] He is inept, his movies are awful, and his business is failing. One of Bedlam's recent pictures, according to the reviewers, is aptly titled *Born to Be Mediocre*. A report from a theater manager in Georgia on another film is equally discouraging: "Your picture, 'It Didn't Mean A Thing,' didn't."[88] The word from Duluth momentarily raises hope: "'Africa Squeaks' does ten thousand in one night." But the crowd came for the Depression gimmicks, Bank Night, Screeno, Beano, Lotto, and Blotto; the manager forgot to show the picture. Business is so bad that Allen himself spends hours in the cutting room—reducing staff salaries. He fires his yes men to save money; in a building with an echo, "I can yes myself."[89] As usual, the perceptive secretary has an unanswerable comeback: "You've made so many turkeys you ought to use a wishbone for a trademark."[90]

His stars are hollow men and untalented women. Allen has to cut copies of Claudette Fadeout's last picture into celluloid mandolin picks for it to produce any revenue. He tells Reginald Fancypants: "Half of the movie fans in America blew the fillings out of their front teeth hissing your last masterpiece."[91] Without her "pearly teeth and . . . big yellow curls," glamour girl Petunia Prim is unattractive. "Those are the property of Stupendous Pictures. They're in the safe."[92] One of Allen's directors begins filming a script he found on the boss's desk. He fills the first scene with characters named Adams, the second scene with Browns, the third scene with Cohens. This "idiot" has "shot the

first 30 pages of the Hollywood Telephone Book" without
wondering why the plot was so thin.[93] Incapable employees, terrible pictures—Allen must cut costs. He scales
down *Hurricane Over Hollywood* to *Breeze Over Brent-
wood*. He recalls *Grapes of Wrath* to "remake it with rai-
sins."[94]

Although they are in the business of communicating
ideas and emotions, Allen's Hollywood professionals are
incapable of communicating anything of substance. One
producer, trying to explain the current slump in atten-
dance, talks doubletalk instead: "The loss of business I am
blaming on a variety of causes. Anyone [*sic*] of which alone
could kill business but together they are off-setting a grad-
ual picking up. If you are catching on to the technical explanation."[95]

The publicity personnel, such as Titanic's Ranton
Rave, spend their days manufacturing bloated adjectives to
puff up the image of a studio celebrity or the stature of a
film, or creating gala public events to attract public attention. With their help, Allen hastily arranges the marriage
of two of his stars in an effort to save the studio. "They can
. . . fall in love in time to make the evening papers," he
decides.

> I'll have the wedding ceremony in front of Grauman's
> Chinese. The bride and groom standing in wet ce-
> ment. I'll have 1000 mixed doves flying overhead
> spelling out Stupendous Pictures. I'll have 2000 peo-
> ple named rice throwing each other at the happy cou-
> ple.[96]

As in radio, movie censorship impeded communication and stifled creativity. The industry's enforcement of a
stricter code of standards in 1934 was especially unfortunate. On one show, it forces producer Allen to make
changes in *Souls in Escrow*, the latest romantic film featuring Devereu Honeypuss and Gloria Devine. When Devereu
beckons to Gloria, he wears "rubber gloves and a gauze

monocle—that makes it sanitary."[97] In another production, the "censors even cut the lace off the valentine . . . they said it's suggestive."[98]

Allen's opinion of Hollywood, advertising, and radio programming, including comedy, entertained his audience and introduced a subject matter unfamiliar to most listeners, and a viewpoint that was largely unavailable on other programs. Through his comedy, Allen also expressed the skeptical view of these powerful businesses born of his own hard experience. Their public influence badly needed the tempering that humor could achieve. Satire was Allen's antidote to arrogance.

Allen's Alley, 1942–1949

Some schnook is knocking on my door.
"FRED ALLEN SHOW,"
March 2, 1947

It was a time of questioning and inquiry, those radio years of the 1930s and 1940s. The communication media intensified the long-standing American hunger for information, and they solicited data from the "mass man" as well as supplying facts to him. Reporters with microphones interviewed "typical" citizens on street corners. Radio listeners mailed questions to the program "Information Please," hoping to win an encyclopedia for stumping well-read panelists Franklin P. Adams and John Kieran. While motion picture and sport celebrities fed their fans' demand for information in countless magazine and newspaper interviews, members of studio audiences appeared on broadcasting's quiz shows, exchanging answers to insignificant questions for fur coats or gift boxes of the sponsor's product. Some of the quizmasters' inquiries entered the language, most notably the phrase "the $64 question." Roper and Gallup pollsters pioneered a field soon refined by university social scientists: quizzing citizen–consumers about their voting behavior and consumption preferences. Employees of the Crossley and Hooper research organizations sampled listeners' program choices to plot radio audience size and composition. The pervasiveness of the rage for questions and answers, expressed in such diverse forums as the presidential press conference and the newspaper cross-word puzzle, invited parody. Fred Allen met the challenge.

From the start of his radio career, Allen drew comedy from current events, often on program segments that asked atypical, eccentric characters to relate their opinions on topics of interest. On programs broadcast between March 1934 and December 1942, for example, Allen simulated movie newsreels to demonstrate that humor was inherent in public affairs, even during depressing times. Some of the titles Allen gave to these interview sessions counseled listeners against taking events too seriously: he translated the screen's *Pathé News* into his own "Passé News" and then "Blazé News" (both 1934); and presented "The March of Trivia" (early 1940s), an unauthorized derivative of radio's pseudodocumentary program "The March of Time." Leaving most stories of national import on the front pages, Allen dug into the newspaper's back sections for "human interest" stories and humorous inquiries into such diffuse issues as wartime resource conservation. As he reflected: "All I know is what Will Rogers doesn't read in the papers. That leaves me the Want Ads and the Business Opportunities."[1] The April 18, 1934, show, for example, included stories on opening day at the baseball park, Mussolini's tax on bachelors, and John Dillinger's robbery of an Indiana police station. The "Town Hall Tonight" show of February 20, 1935, featured hypnotism as a cure for hangovers in the post-Prohibition era, the recent publication of Napoleon's love letters, and the prosecution of British telephone customers who used profanity over the wires.[2] It is interesting that Allen chose to parody the motion picture newsreel, a visual medium, on the radio.

> The screen is lowered
> (sound)

> The studio darkened
> (sound)
> The camera starts
> (sound)[3]

The sound effects used in such openings prompted listeners to visualize a medium that, presumably, most had seen in their local theaters. But Allen replaced the overbearing seriousness of Fox's *Movietone News* and similar short subjects with verbal slapstick and nutty characters, to establish a surreal, most unjournalistic atmosphere.

After eight years of newsreels, Allen suddenly abandoned that format for dealing with current events late in 1942. The appearance of a new feature on December 6 was a benchmark in the evolution of his radio art. Instead of the familiar hybrid of motion picture news and John Q. Citizen interviews, Allen informed Portland that henceforth he would "just drop around to Allen's Alley" to discover what people thought about issues.[4] Until his retirement, Allen continued to burlesque real news stories drawn from the daily press. But now he walked an imaginary byway, playing straight man at the doors of four residents who, although some did yield to replacements of longer tenure as Allen experimented with the best mix of types, contributed a novel element of stability to his program's fantasy world.

The Alley residents contributed a sense of permanence and continuity to Allen's programs of the 1940s. For the first time, Allen's listeners found that their familiarity with a character's traits, voice qualities, and dialect sharpened the aural-induced images on which his comedy depended. Listeners to a situation comedy, which "Amos 'n' Andy," Jack Benny, and "Fibber McGee and Molly" had developed as a mature program type by 1942, relied on the regular use of audible comic devices: Fibber's bragging, Jack's musical *faux pas*, and Andy's malapropisms. Now, as never before, Allen's home audience shared in that com-

edy of the familiar—recognition through repetition. And
the Alley, as much as the McGee residence—even though
both took on a different appearance in each listener's imagination—provided that sense of place essential to humorists. The Alley became Fred Allen's enclosed world of fantasy. The neighbors who lived there, like the patrons of
Mr. Dooley's saloon in turn-of-the-century Chicago or the
denizens of radio's "Duffy's Tavern" and, much later, television's "Cheers," observed and delivered judgments on
life beyond their locale. The Alley residents could not literally have been neighbors. The four with the longest tenure
included a New England farmer, a Bronx housewife, and a
southern senator living side by side! Nor did they function
as a media "family," either natural or intentional, in the
way that the characters on "Father Knows Best" or the
"Mary Tyler Moore Show" or "M*A*S*H" did in the enclosed worlds they shared. The Alley that Allen built with
a few audible clues lacked the unities enforced by poverty
in Hogan's Alley of the 1890s comic strip "The Yellow
Kid" and by blood ties in the 1930s strip "Gasoline Alley."
But Allen's side street did provide tags of identification,
familiar sounds, known characters, features that set apart
the programs beginning in late 1942 from earlier ones and
that gave listeners a feeling of comfortable recognition,
which often spells success for a venture in comedy entertainment.

The ease with which the political became personal
was a second important way in which the Alley enhanced
Allen's radio art. Those who derive comedy from public
issues run several risks: of trivializing the significant for
laughs; of reminding people of painful personal tragedy—
the loss of a farm to the bank during the 1930s or a son on
a foreign battlefield during the 1940s; or of alienating those
of a different persuasion on controversial questions. For the
most part, Allen's Alley avoided such difficulties. Its residents neutralized potentially threatening or divisive subjects when they directed Allen's public questions inward,
transforming world dilemmas or national headlines into idi-

osyncratic anecdotes. Just as members of the listening audience filtered larger issues through personal experience as
they struggled for meaning and relevance, so did the Alley
denizens. When Allen asked one Alley resident, Mrs. Pansy
Nussbaum, for her reaction to the end of meat rationing in
1944, she responded that she never ate meat. One evening,
when she was "a little goil," Pansy went to the kitchen to
cut off a piece of tongue. The tongue shouted, "Stop!" She
had not eaten meat since.[5] A scrap-paper drive threatened
another character, a German-American named Hollister,
with deportation. "My wife gave away my first papers. . . .
I'm an immigrant again."[6] To deal successfully with public
issues in the 1930s and 1940s, a radio comedy show had to
treat subjects indirectly and with a light touch. Allen's job
was not to educate the public, to lecture his audience. If,
by entertaining listeners with material derived from current events he also contributed to reducing rather than
raising tensions, so much the better. He and other comics
reminded people that even serious matters of national survival had ridiculous aspects—a reminder that only humorists could give.

While Allen's Alley expanded the possibilities of its
creator's comic art, the feature also, singly or in league
with other factors, placed restrictions on it. Each occupant
who opened a door to Allen's knock claimed, at most, two
or three minutes of airtime, a temporal constraint that precluded extended commentary on the evening's question
and, more important, the characters' development. Once
Allen had fixed a few stereotyped personality, regional, or
ethnic traits in listeners' minds, the Alley characters failed
to grow. In the short term, that they stopped short of full
individuality was compatible with radio's aesthetics. All
Allen had to do with his Alley residents was to establish
Senator Beauregard Claghorn's loud humor and southern
patriotism, Titus Moody's reserve and gullibility, and Mrs.
Nussbaum's marital irritations and mispronunciation of
words—and then let each audience member's imagination
flesh out a more complete person from those few cues. But

listeners could grow weary of permanent characters who remained static or could tire of the whole Alley concept. Jack Gould, a writer who often praised Allen's creativity, complained after one season of Senator Claghorn's bluster that this southerner "is apparently going to make a life's work out of one routine."[7] William Moyes, during the feature's third year, found "symptoms of chronic mental stasis" in Allen's loyalty to it: "It has got so when he announces his Question for the Day, listeners can tune in to some other show as they can tell in advance just about what gags he'll be pulling."[8] In the Alley, Allen could not develop the fullness of character necessary to sustain the interest of many listeners. They had to tune in to the situation comedy to find radio comedy's fully rounded personalities.

For all its genuine success, the Alley device became a liability to Allen's comedy in another sense. By consuming half of the thirty-minute programs, it helped crowd out features that had filled, and enriched, Allen's hour-long broadcasts of the 1930s. Arthur Frank Wertheim, the historian of radio comedy, contrasts what he calls "the slick comedy of the 1940s" with a more relaxed, less formulaic and sponsor-dominated brand of humor that was standard on the airwaves during the previous decade.[9] Other students of radio may argue with Wertheim's distinctions; that commercial values consistently dominated program decisions throughout radio's pretelevision years is a clear theme of this study, for example. Still, Wertheim's argument establishes a larger context for Allen's Alley. During the 1941–1942 and 1942–1943 seasons, Allen and his sponsor, Texaco, instituted three important changes in program format. The third, in order of occurrence, was Allen's introduction of the Alley. Two months earlier, on the season's premier of October 4, 1942, Allen inaugurated the thirty-minute programs that were to continue for the remainder of his career. And only during the previous season (1941–1942) had the comedian fully committed to the guest-star policy that brought celebrities to his microphone, personalities who consumed the other half of the briefer shows. Allen accommodated the guests in skits that previously had featured his stock company, the Mighty Allen Art Players. The effect of these changes was to restrict what Allen could do. His programs became more hurried, the comedy more compressed. If this produced a "slickness," so did the guest stars, whose frequent lack of radio comedy experience a full orchestra and a polished singing group might help conceal. A changed format reduced Allen's creative freedom—a result for which the Alley was partly responsible.

The Allen's Alley most people recall emerged in the fall of 1945, with the debut of Senator Claghorn, Titus Moody, and Mrs. Pansy Nussbaum. Joining them a year later was Ajax Cassidy.[10] But this combination of residents that has stuck in the public memory was the product of slow evolution rather than an act of startling creativity. The Alley had been a part of the show since 1942, and Allen had drawn on the news for comedy since 1932. Minerva Pious, who played Mrs. Nussbaum, had been in Allen's cast since 1933, frequently doing "Jewish" dialect roles, and the Nussbaum character's first appearance was on the first Alley routine. Claghorn had a predecessor in Senator Bloat, a windy politician who resided in the Alley between January and June 1944. The poet Fallstaff Openshaw, who still recited his silly rhymes in 1945, first appeared in an Allen script in October 1941; Socrates Mulligan also predated the Alley. Like many good ideas, in short, Allen's Alley developed gradually and in parts. The parts converged in the most satisfying configuration for Allen and, apparently, for his audience, beginning in the fall of 1945.

Allen returned to NBC from a year's retirement that October, and so his initial experimentation with the proper mix of character types occurred between December 1942 and June 1943, and again in the illness-shortened 1943–1944 season. In the first of these periods the four regulars were John Doe, the "average man"; Mrs. Nussbaum, housewife; Socrates Mulligan, described as a "Dope" in the

scripts' voice instructions; and poet Openshaw. Allen's
trial-and-error process that season included an interesting
ethnic switch. On four programs, actor Charles Cantor
played the Jewish Mr. Nussbaum, while Minerva Pious,
normally Mrs. Nussbaum, became Mrs. Mulligan, the wife
of the character whom Cantor usually played.[11] Allen's
scripts for 1943–1944 suggest that he knew he had found a
workable comic device but was uncertain about the best
combination of dialects, occupations, and national or regional backgrounds. During that season he introduced his
first politician-in-residence, Senator Bloat, who lacked the
identifiable constituency that helped sharpen the Claghorn
identity later. Allen continued to experiment with ethnics
in 1943–1944, trying out a German, a Greek, and several
Jews. He even briefly portrayed a drunk. Sampson Souse,
played by actor Jack Smart, staggered through only two
programs.

In his last radio season, 1948–1949, Allen experimented once again, this time altering a successful format
in a futile effort to halt the downward slide of his Hooperatings. Instead of mounting the steps of row houses in an
Alley that, notwithstanding its radical diversity of characters, always had the air of New York City about it, Allen
walked down a mythical Main Street. Passing the local
Ford agency (his sponsor was the national organization of
Ford dealers) and other businesses as he met up with some
familiar people from the Alley, Allen drew on the warm
imagery of small-town America in this frightening new
world of Cold War tensions. Allen also, in this last season,
created Sergei Strogonoff, *Pravda* reporter, as a device to
wring comedy from U.S.–Soviet competition. Neither
change succeeded in refreshing the humor or reviving the
ratings.

The "little man" persona that James Thurber, Robert
Benchley, and Clarence Day, Jr., developed in the pages of
the *New Yorker, Vanity Fair*, and other sophisticated publications was a middle-class urban or suburban professional, as Norris W. Yates points out in his authoritative

study of literary humor during the first half of the twentieth century.[12] The little people of Allen's Alley, by contrast, were distinctly lower class in origin, education, and values. Individuals of limited means and humble talents who struggled with life's daily problems resonated with a mass listening audience in the immediate post-Depression years better, one suspects, than affluent but bumbling professionals crafted for the world of literature. And as a satirist, Allen could use lower-class figures to twit the respectable and pretentious.

Allen's scripts located characters such as Socrates Mulligan, Fallstaff Openshaw, Pansy Nussbaum, and Ajax Cassidy in tenements and shacks along the Alley. Allen's own youth gave personal meaning to the term "shanty Irish," and some of the Alley residents fit the mold. The male characters mentioned above had no steady employment. Fallstaff, for example, referred to himself as a "happy bum."[13] Allen satirized high culture and learning through his characters. In his world, the classical names Socrates and Fallstaff belonged to indigents and morons. Poet Openshaw, the Bard of the Bowery, dramatized the cultural distance from Stratford-on-Avon to Lower Manhattan on the East River. Farmer Titus Moody once claimed that "education and common sense don't mix," and cited a neighbor to prove his point. After attending a college of agriculture to learn scientific farming, Mr. Moody's friend purchased the latest equipment. "What finally came up?" Allen asked. "Three men from the bank," Titus replied. "They took the whole place over."[14] Although a member of the Senate, politician Bloat's foolish proposals undermined the respect that normally accrued to one of his position. When his colleagues yielded him the floor, he was to wax it.[15] Mrs. Prawn, an Alley character who appeared briefly in 1944, symbolized all her neighbors: they were shrimps. Clearly, Allen satirized them as well as people of higher status through them.

A notable feature of Allen's Alley was the absence of interaction among the inhabitants. It was only on rare oc-

casions, indeed, that they even betrayed knowledge of their
neighbors' existence. In June 1944, Allen allowed a degree
of interaction that he never repeated. In the Alley spot one
night, Fallstaff's verse answered a poem by Mrs. Nussbaum
on the subject of hot summer weather. Later, in the skit,
guest Peter Lorre, playing Mr. Moto, and Allen as One
Long Pan came to the Alley to solve a murder case, a mystery that the residents helped unravel.[16] This program
prompts speculation. Did Allen miss a chance for the Alley
to become something different, perhaps something better
than it was, when he kept separate those who lived there?
He might have developed a dialogue among New Yorkers
or, as the characters diversified, created discussion across
regional and ethnic lines of items in the news.

The remainder of this chapter discusses three major
categories of American humor to which Allen gave expression in his visits to the Alley: Mrs. Nussbaum and Ajax
Cassidy best expressed the American ethnic humor that
appeared in Allen's comedy, Titus Moody did the same for
the comedy of urban–rural incongruity, and Senator
Claghorn stood for political satire.

Through numerous characters, most notably the Alley's
Pansy Nussbaum and Ajax Cassidy, Allen employed ethnic
humor for decades after it had ceased to be "the dominant
comedic force in [stage] variety entertainment."[17] And he
drew on this venerable strain in American humor while
working in a mass medium whose business managers required of sponsors and ad agencies programs with "the
broadest possible appeal." Allen's program, the most lis-
tened-to network radio show at the time, continued to use
ethnic humor nine years after NBC adopted the following
guideline: "Statements and suggestions which are offensive to religious views, racial characteristics and the like

must not appear in programs."[18] The fact that Allen's comic stereotypes of white religious, regional, and nationality groups, and of racial minorities such as Chinese- and Afro-Americans, were conventional laugh-getters rather than malicious weapons helps explain their persistence in a medium that thrived on the formulaic. In addition, some of his stereotyped characters, especially Mrs. Nussbaum, revealed warm, sympathetic traits that audiences and critics both seemed to appreciate.[19] Nevertheless, to some of his contemporaries, Allen's comic Jews, white southerners, and Irish-Americans were neither benign nor funny. The actress Minerva Pious recalled that Ajax Cassidy "elicited more complaints than any other character" on Allen's Alley, and for good reason: "he was always represented as a no-good drunk."[20] Late in 1948, a listener denounced Allen's ethnics to the president of NBC:

> Mrs. Nussbaum is no longer funny—she is merely a grievous racial stereotype in an age where too many graves attest to the evils of racial stereotypes. Ajax Cassidy is a buffoon who must cast a dubious reflection in the minds of those who know how dissimilar he is to modern-day Irish-Americans.[21]

Scattered listener protest paralleled a changing professional view of radio's role in intergroup relations. In 1944, one writer gave this advice to aspiring script authors:

> Avoid, as though they were the seven plagues, all caricatures of racial and religious types. Radio can do very well without the shuffling, shiftless, unreal Negro, the stereotype distortion of a Jew, the explosive Russian, the sniveling Chinese.[22]

The following discussion illustrates Allen's uses of ethnic humor during his radio career, especially on Allen's Alley. It must also explain why, even in the face of criticism, he helped perpetuate it. The answer is that while remaining within the loose boundaries set by societal and industry expectations, Allen's ethnic humor opened numerous possibilities to his comedy of language.

Henry Popkin has observed that because radio "sprang up in the shadow of Broadway," it inherited a "tradition that could still recognize and present foreigners and foreign accents without excessive self-consciousness or reticence."[23] The vaudeville theater in which Allen matured as a comic was the early twentieth century's most popular manifestation of "Broadway"—the mass entertainment industry that centered in America's preeminent city of immigrants, New York. But ethnic humor, and its close ally, dialect comedy, had been authentic elements of a heterogeneous national culture since the eighteenth century.[24] As a young Irish-American in ethnically conscious Boston at the turn of the twentieth century, Allen took personal lessons in the meaning of an immigrant nation: group differences, including broken English spoken in dialect, produce a humor of accommodation as well as jealousy, misunderstanding, and conflict. Ethnic humor first appeared, and then persisted, in radio comedy because it was a conventional entertainment device that audiences expected to find, and one that, however crudely, reflected the nation's historical experience. Though he played One Long Pan and other ethnic-dialect characters, Fred Allen was not an ethnic comedian. His stage and radio persona was the ethnically neutral, wise-cracking American. His forays into the comedy of group stereotypes was only one laughter-provoking method, which joined wordplay, parody, and others. But Allen knew that ethnic comedy was a ready-made, audience-tested resource, so he used it.

Ethnic humor also allowed the use of dialect, and its advantages in an aural medium of entertainment were obvious. As this study has emphasized, Allen recognized the need for a comedy crafted for a hearing audience. He knew that an Irish, Brooklyn, or hillbilly dialect supplied listeners with funny sounds, mispronounced words, rearranged sentences, hilariously erroneous definitions of words, accents that identified character traits as well as suggested setting and situation. In the absence of the gaudy costume of the stage Jewish tailor or pawnbroker, or the clay pipe, green coat, and shillelagh of the stage Irishman, dialect called to mind humorous group traits that functioned instantly to assemble a mass audience on a common ground of image and association. Although it was by no means indispensable, ethnic humor as represented in spoken language was enormously functional in radio comedy.

Any book on radio comedy suffers from a serious limitation: its pages cannot permit readers to *hear* what made radio audiences laugh decades ago. Merely to read lines that others heard is not enough, although it must suffice. Those who can imagine (or recall) how voice actors, speaking in dialect, transformed words in a script into something vital and humorous may most readily appreciate the program fragments that follow. Mrs. Nussbaum was Allen's most successful ethnic-dialect character, an aural delight whom most critics and listeners thoroughly enjoyed.[25] "To me, sometimes, it seems I am talking with a dialect," she reflected in a moment of innocent self-awareness that highlighted the appeal of this immigrant, whose voice was that of a real Russian-Jewish émigré, Minerva Pious.[26] Each week, Mrs. Nussbaum responded to Allen's greeting with a verbal *faux pas* that brought down the house: "You were expecting maybe Emperor Shapiro-Hito? " she said at war's end. Or, on other occasions, "Dinah Schnorer," "Cecil B. Schlemiel," and "Weinstein Churchill."[27] "When I am least expecting it sometimes—I am Cohning an expression," she admitted.[28] Pansy grew "rutabagels" in her garden; she read the story "Schmo White and the Seven Schwartzes" to Skippy Fogelson, a little neighbor; and she enjoyed the poetry of "Heimie Wadsworth Longfellow" and "Rudyard Kaplan."[29] Verbal surprises like these helped endear Mrs. Nussbaum to Allen's audiences.

Fred Allen drew upon a century-old tradition in popular humor when he moved Ajax Cassidy into the Alley.

Ajax was a latter-day Mose the Bowery 'b'hoy, the uneducated rowdy who became a "tremendously popular" comic persona in antebellum popular culture.[30] As did other radio ethnics, Allen's Irishman possessed an aural distinctiveness, the thick theatrical brogue of actor Peter Donald. Like Pansy Nussbaum in the Bronx, Mr. Cassidy of Third Avenue in Manhattan filtered the world through his ethnic consciousness. This Celtic's favorite dance band was "Guy Lombrady and His Royal Hibernians."[31] The untutored Ajax understood the need for psychiatrists, since "half of the people walkin' the streets today are mental cases. Either they're schizzyphrenics or demented peacocks."[32] The Irishman always stood ready to defend the honor of his native land. On one Alley segment, during the Policeman's Semi-Annual Beefsteak and Ball at Gilhooley's Grotto, a heckler shouted, "Three cheers for Neville Chamberlain" through the open doorway. "Bedlam broke out with pandemonium," Ajax recalled for Allen. "The air was filled with knuckles and bridgework."[33]

Of the other ethnic types that Allen enlisted for roles in his scripts, blacks, Englishmen, Chinese, and mountain hillbillies appeared more than the others. Their dialects justified their presence. Allen is an advertising executive in one skit, and he must prove to government investigators that the cream he promotes really can blanch skin tone. He demonstrates the compound's powers by spreading it on a black man's face. After a pause, listeners hear a "Swede" speak broken English in place of the "Negro" voice present moments before.[34] Allen loved to mock the King's English. When his crew throws the captain of the ship *Bounty* overboard, that worthy objects: "It isn't Ping Pong." The man did not know the game cricket.[35] Allen's frequent appearance as Detective One Long Pan allowed numerous openings for confusion of English and Chinese references. "I'm a Yangtse Doodle Dandy," Pan mutilated one familiar song. "I'm a Yangtse Doodle Boy."[36] Allen filled his hillbilly skits with Lukes and Zekes, feuds, moonshiners, and shotgun weddings. One shy, overprotected backwoods

woman "was 30 years old before she'd take her bubble gum
out in front of a boy."[37]

The ethnics who spoke in dialect were funny not only
because of their pronunciation but also because their language of unbounded verbal slapstick described exaggerated
personalities and experiences. In this, Allen's ethnic characters were one with his whole approach to radio comedy.
Ajax Cassidy, for example, was a one-dimensional character defined by his fondness for drink, pursued with others
in an atmosphere of male fellowship. Through him, Allen
narrowed the original Mose the Bowery 'b'hoy, omitting,
for example, the heart of gold encased in a rough exterior
that gave a positive feature to the image of the show-busi-
ness Irishman. Perhaps Ajax reflected Allen's memory of
his father's frequent, destructive intoxication. It is clear
that radio's casual attitude toward alcoholic excess permitted a Cassidy, as he joined W. C. Fields of the Bergen–Mc-
Carthy program, Phil Harris and his band of the Jack Benny
show, and others whose imbibing the comedians presented
as funny and harmless. The tales Ajax told were as broadly
farcical as his character was narrow. He spoke of Dull
David Dineen, for example, who came from Ireland on a
cattle boat—and felt right at home. This slow-witted immigrant learned to read by studying newspapers, but that
was his downfall. One day, Dull David saw his name in the
obituaries. "He assumed he was dead. . . . He went out and
killed himself."[38] Verbal slapstick could humorously confuse ethnic traits. An Indian named Levine tried to sell a
rube "a blanket with two pairs of pants."[39] Before her marriage to Pierre Nussbaum, Pansy was an attractive young
woman: "For two years at Far Rockaway [a New York
beach] I am Miss Low Tide," she recalled with pride.[40]
Sonny Rappaport, the Knish King, had been one of her
suitors, but Pansy finally chose Pierre, whom she stole
from his girlfriend. "Crime does not pay," she summed up
her twenty years of marriage.[41] Pansy's domestic skills
lacked polish. The soap powder she purchased from a push-
cart vendor turned out to be baking powder. When she

washed her spouse's shirt, "One sleeve is a strudel."[42] Above all, Mrs. Nussbaum was a kind, sensitive person. She gave up mincemeat because she refused to let the butcher kill "a little mince" just for her.[43]

In his use of Alley characters Titus Moody, the New England farmer, and Senator Beauregard Claghorn, "from the South, that is," Fred Allen drew on the comic potential in American regional identity. Of the two, although Claghorn's character and catch phrases quickly captured public attention, Moody was the more enduring and attractive personality. Each of them represented important traditions in American humor.

Like Ajax Cassidy, Senator Claghorn had a nineteenth-century prototype: the backwoods storyteller, the tall-tale exaggerator of the southwestern frontier. Students of American humor use the Greek word *alazon* to describe this persona, one whose immodest traits appear in the rascal Sut Lovingood of George Washington Harris's "yarns," various of Mark Twain's characters, and, in a latter-day incarnation without specific regional content, in the lovable boaster Fibber McGee of radio comedy.[44] Allen's Claghorn, played by Kenny Delmar, was an obsessive Dixie patriot whose blind sectional loyalty and affected southern drawl made him a striking, if ultimately tiresome, study in aural comedy. Claghorn swore off the movies after he saw Ann Sothern married to Cary Grant in one picture. "I couldn't stand to see another Grant takin' anything Sothern."[45] But he liked magicians—if they had "a confederate in the audience."[46] During his reelection campaign, the AFL and CIO endorsed the senator: the "Affectionate Followers of Lee," that is, and "Chattanooga Importers of Okra."[47] The senator's remarkable experience in New York City one day illustrated the benevolent qualities of all that was southern. Struck by a bus while crossing Broadway, he fell to the pavement, expecting to die. But a passing car from Tennessee saved him. As it drove by Claghorn's shattered frame, one of its tires blew out. "That Tennessee air from the tire blew over mah face. . . . Ah revived instantly."[48] While some of the senator's cracks probably alienated northern listeners—the ghost of John Wilkes Booth shooting at the Lincoln Highway, for example—his portrait of southern people as backward and lazy drew protests from the South.[49] Claghorn's New England neighbor, Titus Moody, by contrast, angered no one.

Mr. Moody allowed his creator to draw on urban–rural contrasts as well as New England regional identity. As the Mose persona suggests, American culture nurtured a tradition of urban-based humor, one that shared elements with but also departed from the rural humor of New England and the southwestern frontier.[50] Allen's radio writing built on this heritage. A native of Boston, a resident of New York, and a product of vaudeville's distinctive urban entertainment, Allen not surprisingly filled his scripts with New York City subjects, language, and characters.[51] Critics occasionally commented on Allen's preoccupation with the daily life of the real city that surrounded Radio City, questioning its appropriateness for a national listening audience. After tuning in an Allen broadcast while visiting Schenectady, for example, a *Variety* reviewer criticized some "strictly New Yorkese" lines and "over-localized . . . situations and references" about the city's treatment of World's Fair visitors and the Sixth Avenue "El." Listeners "out in the sticks" found little comedy in "guffaws" crafted for New Yorkers. A second commentator agreed: "Reference to the BMT, Aquarium, subway turnstiles and Flatbush, all familiar things to a New Yorker, may make Joe Doaks in What Cheer, Iowa, miss the kernel of a gag."[52]

Many radio comedy programs, of course, reflected a local bias, but increasingly that of Southern California, as the Bennys and Hopes relocated from New York to Holly-

wood. The golf course and motion picture studio life of
wealthy actors was even less representative of the American norm than that of average New Yorkers, although
probably more attractive to listeners in "What Cheer."[53]
While he made movies on the West Coast, Allen chose not
to join the colony of entertainers living there, for
professional and personal reasons. In New York, he told
Arnold Auerbach during the war, "i may be better off with
the writing troubles. i can use more topical things and the
[news]papers are better for items that can be turned into
bits."[54] Indeed, Allen's New York orientation encouraged
his creation of local characters like Mrs. Nussbaum, and it
contributed local dialects to Allen's verbal menu. And his
urban bias permitted Allen to employ the venerable literary and stage convention of the naive and innocent rube, in
this case Titus Moody, let loose in the evil city.

Ever since Benjamin Franklin created Poor Richard
Saunders, Americans have laughed with, and at, the wise-
fool character. Sometimes called the *eiron*—since, ironically, this foolish simpleton occasionally does speak with
common sense and native wisdom—the persona has appeared for a century and a half in such diverse characters as
James Russell Lowell's Hosea Biglow, Charles Farrar
Browne's Artemus Ward, Langston Hughes's Jesse Semple,
and even in Norman Lear's Archie Bunker. Created as a
Yankee rustic, the character type has assumed other regional garb and appeared in media other than literature.[55]
True to type, Allen's Titus Moody was a farmer from New
England. Clearly, this wise fool's personality stressed the
second half of the coupled traits. Titus's humor derives
from the bizarre people and absurd experiences that fill his
life, which he relates to Allen in a lean, carefully measured
vernacular colored with earthy sayings. The actor Parker
Fennelly played Mr. Moody to perfection. Type-cast as a
rural New Englander as early as 1930 in the radio series
"Snow Village Sketches," Fennelly portrayed an elderly
country character in television ads for Pepperidge Farm
products into the 1970s. "I was born old," Fennelly com-

mented on his ninetieth birthday, "and I played old parts most of my life."[56]

Ajax Cassidy once disparaged the countryside because farm houses lacked fire escapes. "On a hot day where else can a man sit in his underwear?" Titus Moody, lifelong ruralite, boosted that same environment: "A man that stays in a small town'll live twice as long." But the slower pace had drawbacks, for "it'll seem twice as long, too."[57] A simple man, Titus spoke in an unaffected, literal manner. If Ajax sat on fire escapes, Titus once sat at the bottom of his well writing a letter. "A city feller gave me one of them pens that writes under water," and Titus had to try it.[58] Moody complained that he had "had tough sleddin' all week." Why? Allen sympathized. "No snow," Titus reported.[59] Allen's theatrical version of rural speech peppered Mr. Moody's dialogue. When the electricity failed his farmhouse was "darker than two feet down a bear's throat."[60] The winter weather "was colder than an Eskimo's immediate vicinity."[61] People in Titus's area, lacking commercial amusements, made their own fun. His own hobby was collecting deer ends: "Everybody was mountin' deer-heads. I started collectin' what was left over."[62] His neighbors once feted the old codger at a silo warming, where the folks feasted on "roast owl—country style."[63] For years, Mr. Moody sang duets at public functions with Miss Mona Boone. One night, while assisting her out of the buggy, he inadvertently glimpsed her shinbone. "I done the decent thing. I married her."[64] A man of honor, indeed.

If farming was God's special calling, divine guidance lost track of Titus's place. The weather, new-fangled technology, and low commodity prices combined with Mr. Moody's naiveté to undermine his best efforts. He was gullible. Once he responded to a magazine ad that offered "Big Bargain—Dirt Cheap" by mailing $20 to an address. He received a box of dirt.[65] Titus's experience with farm machinery made the twelfth century seem attractive. His "self-operatin', short-wave plow" broke loose and disappeared over the horizon. "All I know is that from here to

Syracuse there's a rut that belongs to me."[66] Weather ruined what little would grow on his poor land. During one
dry summer, Titus's pump could draw only "two feet of
dirt and a thirsty gopher" out of the ground.[67] A windstorm
blew Moody's razorback hog into the woods. "Before he got
dull he cut down twenty-eight trees."[68] Another wind
whistled through the rack of moose calls at the sporting
goods store. "The Elks Club House jumped off its foundation and came waddlin' down Main Street" in response.[69]
Farming, this agrarian concluded, was like communism:
"Nobody's got nothin' but everybody's workin'."[70]

   "Effen I ain't a rube I'll do till one gets here," Titus
admitted—a reality most often exposed during his visits to
New York City.[71] Mr. Moody was a good example of the
folklore type that Richard Dorson has called the Yankee
"greenhorn," duped of his savings, if not his good humor,
while in the big city.[72] While Titus was in New York to
buy a car, for example, a sharper led him from a display
window to a junkyard filled with fenders, doors, and other
auto parts. The man "was puttin' cars together by appoint-
ment" at this "car cafeteria," and the Alley's rube exchanged his money and a custom order for a car's horn and
a promise. The horn turned out to be an expensive one, of
course.[73] Titus took his goose to New York on one trip,
after a "feller" advised him to "take a gander" at Radio
City.[74] Warned about pickpockets, Titus cut the bottoms
out of his pants pockets.

Moody: I was walkin' down Broadway—I felt a hand in
     my side pocket.
Allen: What did you do?
Moody: I put my hand through t'other side pocket—and
     shook hands with the feller. . . . Met some nice people
     that way.[75]

Another time, someone reached through his bottomless
pockets and stole Moody's underwear.[76] Hoping to acquire
financial security in his old age, this already aged hayseed

bought his own toll bridge from a con man. Locals called it
the George Washington Bridge. "When they're comin'
across," the slicker assured him, "they'll be comin' across
for you."[77] Moody would have been better off if he had
stayed on the farm, waiting for the only safe trip he would
ever take, across the road from his house to the cemetery.[78]

By means of questions posed during news-of-the-week and
Alley segments, but also in prepared comments and ad-libs
scattered throughout skits and other features, Allen moved
from the back pages of newspapers' human-interest stories
to the front page of headline news. Comedians, of course,
had to tread carefully through the censors' restrictions on
political material. Allen's style of comment helped ease his
satire past Janet MacRorie and other continuity watchdogs.
He never gave extended treatment to national or international issues, for example, preferring instead the brief,
off-handed quip, which was less likely to offend than a ten-
minute skit. Allen avoided criticism of actual public officials; his senators might resemble real types, but not specific individuals. Allen's skepticism toward those who
wielded power, moreover, whether New Deal bureaucrats
or Joe Stalin, was one with which few could quarrel, including, one guesses, his corporate sponsors.[79] As was true
of his treatment of broadcasting executives and Hollywood
studio heads, a major achievement of Allen's political commentary was the exposure of powerful individuals as fallible. Indeed, Senator Claghorn's most useful function as an
Alley resident was his weekly demonstration that authority figures were fools. Through his Dixie drawl and southern chauvinism came a message that sensitive defenders of
the South missed: a healthy skepticism about political
leaders, especially when expressed with a smile, is essential in a democratic culture. The domestic demagogues and

foreign dictators of Allen's radio years were sufficient reminder of that.

Among the public figures made humble by Allen's
commentary, pompous and incompetent senators ranked
first. Their names—Senator Ranton Bore, Senator Fuller
Zephyr, and Senator "Fightin' Luke" Allen, "the Militant
Windbag"—announced their dominant quality.[80] After listening to another insane legislative proposal from Senator
Bloat, Allen observed: "There are no flies on the Senator.
There are some things a fly won't stoop to."[81] On one Alley
visit, Claghorn reported that to honor George Washington's birthday, members of the Senate vowed to tell the
truth all day on February 22; "it was the quietest day ah've
ever spent in the senate."[82] The Dixie Democrat could not
conceal his ignorance about international relations. "I ain't
got not Foreign Policy. . . . Ah buy all of mah insurance in
this country. Mississippi Mutual."[83] But the Congress did
not monopolize errant policy. After encouraging egg conservation, administrators of the War Food Administration
found that the nation had an embarrassing surplus of eggs
in 1944. Fallstaff Openshaw's poem chuckled over their
discomfort:

> "These eggs must stop" bureaucrats cry
> Or there will be arrests
> We'll subpena [sic] every Plymouth Rock
> And padlock all the nests.[84]

Military officers and diplomats also looked foolish. "This
has been a war to end wars. Democracy is saved!" That
had been the rhetoric of Armistice Day 1918, Allen recalled two decades later. But what did world leaders tell
the people in 1938? "The world will spend billions to arm.
Democracy must be saved!"[85] Noting recent disclosures of
waste in military spending in 1949, Senator Claghorn advised that, in the next war, rather than pay for armaments,
"It'll be cheaper to jest throw the money at the enemy."[86]

During the 1930s and 1940s, while both Franklin

Roosevelt and Harry Truman frustrated Republican aspirations to govern, Allen made the minority party seem ridiculous. The southern Democrat Claghorn was an effective device to lambast the GOP. To get out the southern vote in 1946, the senator traveled from town to town exhibiting "a Republican in a revival tent." Under this rare specimen he placed a sign: "Don't Let This Happen to You."[87] Emotionally disturbed Republicans, distraught by Roosevelt's election victories and New Deal policies, reacted to his "fireside chats" by standing in fireplaces and "talking back to the President."[88] In a Freudian treatment of the nursery rhyme "Jack and Jill," indecision immobilizes Jack. He is incapable of speech or action. "Gentlemen," a party official announces, "I nominate Jack as the next Republican candidate for President!"[89] Television brought the 1948 party conventions to voters in some cities, with disturbing consequences for Republicans if Allen was correct. Seated at a bar in Philadelphia, one man recognizes Herbert Hoover on the television screen, addressing his party's delegates. "If Hoover is President—what am ah doin' with three dollars in my pocket?"[90]

On two occasions during the 1930s, Freeman Gosden and Charles Correll—radio's "Amos 'n' Andy"—requested White House permission to include morale-boosting, pro–New Deal messages in their comedy shows. Roosevelt's staff complied.[91] That Allen sent similar telegrams to Washington, or even imagined himself as a restorer of national confidence, is highly doubtful. His references to Roosevelt were infrequent, and incidental to other comic purposes. In a skit about the famous nineteenth-century reporter Henry M. Stanley's search for the elusive Dr. David Livingstone, an African runner travels a thousand miles to ask the journalist the question of the hour: "You think he'll run for a third term?"[92] Early in 1944, when Roosevelt won a fourth presidential term, Allen quipped: "You don't have to be earnest to get in the White House. You have to be Frank."[93] With the aid of Senator Claghorn, a confidant of "little ole Harry," Allen wrote more fre-

quent and familiar references to President Truman.[94] For
Truman's whistlestop tour of 1948, Claghorn wrote a campaign song to the tune of "Home on the Range."

> Let me keep mah home—near the Capital [sic] dome
> It is there my affections I'll fasten
> In this year '48—Oh, how I would hate
> To move out for Dewey or Stassen
>
> Home, home near the dome
> With Bess and Margaret and me
> Where seldom is heard—a discouragin' word
> Except from the G-O-P[95]

When Truman won in November, Claghorn gloated: "This
is one thing the elephant will never forget." The public
opinion pollsters looked as foolish as the publishers of the
Chicago Tribune who had prematurely announced
Dewey's victory. For the first time, "the polls" went to the
dogs, rather than vice versa.[96]

During the New Deal–Fair Deal years, Allen found
opportunities for casual comment on domestic problems
and programs, of which the following examples are representative. He fed the public skepticism about business during the Depression. When the U.S. Chamber of Commerce
claimed in 1936 that prosperity had returned, the "Town
Hall News" showed that retailers, no longer so desperate
for business, would return to their normally rude treatment of customers.[97] Allen had his doubts about organized
labor as well. Lumberjacks picket as George Washington
chops down the cherry tree; he lacks a union card.[98] In his
annual Christmas skit, Allen had Santa Claus begin a sit-
down strike on December 24. A fractious humanity rejects
the goodwill that the old gentleman symbolizes.[99] New
Deal spending to assist beleagured economic groups attracted Allen's interest, especially farm programs that paid
producers not to grow. In one skit, a farmer tallies the
year's harvest: "Biggest crop I ain't growed under this administration. . . . 50 acres of no corn. 75 acres of no oats.

And a cool 25 acres of no barley." A man from Washington rewards the agrarian with a check for $3,000 for not farming.[100] In 1946, Portland announced that United Mine Workers head John L. Lewis was writing a sequel to Eugene O'Neill's play *The Iceman Cometh—The Coal Man Isn't*.[101] And what was Truman's Fair Deal? Senator Claghorn knew. "The Fair Deal is like a game of cards. Everybody lives like a king but nobody's got no jack."[102]

As did other radio humorists, Allen harnessed his comedy to the war effort after Pearl Harbor. But unlike many others, including his feuding friend Jack Benny, Allen did not journey abroad to entertain troops. His high blood pressure prevented that. But the Armed Forces Radio Service rebroadcast Allen's shows wherever American personnel served. Allen used the news feature and, beginning in December 1942, Allen's Alley, to promote civilian cooperation with scrap metal and paper drives and acceptance of plans for rationing scarce consumer goods. Fallstaff's poems carried the most effective of Allen's messages denouncing the hoarder and ration-book cheater, and praising citizen sacrifice. When the government limited Americans to one cup of coffee each per day, Fallstaff offered these stanzas

> I'm going to miss that steaming cup
> I held under my schnozzola
> A donut will never taste the same
> Dunked in Pepsi-Cola
> . . . .
>
>
> Give my coffee to some soldier-boy
> Who is fighting for our rights
> And instead of me, Herr Hitler
> Will be having sleepless nights.[103]

Fallstaff took frequent swipes at Axis leaders, especially Hitler, as a means of generating war enthusiasm in the mass audience. Concluding a discussion of Britain's cradle-to-the-grave welfare system, the Bowery Bard promised: "We missed Hitler in his cradle/But we'll see him in his grave."[104] And after a German military disaster on the eastern front, listeners heard this poemless title: "Everyone said they saw Hitler's end. When he lost his panzers in the Dneiper Bend."[105] Other Alley characters echoed Fallstaff's message. In 1943, Mrs. Nussbaum explained the point system of rationing to the radio audience. You go to the market for two pounds of coffee, she began.

Mrs. N.: You are pointing to the coffee grinder.
Allen: Yes.
Mrs. N.: The grocer is pointing to an empty shelf.
Allen: Yes.
Mrs. N.: You are pointing to your rationing book.
Allen: And?
Mrs. N.: The grocer is pointing to the door.
Allen: That's all there is to the point system?
Mrs. N.: You are getting the point.[106]

After the war, Allen visited the Alley and Main Street for opinions on the Cold War—in Europe and in Washington. A newcomer to the Alley, Sergei Strogonoff, *Pravda* journalist, offered revealing insights into Russian life. He assured Americans that his nation wanted peace: a piece of Austria, a piece of Poland, and a piece of other neighbors.[107] Sergei explained that, like the United States, the USSR had a two-party system and the secret ballot. What party opposed the Communists? Allen asked. "That is the secret," the Russian admitted.[108] According to Strogonoff, Russian technology led the world. His nation had developed the light bulb a century before Thomas Edison "invented" it. Why was the world unaware of this advance? "We are not knowing how to turn it on."[109] A wistful longing for international comity coexisted with jokes at Russia's expense on Allen's programs of the late 1940s. As Humphrey Titter, a greeting-card rhymster and Main Street character from Allen's final season, appealed to Joseph Stalin in 1948:

Come help us make the UN work
Bring your hammer and your sickle
Let's go, Joe Tovarich
The world is in a pickle.[110]

Allen seemed to fear more for the world's peace than from internal subversion in these years of red-baiting in Washington. On one Alley segment, Senator Claghorn made light of congressional inquiries into communist influence in the motion picture and broadcasting industries. The senator ridiculed through exaggeration; he recalled seeing a subversive scene in a Lum and Abner movie, as Lum used the "party line" to telephone his friend.[111] Mr. Moody's farm also came under investigation. Forty of his chickens—Rhode Island Reds—traveled to the nation's capital for questioning by a congressional committee. Allen's comment: "Who'll notice a few more clucks in Washington."[112]

The last three chapters have drawn a distinction between radio comedy that began and ended with the easy conventions of show business, and another variety that reached into American life in the 1930s and 1940s for its subject matter. Allen used both. But the strength of his work derives largely from his ability to rise above the easy solutions to the challenge of entertaining a large, remote audience. If, more than forty years after his last weekly broadcast Allen's satire has lost its immediacy, it has not become irrelevant. The arrogance of powerful individuals and institutions will plague the American economic and political systems as long as those systems exist, and so deflaters like Allen will continue to have a job, an audience, and a useful social function.

An Epilogue

that was why i liked radio. we had some fun.

FRED ALLEN,
Theatre Arts, 1953

If "Stop the Music's" popularity and the giveaway shows' cost advantages were the proximate cause of Allen's professional demise, television's rapid displacement of radio would very likely have ended his career soon anyway. For Allen created a comedy uniquely aural in achievement and appeal, one crafted to meet radio's technical qualities and aesthetic demands, but one that was inappropriate for television. His talents as a writer and performer were particularly unsuited to the comedy vehicle that dominated television by the time of his death in 1956, the situation comedy.

Continuing under contract to NBC after his final radio show on June 26, 1949, Allen made several flawed attempts to adjust to the new world of video. His failure in television supports the argument that each medium of entertainment presents unique opportunities and limits to comedy's creators and performers. Allen hosted an hour-long, once-monthly variety show on television in the fall of 1950. A variety format had worked for Allen on radio. But the ill-conceived attempt to reincarnate Allen's Alley

characters as puppets on the "Colgate Comedy Hour" symbolized Allen's inability to transfer his talents to the new
medium.[1] In truth, Allen did not expect the show to succeed. To resurrect the Alley for the visual medium would
create "the impression that we were merely putting the old
radio devices before the cameras," he realized.[2] All the radio comedians "have a great problem," Allen commented
in 1949. "We don't know how to duplicate our success in
radio. . . . Those things won't work in television."[3]

Allen's second attempt to break into television, this
time via a panel, or game, show in the fall of 1953, was
even more discouraging. He had not been optimistic about
this venture either: "i start on a quiz show this fall," he
wrote to H. Allen Smith. "this can well be the artistic end
of me."[4] The strength of "Judge for Yourself" was supposed
to be Allen's witty banter with amateur talent, but his ad-
libbing was lost in the confusion of a half hour filled with
too many people and too much activity. Groucho Marx,
whose television success rested on exactly the sort of interaction with average people that Allen hoped to achieve, located the show's problem after one viewing: "There isn't
enough of Fred Allen." Allen agreed: "there was no opportunity to ad lib. i had so many ad libs left over when the
show finished i talked to myself for two hours."[5] If Allen's
willingness to try a quiz show created comic incongruity,
given his criticism of that kind of entertainment, his even-
tual success on such a program was even more ironic. At
the time of his death, he was a member of the celebrity
panel on "What's My Line," a program he defended as a
witty and entertaining game show, not at all like the
numbskull quiz shows he opposed.[6] But Allen's established
brand of humor was unsuited to the giveaway programs
and the sitcoms that predominated on early television. By
1956, the lighthearted domestic drama, as modeled by "Father Knows Best" and "Ozzie and Harriet," had become
the major vehicle for television comedy. But what television would do best, Allen never tried. When his radio years
ended, so too did his career as a regular comedy writer and
performer.

Allen's video failure did not derive from his "dour expression," as Steve Allen once suggested,[7] or from NBC's unsuitable program formats and weak scripts. The fundamental problem, one Allen clearly recognized, was that the new visual medium radically altered broadcast comedy. Allen was simply unable or unwilling to adjust once again to new technical and artistic demands. Just as the "talkies" had disrupted the motion picture's comedy empire in the late 1920s, visual broadcasting shattered radio's comedy establishment in the late 1940s and early 1950s.

In radio, the eye of the imagination, stimulated by sound, created worlds of laughter for listeners. Radio comedy feasted on dialogue; in dialect, it transported listeners to Titus Moody's New England farm and Pansy Nussbaum's neighborhood in the Bronx. Allen's verbal slapstick, his burlesques-in-sound of Hollywood studios and broadcasting bureaucrats, rested on techniques of language that took advantage of radio's audible opportunities, as opposed to such devices as the garish costume, distorted facial expression, or pratfall on which video comics Milton Berle, Sid Caesar, and Lucille Ball would later capitalize. Those who mourned the end of silent film comedy after 1927 had counterparts in broadcasting a quarter-century later. Even the theologian Reinhold Niebuhr lamented television's need for "the most obvious kind of [visual] slapstick. . . . The descent from Fred Allen to Milton Berle is, for the moment at least, the measure of the difference between radio and television humor."[8]

Television was a closed rather than an open system, Allen thought. It made all the decisions for audience members, frustrating possibilities for diversity of response among viewers. "In radio, even a moron could visualize things his way; an intelligent man, his way. It was a custom-made suit. Television is a ready-made suit. Everyone has to wear the same one."[9] In contrast to television, Allen wrote in 1953, radio had been "an instrument of wit" because it was verbal rather than visual; "on radio you could do subtle writing because you had access to the imagination. that was why i liked radio. we had some fun."[10]

Allen *did* enjoy his radio work; that point is worth reiterating. His well-publicized complaints about radio's bureaucratic complexity and programming constraints grew out of the pride with which he regarded his work. A writer as well as a performer, Allen defended his scripts from those who would shape and edit them for reasons unrelated to the art of entertaining a vast, nationwide audience. An individualist in a medium where entertainment grew from collective effort, Allen's fights with corporate censors were ultimately over control of the creative process. That he won many of these otherwise petty battles over words shows that, even in the mass media, the individual comic vision can find a place. Had Allen limited his comedy to wordplay, or to insult or gender jokes, he would not have experienced the heavy-handed censorship of the networks. But he was a satirist in a commercial mass medium, one who commanded the world of current events as his domain. If he exaggerated when he claimed that his scripts contained "a history of this country done in a comedy manner," it is true that, unlike most radio or television comedians of his era, Allen set for himself the difficult task of contemporary commentary.[11]

The case of Fred Allen is only one of many that reveal the ways in which artists may bridge such judgmental categories as "humorist" and "comedian," or "popular" and "high" art. This book has taken Allen's radio comedy seriously and has attempted to place it in larger contexts: not only of American popular entertainment and broadcasting but also of American humor. Allen learned to write and perform in the popular theaters. Vaudeville and Broadway revues schooled him in the arts of parody and satire. The live theater of the early twentieth century confirmed the urban and ethnic influences of Allen's youth, and these helped to flavor his comedy as long as he performed. But though he grew up in show business, Allen also knew humorous American writing of more earnest intent. His radio scripts parallel literary humor in their expression of broad tendencies, such as the emergence of the "little man" persona. That representative twentieth-century figure found a home in Allen's radio comedy. Of course, Allen's comedy drew on diverse sources not to carry forward cultural traditions or provide material for scholarly studies; if those sources fit his personal comedic vision and worked with audiences, he used them.

In a career that lasted from 1912 into the 1950s, Fred Allen experienced dramatic changes in the business of creating and performing comedy. While he ventured into three electronic media of amusement—radio, motion pictures, and television—he succeeded only in one. In radio, Allen did more with less. The medium forced Allen and other creators to concentrate their resources on sound and language. If art results from a process of reduction, as Walter Kerr maintains, then Allen became an artist of sound in the early 1930s, and he always remained one. He constructed a comedy of language for which television and motion pictures had little use. But as long as radio ruled broadcasting, Allen was among the few artists who mastered its possibilities. From October 1932 until June 1949 Allen, the one-time comic juggler from Boston, "had access to the imagination" of a vast audience. He put it very simply: "that was why i liked radio. we had some fun."

Notes

Throughout the notes, abbreviations have been used for citations to the variously titled Fred Allen programs broadcast from 1932 until 1949. (The program scripts, on microfilm, are found in the Fred Allen Papers, Manuscript Division of the Library of Congress, Washington, D.C.) The shows, in chronological order, and their abbreviations are as follows:

LBC	Linit Bath Club Revue	October 23, 1932–April 16, 1933
SBR	Salad Bowl Revue	August 4–December 1, 1933
SHR	Sal Hepatica Revue	January 3–March 14, 1934
HOS	Hour of Smiles	March 21–July 4, 1934
THT	Town Hall Tonight	July 11, 1934–June 28, 1939
FAS	Fred Allen Show	October 4, 1939–June 26, 1940
		October 7, 1945–June 26, 1949
TST	Texaco Star Theatre	October 2, 1940–June 25, 1944

Chapter 1

1. John J. Pullen, *Comic Relief: The Life and Laughter of Artemus Ward, 1834–1867* (Hamden, Conn.: Archon Books, 1983), 77.

2. Students of American humor maintain that such nineteenth-century comic personae as the rural storyteller have not yielded fully to the insecure, neurotic "little man" of the twen-

tieth century, but along with such themes as "black humor" represent the dominant trends in recent American humor. For broad assessments of our humor over time, see Hamlin Hill, "Black Humor and the Mass Audience," in *American Humor: Essays Presented to John C. Gerber,* ed. O. M. Brack (Scottsdale, Ariz.: Arete, 1977), 1–2; Hamlin Hill, "Modern American Humor: The Janus Laugh," *College English* 25 (December 1963): 170–176; Walter Blair, " 'A Man's Voice Speaking': A Continuum in American Humor," in *Veins of Humor,* ed. Harry Levin, Harvard English Studies no. 3 (Cambridge: Harvard University Press, 1972), 185–204; Sanford Pinsker, "On or about December 1910: When Human Character—and American Humor—Changed," in *Critical Essays on American Humor,* ed. William Bedford Clark and W. Craig Turner (Boston: Hall, 1984), 184–199; Lawrence E. Mintz, "American Humor in the 1920s," *Thalia: Studies in Literary Humor* 4, no. 1 (Spring and Summer 1981): 26–32. Most discussions of American humor suffer from a gender bias, which Nancy Walker challenges and corrects in *A Very Serious Thing: Women's Humor and American Culture* (Minneapolis: University of Minnesota Press, 1988). Other discussions of trends and transitions in American humor include Walter Blair and Hamlin Hill, *America's Humor: From Poor Richard to Doonesbury* (New York: Oxford University Press, 1978), 367–387; Albert F. McLean, Jr., *American Vaudeville as Ritual* (Lexington: University of Kentucky Press, 1965), chap. 6, "The New Humor"; James DeMuth, *Small Town Chicago: The Comic Perspective of Finley Peter Dunne, George Ade, Ring Lardner* (Port Washington, N.Y.: Kennikat Press, 1980), 3–5 and passim; Norris W. Yates, *The American Humorist: Conscience of the Twentieth Century* (Ames: Iowa State University Press, 1964), 12, 27, 38; Enid Veron, ed., *Humor in America: An Anthology* (New York: Harcourt Brace Jovanovich, 1976), 201–203; Robert C. Toll, *The Entertainment Machine: American Show Business in the Twentieth Century* (New York: Oxford University Press, 1982), chap. 8, "'Leave 'Em Laughin': Comedy and the Media."

3. Quoted in Toll, *Entertainment Machine,* 23.

4. William C. deMille, *Hollywood Saga* (New York: Dutton, 1939), 60.

5. Kalton Lahue, *World of Laughter: The Motion Picture Comedy Short, 1910–1930* (1966; reprint, Norman: University of Oklahoma Press, 1972), 96.

6. Gilbert Seldes, *The Seven Lively Arts* (1924; reprint, New York: Sagamore Press, 1957), 16.

7. James Agee, "Comedy's Greatest Era," in *Agee on Film: Essays and Reviews by James Agee* (New York: Grosset and Dunlap, 1969), 1:2–19, is a classic affirmation of silent film comedy's achievement; on p. 6, Agee describes the "anarchic motion" of a Sennett film chase. William K. Everson, *American Silent Film* (New York: Oxford University Press, 1978), offers a brief assessment of comedy on pp. 260–280. Gerald Mast, *The Comic Mind: Comedy and the Movies*, 2nd ed. (Chicago: University of Chicago Press, 1979), discusses "assumptions, definitions, and categories" on pp. 3–27; pp. 43–58 all on Mack Sennett.

8. Robert Sklar, *Movie-Made America; A Social History of American Movies* (New York: Random House, 1975), 107.

9. Vachel Lindsay, *The Art of the Moving Picture* (1915; reprint of 1922 ed., New York: Liveright, 1970), 189.

10. Charles Chaplin, "Pantomime and Comedy," *New York Times*, January 25, 1931, sec. 8, p. 6, reprinted in Donald W. McCaffrey, ed., *Focus on Chaplin* (Englewood Cliffs, N.J.: Prentice Hall, 1971), 63–65; Lahue, *World of Laughter*, x. An advertisement of the Universal Film Manufacturing Company of the period (1910 to 1912) emphasized the unrestricted appeal of the firm's "stories told in pictures": "Regardless of creed, color, race, or nationality, everyone in the universe understands the stories told by Universal Pictures." Reprinted in Everson, *American Silent Film*, 25.

11. Ibid., 10.

12. deMille, *Hollywood Saga*, 276.

13. Andrea S. Walsh, "Of Strong Mothers and Terrified Wives: 'Women's Films' in the World War II Era," *Clark Now: The Magazine of Clark University*, Winter 1985, 20.

14. Benjamin McArthur, *Actors and American Culture, 1880–1920* (Philadelphia: Temple University Press, 1984), 209. Lawrence Levine makes the same point in "William Shakespeare and the American People: A Study in Cultural Transformation," *American Historical Review* 89 (February 1984): 50, 57. See also Paul M. Zall, ed., *Mark Twain Laughing: Humorous Anecdotes by and about Samuel L. Clemens* (Knoxville: University of Tennessee Press, 1985), x; and Richard Hughes, "The Second Revolution: Literature and Radio," *Virginia Quarterly Review* 23 (Winter 1947): 34–43.

15. Nicholas Vardac, *Stage to Screen: Theatrical Method from Garrick to Griffith* (Cambridge: Harvard University Press, 1949), xxi–xxvi, 67, 87–88, 108, 134–135, 137, and passim.

16. John Dunning, *Tune in Yesterday: The Ultimate Ency-

clopedia of Old-Time Radio, 1925–1976 (Englewood Cliffs, N.J.: Prentice Hall, 1976), 141–145, 407–413; Erik Barnouw, *The Golden Web: A History of Broadcasting in the United States, 1933–1953* (New York: Oxford University Press, 1968), 65–73, 84–89, 116–120, 151–154, 210–214; J. Fred MacDonald, *Don't Touch That Dial: Radio Programming in American Life from 1920 to 1960* (Chicago: Nelson-Hall, 1979), 52–60. On Corwin's career, see R. LeRoy Bannerman, *Norman Corwin and Radio: The Golden Years* (University: University of Alabama Press, 1986); Arch Oboler, *This Freedom: Thirteen New Radio Plays*, with a "Foreword" by Robert J. Landry (New York: Random House, 1942); Erik Barnouw, ed., *Radio Drama in Action; Twenty-Five Plays of a Changing World* (New York: Rinehart, 1945).

17. Lee De Forest, *Television Today and Tomorrow* (New York: Dial Press, 1942), 349; see p. 350 for Sarnoff's view.

18. Landry, "Foreword," viii–ix; *Columbia Workshop Plays*, selected and edited by Douglas Coulter (New York: Whittlesey House, 1939), ix.

19. *Thirteen by Corwin: Radio Dramas by Norman Corwin*, with a "Preface" by Carl Van Doren (New York: Henry Holt, 1942), vii–ix.

20. Archibald MacLeish, *The Fall of the City: A Verse Play for Radio* (New York: Farrar and Rinehart, 1937), ix–x. For an interesting exploration of "radio's startling impact of sensibility" in broadcasting's first era of widespread influence, see Catherine L. Covert, "'We May Hear Too Much': American Sensibility and the Response to Radio, 1918–1941," in *Mass Media between the Wars: Perceptions of Cultural Tension, 1918–1941*, ed. Catherine L. Covert and John D. Stevens (Syracuse: Syracuse University Press, 1984), 199–220.

21. Ross Firestone writes: "The comedian compares to the poet in his sensitivity to the creative possibilities of language and in his ability to deploy it with precision, economy and effect." Ross Firestone, ed., *The Big Radio Comedy Program* (Chicago: Contemporary Books, 1978), ix.

22. Walter Kerr, *The Silent Clowns* (New York: Knopf, 1975), 3, 4.

23. Rudolph Arnheim, *Radio* (London: Faber and Faber, 1936), 14.

24. Arch Oboler, "The Art of Radio Writing," in his *Fourteen Radio Plays* (New York: Random House, 1940), xv.

25. Leonard Maltin, "They're Tuned in to the 'Thrilling Days of Yesteryear,'" *Smithsonian* 17, no. 12 (March 1987): 73.

26. Joseph Julian, *This Was Radio: A Personal Memoir* (New York: Viking Press, 1975), 232.

27. Arnold Auerbach, *Funny Men Don't Laugh* (Garden City, N.Y.: Doubleday, 1965), vii.

28. Fred Allen, *Treadmill to Oblivion* (Boston: Little, Brown, 1954), 239; see also 4–5.

29. Arthur Frank Wertheim, *Radio Comedy* (New York: Oxford University Press, 1979), 14, 63, 90–91, 93, 95–96; Barnouw, *Golden Web*, 99–100; John E. DiMeglio, "Radio's Debt to Vaudeville," *Journal of Popular Culture* 12 (Fall 1978): 232–234.

30. LBC script, October 23, 1932.

31. DiMeglio, "Radio's Debt to Vaudeville," 230–232, 234; see John E. DiMeglio, *Vaudeville, U.S.A.* (Bowling Green, Ohio: Bowling Green University Popular Press, 1973), 15–16, for Allen's comment. See also Robert C. Toll, *On with the Show: The First Century of Show Business in America* (New York: Oxford University Press, 1976), 286–287, 292–293.

32. Until recently, literary scholars dominated the formal study of humor in this country. College courses in humor almost invariably appeared in English Department listings, although even there the subject was a minor specialty. Today the study of humor is developing into a lively interdisciplinary field. The work of anthropologists and folklorists is becoming more widely known to scholars in other areas. Physiologists and psychologists—those interested in personality development and those interested in counseling—and students of popular culture are among the people pursuing aspects of the subject.

33. Constance Rourke was among the first to demonstrate that classic nineteenth-century American literature drew heavily on the comic spirit in folk and commercial popular culture; see Constance Rourke, *American Humor: A Study of the National Character* (1931; reprinted, New York: Doubleday, 1953). Of Walt Whitman she writes: "To enter the world of Whitman is to touch the spirit of American popular comedy, with its local prejudices, its national prepossessions, its fantastic beliefs; many phases of comic reaction are unfolded there" (p. 142). And: "The impact of popular comic story-telling in America must have reached Poe" (p. 145). See Gene Bluestone, "Constance Rourke and the Folk Sources of American Literature," *Western Folklore* 26 (1967): 77–87; Joan Shelly Rubin, *Constance Rourke and American Culture* (Chapel Hill: University of North Carolina Press, 1980), 57–58. For other instances of modern authors drawing on the oral folk tradition of the South, see Robert D. Jacobs, "The Humor of Tobacco Road," in *The Comic Imagination in*

American Literature, ed. Louis D. Rubin (New Brunswick, N.J.: Rutgers University Press, 1973), 286–287; and Jacobs, "Faulkner's Humor," in ibid., 306. A recent study of interest is Alan Dundes, *Cracking Jokes: Studies of Sick Humor Cycles and Stereotypes* (Berkeley, Calif.: Ten Speed Press, 1987).

34. Herbert J. Gans, *Popular Culture and High Culture: An Analysis and Evaluation of Taste* (New York: Basic Books, 1974), 21, 22; Ray B. Browne, "Popular Culture: Notes toward a Definition," in *Popular Culture and the Expanding Consciousness,* ed. Ray B. Browne (New York: Wiley, 1973), 16–18, 21–22; Russel Nye, *The Unembarrassed Muse: The Popular Arts in America* (New York: Dial Press, 1970), 1–7, 417–420. See also Robert E. Faulkner's sociological study of classically trained musicians who performed in movie studio orchestras, *Hollywood Studio Musicians: Their Work and Careers in the Recording Industry* (Chicago: Aldine-Atherton, 1971).

35. Kenneth S. Lynn, *Mark Twain and Southwestern Humor* (1960; reprinted, Westport, Conn.: Greenwood Press, 1972); Bernard DeVoto, *Mark Twain's America* and *Mark Twain at Work* (Boston: Houghton Mifflin, 1967); Paul Fatout, *Mark Twain on the Lecture Circuit* (Bloomington: Indiana University Press, 1960); Zall, *Mark Twain Laughing,* xv.

36. Pullen, *Comic Relief;* on Ward the showman–lecturer, see pp. 27–29, 38–56, 64–68, 74– 77, 93–95, 112–122, 130–132, 135–136, 151–156, 169–174; Curtis Dahl, "Artemus Ward: Comic Panoramist," *New England Quarterly* 32 (Winter 1959): 476–485; DeMuth, *Small Town Chicago;* Kenny J. Williams and Bernard Duffey, eds., *Chicago's Public Wits: A Chapter in the American Comic Spirit* (Baton Rouge: Louisiana State University Press, 1983); Sinda Gregory, *Private Investigations: The Novels of Dashiell Hammett* (Carbondale: Southern Illinois University Press, 1985), 11.

37. See Tom Dardis, *Some Time in the Sun* (New York: Scribner's, 1976); Richard Fine, *Hollywood and the Profession of Authorship, 1928–1940* (Ann Arbor: UMI Research Press, 1985), passim.

38. Howard Teichmann, *Smart Aleck: The Wit, World, and Life of Alexander Woolcott* (New York: Morrow, 1976), 180–207; Norris W. Yates, *Robert Benchley* (New York: Twayne, 1968); Robert Redding, *Starring Robert Benchley: "Those Magnificent Movie Shorts"* (Albuquerque: University of New Mexico Press, 1973), xviii, 2, and passim.

39. Joan Shelly Rubin, "Swift's Premium Ham: William Lyon Phelps and the Redefinition of Culture," in Covert and Stevens, *Mass Media between the Wars*, 3–19.

40. Ruth R. Wissen, *The Schlemiel as Modern Hero* (Chicago: University of Chicago Press, 1971), 73.

41. Fred Allen, *Much Ado about Me* (Boston: Little, Brown, 1956), 165–166.

42. Herman Wouk, "Foreword," in *Fred Allen's Letters*, ed. Joe McCarthy (Garden City, N.Y.: Doubleday, 1965), n.p.

43. Quoted in "Aristides," "What's So Funny?" *American Scholar* 53, no. 4 (Autumn 1984): 441.

44. James Thurber to Edward Weeks, August 20, 1954, in McCarthy, *Letters*, 346.

45. On the use of broadcast programming as texts, see David Marc, *Demographic Vistas: Television in American Culture* (Philadelphia: University of Pennsylvania Press, 1984), xi–xii; Rubin, "Swift's Premium Ham," 3.

46. Andrew Bergman, *We're in the Money: Depression America and Its Films* (New York: New York University Press, 1971), xii. Lawrence W. Levine has made the same point in his "American Culture and the Great Depression," *Yale Review* 74 (Winter 1985): 208–209. Stephen Fox represents those who believe that radio listeners in the 1930s "were seeking not reality but escape." See Stephen Fox, *The Mirror Makers: A History of American Advertising and Its Creators* (New York: Vintage, 1984), 151.

47. Lahue, *World of Laughter*, xi.

48. Marc, *Demographic Vistas*, 39–40.

49. "A Note on the Movie Industry and the Depression," in Bergman, *We're in the Money*, xix–xxiii; xxi and xxii quoted.

50. *Variety*, July 12, 1932, 1.

51. On vaudeville's decline, see McLean, *American Vaudeville as Ritual*, 24; Anthony Slide, *The Vaudevillians: A Dictionary of Vaudeville Performers* (Westport, Conn.: Arlington House, 1981), xii; Charles W. Stein, ed., *American Vaudeville as Seen by Its Contemporaries* (New York: Knopf, 1984), 335–337; DiMeglio, "Radio's Debt to Vaudeville," 228; *Variety*, August 16, 1932, 1, 23.

52. *Variety*, December 6, 1932, 32, and December 20, 1932, 1; and special Radio City section of the paper on pp. 56–162. Carol Herselle Krinsky, *Rockefeller Center* (New York: Oxford University Press, 1978), chap. 11, "The RCA Building"; Richard

B. Jewell, "Hollywood and Radio: Competition and Partnership in the 1930s," *Historical Journal of Film, Radio and Television* 4 (October 1984): 126; Erik Barnouw, *The Sponsor: Notes on a Modern Potentate* (New York: Oxford University Press, 1978), 27.

53. Stein, *American Vaudeville*, 335; Slide, *Vaudevillians*, xii.

54. William McKinley Randle, Jr., "History of Radio Broadcasting and Its Social and Economic Effect on the Entertainment Industry, 1920–1930," doctoral dissertation, Western Reserve University, 1966, 1:94. Randle says that the touring company appeared on WGM, but I find no record of a station with those call letters. Because "The Passing Show" appeared in Chicago, the station may have been that city's WGN.

55. Allen, *Much Ado about Me*, 349.

56. Teichmann, *Smart Aleck*, 82.

57. Jo Ranson, "Out of a Blue Sky," *Brooklyn Daily Eagle*, June 6, 1937, in Fred Allen clipping file, Billy Rose Theatre Collection, New York Public Library at Lincoln Center. Hereinafter cited as Billy Rose Collection.

58. The production appeared in theaters of the Paramount-Publix chain, which presented a mix of live and film entertainment. See John L. Marsh, "Vaudefilm: Its Contribution to a Moviegoing America," *Journal of American Culture* 7 (Fall 1984): 80.

59. Allen's experience with *Three's a Crowd* may be glimpsed in his letters of 1931 and early 1932, as collected in McCarthy, *Letters*; his letter to Mrs. Frank Rosengren, May 6, 1931 (114–115), is quoted. See also Allen, *Treadmill to Oblivion*, 3.

60. *Variety*, September 27, 1932, 55; Roland Marchand, *Advertising the American Dream: Making Way for Modernity, 1920–1940* (Berkeley: University of California Press, 1985), 20.

61. *Variety*, November 15, 1932, 55.

62. See the following issues of *Variety*: November 1, 1932, 50; December 27, 1932, 1; February 28, 1933, 47.

63. Edwin O'Connor, "Epilogue," in Allen, *Much Ado about Me*, 363.

64. Allen to James R. Naulty, April 15, 1933, 71; to Joe Kelly, November 1, 1932, 87; and to Val Eichen, March 20, 1933, 281; all in McCarthy, *Letters*.

65. Allen to Naulty, ibid.

66. Allen to Eichen, ibid.

Chapter 2

1. Quoted in William V. Shannon, *The American Irish* (New York: Macmillan, 1963), 99–100.

2. For a description of Somerville's economic and social landscape, see Reed Ueda, "The High School and Social Mobility in a Streetcar Suburb: Somerville, Massachusetts, 1870–1910," *Journal of Interdisciplinary History* 14, no. 4 (Spring 1984): 751–756. Allen's joke is in the script of "The Pepsodent Show," starring Bob Hope, October 29, 1946, Fred Allen Papers, Library of Congress, Washington, D.C.; until he applied for a passport to work abroad in 1916–1917, Allen believed he had been born in Cambridge, and many journalistic accounts of his life repeated the error. Allen was born in the family home on Union Street, the boundary between Cambridge and Somerville, on the Somerville side of the street. See Fred Allen, *Much Ado about Me* (Boston: Little, Brown, 1956), 179–180. Allen's account of his life to 1930 is the best memoir written by a vaudevillian and the basic source for factual material about Allen's life.

3. Allen, *Much Ado about Me*, 4–5, 18. According to one occupational ranking of Boston's workers, bookbinders were categorized as "skilled blue-collar." Stephen Thernstrom, *The Other Bostonians: Poverty and Progress in the American Metropolis, 1880–1970* (Cambridge: Harvard University Press, 1973), 291. Allen's father earned $1,000 annually around the turn of the century.

4. Allen, *Much Ado about Me*, 7, 13; *Variety*, May 29, 1934, 34.

5. Quoted in Shannon, *American Irish*, 142.

6. Mary Braggiotti, "Fred Allen and Portland Hoffa," *New York Post Weekend Magazine*, November 2, 1946, clipping in Al Durante Collection, Archive of Contemporary History, University of Wyoming, Laramie. Hereinafter cited as Durante Collection. Allen included the same statement in a THT script for the program of November 2, 1938.

7. For example, John K. Hutchens, "On Books and Authors: Ex-Juggler," *New York Herald Tribune Book Review*, December 19, 1954, 2. Journalist Beverly Smith called this quip his "best and most characteristic ad lib" in "Want a Job at a Million a Year?" *American Magazine* 140 (December 1945), 124. The quote is also noted in J. Bryan III, "Eighty Hours for a Laugh," *Saturday Evening Post* 214 (October 4, 1941): 23. And it lived on

in the 1980s: see Maurice Zolotow, "Unforgettable Fred Allen," *Reader's Digest*, October 1987, 56.

8. S. J. Perelman, "The Great Sourpuss; or, Should Auld Acquaintance Be Exhumed?" *Holiday* 12 (December 1952): 95; see also *Variety*'s review of the "Texaco Star Theatre," October 8, 1941, 26.

9. Shannon, *American Irish*, 8–11, discusses the world view of the Irish people.

10. Harold E. Stearns, *The Street I Know* (New York: Lee Furman, 1935), 63–69, 93.

11. Allen, *Much Ado about Me*, 13.

12. For example, the scripts of Fred Allen's shows for October 26, 1947, and April 11, 1948.

13. Norris W. Yates, *Robert Benchley* (New York: Twayne, 1968), 18.

14. John E. DiMeglio, *Vaudeville, U.S.A.* (Bowling Green, Ohio: Bowling Green University Popular Press, 1973), 63. On immigrant mobility through mass culture, see John Higham, "Immigration," in *The Comparative Approach to American History*, ed. C. Vann Woodward (New York: Basic Books, 1968), 102–103; Irving Howe, *World of Our Fathers* (New York: Harcourt Brace Jovanovich, 1976), 556–573.

15. Robert C. Toll, *The Entertainment Machine: American Show Business in the Twentieth Century* (New York: Oxford University Press, 1982), 7. John Kasson, *Amusing the Million: Coney Island at the Turn of the Century* (New York: Hill and Wang, 1978), discusses the American public's hunger for amusements; on Boston's relative lack of opportunity, particularly for the Irish, see Shannon, *American Irish*, 183–187; Lawrence J. McCaffrey, "Irish America," *Wilson Quarterly* 9 (Spring 1985): 84–85; Thernstrom, *The Other Bostonians*, chaps. 6 and 7.

16. Allen, *Much Ado about Me*, 35–41, 53; Bryan, "Eighty Hours for a Laugh," 108.

17. Bill Smith, "Vaudeville: Entertainment of the Masses," in *American Popular Entertainment: Papers and Proceedings of the Conference on the History of American Popular Entertainment*, ed. Myron Matlaw (Westport, Conn.: Greenwood Press, 1979), 14. See also DiMeglio, *Vaudeville, U.S.A.*, 64–69, on amateur nights; Bryan, "Eighty Hours for a Laugh," 108.

18. John B. Kennedy, "Wisecracker," *Colliers'* 85 (June 7, 1930): 64.

19. Allen, *Much Ado about Me*, 53–66, 60 quoted. See also Jack Haley, "I Knew Fred Allen When," *Cosmopolitan*, May

1948, 8; Alton Cook, "Fred Allen's Amateur Days," *New York World Telegram*, April 30, 1935, clipping in Billy Rose Collection; Irving Wallace, "Fred Allen: Never without a Gag," *Liberty*, February 28, 1942, reprinted in *Liberty* 1 (Winter 1972): 77–78.

20. Albert F. McLean, *American Vaudeville as Ritual* (Lexington: University of Kentucky Press, 1965), 1; see also DiMeglio, *Vaudeville, U.S.A.*, 11.

21. DiMeglio, *Vaudeville, U.S.A.*, 195; "Fortunes for Entertainments," *New York Times*, September 7, 1913, sec. 7, p. 1.

22. Rowland Haynes, *Recreation Survey, Milwaukee*, Bulletin no. 17 (Milwaukee: Milwaukee Bureau of Economy and Efficiency, 1911), 8–10; Rowland Haynes, "Recreation Survey of Kansas City, Mo.," in *Second Annual Report of the Recreation Department of the Board of Public Welfare* (Kansas City, 1912), 29–32; Rowland Haynes, *Recreation Survey, Detroit, Michigan* (Detroit, 1913), 47; *Public Recreation: Transactions of the Commonwealth Club of California* 8, no. 5 (San Francisco, 1913), 227–228.

23. DiMeglio, *Vaudeville, U.S.A.*, 155–157. On the national circuits and major booking agencies, see ibid., 19–27; and McLean, *American Vaudeville as Ritual*, 20–21.

24. "The Amusement Situation in the City of Boston," Drama Committee of the Twentieth Century Club, Boston, 1910, 4–7, 10; Douglas Gilbert, *American Vaudeville, Its Life and Times* (1940; reprinted New York: Dover, 1968), 206.

25. Allen, *Much Ado about Me*, 57, 70, 109. A case study of the rise of the movies in Boston and that city's mass amusement market can be found in Russell Merritt, "Nickelodeon Theaters 1905–1914: Building an Audience for the Movies," in *The American Film Industry*, ed. Tino Balio (Madison: University of Wisconsin Press, 1976), 67–79; on theaters that mixed vaudeville and motion picture showings, see John L. Marsh, "Vaudefilm: Its Contribution to a Moviegoing America," *Journal of American Culture* 7 (Fall 1984): 77–84.

26. Allen borrowed his first stage name from the St. James Hotel on Bowdoin Square in Boston; see Allen, *Much Ado about Me*, 71, 78, 93, 103. Will Rogers's vaudeville act evolved as did Allen's; Rogers's popularity grew as he added joking patter to his lariat tricks. See Walter Blair, *Horse Sense in American Humor: From Benjamin Franklin to Ogden Nash* (Chicago: University of Chicago Press, 1942), 262.

27. See Blair, *Horse Sense*, 94, 101–102, 110; Kennedy, "Wisecracker," 64; Bryan, "Eighty Hours for a Laugh," 109; Di-

Meglio, *Vaudeville, U.S.A.*, 34, on comedy's central role in vaudeville. Douglas Gilbert calls "comedy . . . the essence of American vaudeville" in *American Vaudeville*, 251.

28. Allen, *Much Ado about Me*, 114–118. In his memoirs, Allen identified his friend as John Murphy (p. 117); Beverly Smith also identifies John Murphy as the friend in his "Want a Job at a Million a Year?" 122. In 1948, Jack Haley, boyhood friend of Fred Allen, claimed to have been the one who agreed to send the train fare; see Haley, "I Knew Fred Allen When," 108. See DiMeglio, *Vaudeville, U.S.A.*, 133–134, on the importance of New York to a successful vaudeville career.

29. For his experience in the bigtime, see Allen, *Much Ado about Me*, 212–213, 228, 258–294, 314–351.

30. Ibid., 237. For a contemporary discussion of vaudeville circuits, see Alfred L. Bernheim, "The Facts of Vaudeville," *Equity News* 9 (November 1923): 33–40, reprinted in *American Vaudeville as Seen by Its Contemporaries*, ed. Charles W. Stein (New York: Knopf, 1984), 124–130. One contemporary account of the smalltime is George Jean Nathan, *The Popular Theatre* (New York: Knopf, 1918), chap. 15, "It's 'Small Time' Vaudeville."

31. Allen, *Much Ado about Me*, 186–187; Mark Leddy, the young vaudeville agent who helped promote Allen's vaudeville career as early as 1914, suggested the name change. Allen's last name was borrowed from Fox booker Edgar Allen. See ibid., 203, and Leddy's obituary in *Variety*, June 27, 1984, 94.

32. Allen, *Much Ado about Me*, 237; on his foreign tour, see pp. 144–185.

33. Ibid., 226.

34. Ibid., 226–228; James Agee, "Comedy's Greatest Era," in *Agee on Film: Essays and Reviews by James Agee* (New York: Grosset and Dunlap, 1969), 1:14.

35. Allen, *Much Ado about Me*, 291.

36. On this problem, see DiMeglio, *Vaudeville, U.S.A.*, 77–78.

37. Allen, *Much Ado about Me*, 279; see also p. 258.

38. Ibid., 293.

39. Ibid., 285–288, 314–330, 338–348. Like Allen, Savo came to professional vaudeville from amateur nights, turned professional in 1912, and tried juggling before he became a comic. See Jimmy Savo, *I Bow to the Streets: Memories of a New York Childhood* (New York: Howard Frisch, 1963); Jackson Harvey, "Mr. Savo Steps Up among the Artists," *Theatre Magazine* 52

(October 1930): 20. In the Fred Allen clippings in the Billy Rose Collection there is a "Program Magazine" from B. F. Keith's Palace Theatre for the "Week Commencing Mon. Mat., October 4"; Allen and Yorke's act, "The Efficiency Men," was on the bill. Yorke's obituary is in *Variety*, October 8, 1958.

40. Gilbert, *American Vaudeville*, 251; for a discussion of this strain of American humor in several media, see Gerald Weales, *Canned Goods as Caviar: American Film Comedy of the 1930s* (Chicago: University of Chicago Press, 1985), 55–59, in a chapter on the Marx Brothers' *Duck Soup*.

41. Gilbert, *American Vaudeville*, 262–263; *Variety*, April 29, 1925, 5.

42. "The Argot of Vaudeville," *New York Times*, December 23, 1917, sec. 4, p. 6.

43. According to John B. Kennedy, Allen made the remark during the first performance of *The Little Show* in 1929; see "Wisecracker," 66. The remark is quoted in Wallace, "Fred Allen: Never without a Gag," 78. And it appears in Zolotow's 1987 article "Unforgettable Fred Allen," 55.

44. McLean, *American Vaudeville as Ritual*, chap. 6, "The New Humor."

45. Ibid., 112, 119; Toll, *Entertainment Machine*, 213.

46. McLean, *American Vaudeville as Ritual*, 112.

47. Ibid., 137 quoted; see also 107, 109, 110, 117, 131. Others have found the use of humor to attack authority to be characteristic of such ethnic minorities as the Irish and the Jews. See Joseph Boskin and Joseph Dorinson, "Ethnic Humor: Subversion and Survival," *American Quarterly* 37 (Spring 1985): 85.

48. *Variety* printed the January 4, 1918, review in its issue of January 16, 1934, 33.

49. Allen, *Much Ado about Me*, 200, 266.

50. Jimmy Lyons, *Encyclopedia of Stage Material* (Boston: Walter H. Baker, 1925), 123.

51. The first two are from Allen, *Much Ado about Me*, 102, and were used before 1914 while Allen was still in Boston; the second two jokes are in Kennedy, "Wisecracker," 66. For other examples, see Bryan, "Eighty Hours for a Laugh," 108.

52. Perelman, "Great Sourpuss," 95.

53. Allen, *Much Ado about Me*, 228; after Allen's death, his friend H. Allen Smith criticized the compiler of *The Home Book of Humorous Quotations* for insulting the comedian's memory by including "a long series of vapid, senseless, and unfunny gags largely out of Mr. Allen's beginning days in vaudeville." Smith

clearly believed that Allen's talents had improved with maturity. See H. Allen Smith, *Low Man Rides Again* (Garden City, N.Y.: Doubleday, 1973), 203.

54. *Variety*, October 13, 1926, 24; see also *Variety*, October 6, 1926, 58.

55. Allen, *Much Ado about Me*, 165–166.

56. Ibid., 163–164, 177–185, 187, 201–205, 227–228, 259–260, 280–290, 292–294; *Variety*, October 13, 1926, 24. Burton Lane, who knew Allen while both worked in *Three's a Crowd*, commented later: "Fred Allen was the best comedian that I know of, and he was a creative comedian: he didn't depend on writers to give him material, he wrote most of it himself. I remember on the road, trying out material, every performance would be a completely different routine, until we got set on one that he liked." Memoir of Burton Lane, Oral History Collections, Columbia University, New York.

57. Gilbert, *American Vaudeville*, 3; see also 385.

58. The historian Gunther Barth has explored the "intimate relation between the [vaudeville] show and urban life." See Gunther Barth, *City People; The Rise of Modern City Culture in Nineteenth-Century America* (New York: Oxford University Press, 1980), 219; see also 191, 193–194, 228, 232.

59. Michael M. Davis, Jr., *The Exploitation of Pleasure: A Study of Commercial Recreations in New York City* (New York: Russell Sage Foundation, 1910), 32–33.

60. Gilbert, *American Vaudeville*, 61.

61. On the roots and use of ethnic stage humor, see David Grimsted, *Melodrama Unveiled: American Theater and Culture, 1800–1850* (Chicago: University of Chicago Press, 1968), 189–190; Robert C. Toll, *Blacking Up: The Minstrel Show in Nineteenth-Century America* (New York: Oxford University Press, 1974), passim on the uses whites made of black stereotypes for humorous purposes, and pp. 175–180 for the portrayal of the stage Irishman by blackface minstrel characters; Richard Moody, *Ned Harrington: From Corlear's Hook to Herald Square* (Chicago: Nelson-Hall, 1980), 11–18, 21–28, 51–53, 85–96, and passim for the career of a nineteenth-century show business entrepreneur and performer who assumed black, Irish, and German stage personae; McLean, *American Vaudeville as Ritual*, 109, 114, 120–121, and 122–130 on the German and Jewish influence on vaudeville humor; Gilbert, *American Vaudeville*, 61–72 on ethnic humor, 291–292 on Jewish comics.

62. Nathaniel Benchley, *Robert Benchley, a Biography*

(New York: McGraw-Hill, 1955), 39; Weales, *Canned Goods as Caviar*, 62.

63. Allen, *Much Ado about Me*, 233.

64. "Don't Trust Midgets," *New Yorker* 6 (January 10, 1931): 53–54. A good overview that includes a discussion of the *New Yorker* humorists and Algonquin Wits is Lawrence E. Mintz, "American Humor in the 1920s," *Thalia: Studies in Literary Humor* 4, no. 1 (Spring and Summer 1981): 26–32. Robert E. Drennan, ed., in *The Algonquin Wits* (New York: Citadel Press, 1968), 11, lists these as the "lead" characters: George S. Kaufman and Robert E. Sherwood (playwrights), Franklin Pierce Adams (FPA) and Heywood Broun (columnists), Ring Lardner, Robert Benchley, Alexander Woollcott, and Dorothy Parker (writers and critics), and Edna Ferber (novelist and playwright). A larger list contains the "supporting players."

65. See James Thurber to Edward Weeks, August 20, 1954; Thurber to Allen, September 3, 1954; Thurber to Portland Hoffa, August 29, 1961; Allen to Thurber, November 19, 1953; all in Joe McCarthy, ed., *Fred Allen's Letters* (Garden City, N.Y.: Doubleday, 1965), 345–346, 347, 342–344, 344–345.

66. Allen to H. Allen Smith, August 16, 1945, in ibid., 27.

67. Haley, "I Knew Fred Allen When."

68. Allen to Tishman, December 25, 1920, in McCarthy, *Letters*, 49, 50.

69. Allen, *Much Ado about Me*, 253.

70. Ibid., 251.

71. TST script, March 19, 1944.

72. THT script, December 14, 1938.

73. TST script, May 21, 1941. Arnold M. Auerbach quotes a similar statement by Allen in his *Funny Men Don't Laugh* (Garden City, N.Y.: Doubleday, 1965), 165.

74. For Silverman's editorial tribute to Gray, see *Variety*, December 3, 1924, 11.

75. The dates of publication were January 21 and 28, February 4, 11, 18, 25, and March 4 and 11.

76. For Allen's story of his brief career as a newspaper humorist, see *Much Ado about Me*, 306–313.

77. They are "A Small Timer's Diary," *Variety*, September 6, 1923, 7, 36–38; "The Acrobat's Christmas; Or, a Tight Episode," *Variety*, January 3, 1924, 6; "The Sharpshooter's Revenge; 'A Shot Story,'" *Variety*, December 30, 1925, 24; "Don't Trust Midgets," *New Yorker* 6 (January 10, 1931): 53–54; "Proving That a 'Variety Mugg' Is a Mugg," *Variety*, January 8, 1941, 40;

"The Confession," *Variety*, January 5, 1944, 23; "The Vaude Elephant That Didn't Remember," *Variety*, January 3, 1945, 14.

78. "Down to the Sea in Quips," *New York Times*, June 30, 1929, sec. 8, p. 1; " 'How I Got That Way,' " *Theatre Magazine* 50 (July 1929): 31, 66; a third piece, published while Allen performed in *Three's a Crowd* sometime in 1930, 1931, or 1932, is "Fred Allen Gets a Letter." It is an unidentified clipping in the box of Allen newspaper clippings, Billy Rose Collection; Kennedy, "Wisecracker," 19, 64, 66.

79. Margaret M. Knapp, "Theatrical Parodies in American Topical Revues," *Journal of Popular Culture* 12, no. 3 (Winter 1978): 482–483.

80. Ibid.; David Ewen, *The New Complete Book of the American Musical Theater* (New York: Holt, Rinehart and Winston, 1970), 310. On the revue form, see also Richard Kislan, *The Musical: A Look at the American Musical Theater* (Englewood Cliffs, N.J.: Prentice Hall, 1980), 79–92; Donald Oliver, "Preface," in *The Greatest Revue Sketches*, ed. Donald Oliver (New York: Avon, 1982), xi–xv. On Broadway during the postwar decade, see Allen Churchill, *The Theatrical 20s* (New York: McGraw-Hill, 1975).

81. Review of *The Little Show*, *Theatre Magazine* 50 (July 1929): 42; *New York Times*, May 1, 1929, 28.

82. On *Three's a Crowd*, see *Theatre Magazine* 52 (December 1930): 2, and January 1931, 2; *New York Times*, October 16, 1930, 28, and October 26, 1930, sec. 8, p. 1; Ewen, *American Musical Theater*, 529–531; Max Wylie, ed., *Best Broadcasts of 1938–39* (New York: Whittlesey House, 1939), 212; Ben Gross, *I Looked and I Listened: Informal Recollections of Radio and TV* (1954; reprint, New Rochelle, N.Y.: Arlington House, 1970), 134; Russell Lynes, *The Lively Audience: A Social History of the Visual and Performing Arts in America, 1890–1950* (New York: Harper & Row, 1985), 143, 145.

Chapter 3

1. Quoted in "The World's Worst Juggler," *Time* 49 (April 7, 1947): 71. See *Variety*, December 25, 1935, 28, for Studio 8-H size.

2. Quoted in Arnold M. Auerbach, *Funny Men Don't Laugh* (Garden City, N.Y.: Doubleday, 1965), 130–131.

3. Ibid., 131; Al Hirschfeld, "Fred Allen a Grim Success Story," *New York Times Magazine*, July 2, 1944, 53.

4. "Watching an Hour of Smiles," *New York Times*, August 12, 1934, sec. 8, p. 15.

5. This paragraph draws on the sources cited in notes 1 through 4 plus the following: *Variety*, November 28, 1933, 40; Carroll Nye, "Gags Flow Swiftly at Fred Allen Show," *Los Angeles Times*, June 28, 1936, sec. 3, p. 10; Robert Eichberg, *Radio Stars of Today; Or, Behind the Scenes in Broadcasting* (Boston: L. C. Page, ca. 1937), 28–32. Since Allen's programs evolved over time, there were variations in procedure that these paragraphs cannot capture. Allen's broadcasts were heard on both Wednesdays and Sundays, for example, and at times the show's announcer performed the warm-up function.

6. Quote from James Cannon, "Hermit Fred Allen Emerges," *New York World-Telegram*, July 19, 1933, clipping in Fred Allen file, Billy Rose Collection.

7. Authors have contrasted the comedy–variety format with the situation-comedy formula, which Allen did not employ. See J. Fred MacDonald, *Don't Touch That Dial! Radio Programming in American Life from 1920 to 1960* (Chicago: Nelson-Hall, 1979), 115–132; David Marc, *Demographic Vistas: Television in American Culture* (Philadelphia: University of Pennsylvania Press, 1984), 21–29. Marc shows that the sitcom has dominated television comedy since the 1950s. See David Marc, *Comic Visions: Television Comedy and American Culture* (Boston: Unwin Hyman, 1989).

8. "Radio II: A $45,000,000 Talent Bill," *Fortune* 17 (May 1938): 122.

9. Nathan Norman Weiss, "Long Pan Alley—III," *Jewish Advocate* (Boston), March 4, 1948, clipping in Durante Collection.

10. Fred Allen, *Treadmill to Oblivion* (Boston: Little, Brown, 1954), 19–21.

11. *Variety*, December 12, 1933, 37. On the importance of drug and cosmetic sponsors, see the following issues of *Variety*: March 13, 1934, 39; September 25, 1935, 45; October 2, 1935, 36; January 17, 1940, 26. An early assessment of World War II's effect on radio advertising noted: "Eighty per cent of radio's advertising revenue comes from four principal commodities: foods, drugs, toiletries, tobacco." Sherman H. Dryer, *Radio in Wartime* (New York: Greenberg, 1942), 27.

12. William McKinley Randle, Jr., "History of Radio Broadcasting and Its Social and Economic Effects on the Entertainment Industry, 1920–1930," doctoral dissertation, Western Reserve

University, 1966, 1:146, 156; *Variety*, July 14, 1943, 30; memo from I. E. Showerman to Janet MacRorie, December 19, 1938, Box 59, folder 28, "Bristol-Myers" (1938), National Broadcasting Company Records, State Historical Society of Wisconsin. Hereinafter cited as NBC Records.

13. Both quotes from W. B. Benton to R. C. Patterson, Jr., March 13, 1934, Box 24, folder 24, "Bristol-Myers" (1934), NBC Records.

14. See ibid. for Benton's comments; see also *Variety*, March 13, 1934, 39 (for quote), 40. For Allen's reaction to the situation, see Allen, *Treadmill to Oblivion*, 29.

15. See HOS scripts, March 21 and 28, 1939.

16. "33 Hit Programs in '33–'34," *Variety*, June 12, 1934, 41; a review of the show is in the issue of March 27, 1934, 38.

17. "Gag Writers Wanted," *Newsweek* 24 (November 6, 1944): 88.

18. Arthur Frank Wertheim, *Radio Comedy* (New York: Oxford University Press, 1979), makes a similar judgment in his contrast of the Allen programs of the 1930s and 1940s; see chaps. 8 and 15.

19. Allen, *Treadmill to Oblivion*, 30. Vaudeville actor Will Cressy wrote and apparently acted in a rural sketch prior to 1910 entitled "Town Hall To-Night." Allen may have named his radio program after the skit; surely he knew Cressy, at least by reputation. See Shirley Louise Staples, "From 'Barney's Courtship' to Burns and Allen: Male–Female Comedy Teams in American Vaudeville, 1865–1932," doctoral dissertation, Tufts University, 1981, 233.

20. Reported in *Variety*, June 2, 1937, 28; and *New York Times*, June 6, 1937, sec. 11, p. 10.

21. "Radio II: A $45,000,000 Talent Bill," 55. For other estimates of program costs, see Warren B. Dygert, *Radio as an Advertising Medium*, 1st ed. (New York: McGraw-Hill, 1939), 18; *Variety*, June 19, 1940, 20.

22. Quote from memo, Edward R. Hitz to Roy C. Witmer, May 6, 1940, Box 74, folder 90, "Bristol-Myers" (1940), NBC Records. See also the following issues of *Variety*: September 20, 1939, 42; February 7, 1940, 25; March 20, 1940, 26; April 10, 1940, 20; May 8, 1940, 2; May 15, 1940, 2; May 22, 1940, 2; August 28, 1940, 38; September 25, 1940, 24; and see Hugh Pentecost and Virginia Faulkner, "Murder on the Fred Allen Program," *American Magazine* 136 (July 1944): 140–160.

23. TST script, March 8, 1942.

24. *Variety*, August 26, 1942, 33.

25. On the change of days, see *Variety*, January 21, 1942, 22; for Allen's comment, see TST script, March 8, 1942; for the listener's comment, see Reynold M. Wik, *Henry Ford and Grass-Roots America* (Ann Arbor: University of Michigan Press, 1972), 56. For a critique of the Ford ideology presented by Cameron, see Ruth Brindze, *Not to Be Broadcast: The Truth about Radio* (New York: Vanguard Press, 1937), chap. 9, "His Master's Voice."

26. Allen, *Treadmill to Oblivion*, 154; *Variety*, June 3, 1942, 3. A review of Allen's program is in *Variety*, October 7, 1942, 38.

27. Josephine H. MacLatchy, ed., *Education on the Air: Thirteenth Yearbook of the Institute for Education by Radio* (Columbus: Ohio State University, 1942), 21.

28. "Back in Allen's Alley," *Newsweek* 26 (October 15, 1945): 99.

29. See the following issues of *Variety*: March 31, 1943, 1; May 12, 1943, 33; May 26, 1943, 1; November 3, 1943, 19; May 17, 1944, 1; May 24, 1944, 2.

30. *New York Times*, April 15, 1945, sec. 2, p. 7; *Variety*, March 21, 1945, 26.

31. On Allen's return, see the following issues of *Variety*: May 2, 1945, 2; May 16, 1945, 23; May 23, 1945, 30; June 13, 1945, 31; September 5, 1945, 24; September 19, 1945, 26; September 26, 1945, 33; and see Sidney Lahman, "Radio Row: One Thing and Another," *New York Times*, May 20, 1945, sec. 2, p. 5; *New York Times*, December 13, 1948, 38.

32. See the following issues of *Variety*: May 16, 1945, 23; August 14, 1946, 26; August 13, 1947, 30.

33. *New York Times*, November 4, 1947, 50; *JWT Weekly News* (Newsletter), November 3, 1947, archives of the J. Walter Thompson Company, New York City.

34. Collie Small, "Biggest Man in Radio," *Saturday Evening Post* 220 (November 22, 1947): 25ff.; Arthur D. Morse, "Radio: Battle of the Ratings," *Nation* 167 (October 2, 1948): 372–373; Mark James Banks, "A History of Broadcast Audience Research in the United States, 1920–1980, with an Emphasis on the Rating Services," doctoral dissertation, University of Tennessee, 1981, 60–65, 92–97, and passim.

35. On Allen's high Hoopers, see *JWT Weekly News*, October 28, 1946; see also the following issues of *Variety*: October 23,

1946, 97; December 4, 1946, 28; November 5, 1947, 26; February 4, 1948, 30; and see Gould, "Mr. Allen's Comeback," *New York Times*, October 14, 1945, sec. 2, p. 5.

36. See the following issues of *Variety*: February 4, 1948, 30; May 19, 1948, 22; March 23, 1949, 24.

37. *Variety*, June 30, 1948, 29.

38. *Variety*, November 10, 1948, 28, 30; George Rosen, "Low-Cost Radio in Big Payoff," *Variety*, May 25, 1949, 1.

39. "Mr. Allen Regrets," *Time* 52 (December 13, 1948): 51–52; see also the following issues of *Variety*: December 1, 1948, 23; February 9, 1949, 24; May 25, 1949, 23; August 3, 1949, 1; and *New York Times*, March 19, 1949, 28.

40. MacDonald, *Don't Touch That Dial!*, 121–122.

41. Ibid., 122.

42. For examples of revue comedy, see Donald Oliver, comp. and ed., *The Greatest Revue Sketches* (New York: Avon, 1982).

43. Allen, *Treadmill to Oblivion*, 75, 135–136. The first mention of the Mighty Allen Art Players was on the program of May 23, 1934; Allen used that title, with the exception of the Texaco period, during most of the next fifteen years. The group's spiritual successor, the Mighty Carson Art Players, survives on television's "Tonight Show" more than a half century after Allen coined the title.

44. Allen, *Treadmill to Oblivion*, 33–35; White's obituary in *Variety*, November 25, 1942, clipping in Fred Allen file, Billy Rose Collection.

45. THT script, October 2, 1935.

46. THT script, December 23, 1936.

47. The phrase is from MacDonald, *Don't Touch That Dial!*, 47; THT script, January 2, 1935. Aaron Stein, "Beginners on the Networks; Fred Allen Adds Amateur Night Spot to His Show," clipping in Box 52, folder 24, "Bristol-Myers" (1937), NBC Records.

48. *Variety*, September 18, 1935, 46. On the first program to feature amateurs, Allen recalled his own origins: "Years ago, Ladies and Gentlemen, this amateur business was more dangerous. Say, when I first went on at an amateur night we used to come on the stage wearing a big smile and walk off wearing a tired-tomato or a matured egg rampant. It goes to show how things have improved." THT script, January 2, 1935.

49. Harry Leon Wilson, *Merton of the Movies* (New York: Grosset and Dunlap, 1922), is the best of many novels and films

that told the story of Hollywood's naive hopefuls. See also Mary Margaret McBride, *Tune in for Elizabeth: Career Story of a Radio Interviewer* (New York: Dodd, Mead, 1946).

50. *Variety*, October 16, 1935, 41.

51. Jo Ranson, "Out of a Blue Sky," *Brooklyn Daily Eagle*, June 6, 1937, clipping in Fred Allen file, Billy Rose Collection.

52. MacDonald, *Don't Touch That Dial!*, 48.

53. Nye, "Gags Flow Swiftly at Fred Allen Show," 10; review in *Variety*, October 16, 1935, 44; Aaron Stein, "One Show Too Many," *New York Evening Post*, February 23, 1935, clipping in Fred Allen file, Billy Rose Collection. See also Eichberg, *Radio Stars of Today*, 29, for an observer's account of the amateur spot on Allen's show.

54. On the contest at the University of Cincinnati, see *Variety*, April 1, 1942, 28.

55. John K. Hutchens, "Fred Allen: Comedian's Comedian," *Theatre Arts* 26 (May 1942): 311.

56. *Variety*, January 27, 1943, 3; January 5, 1944, 1.

57. Ibid.

58. Jack Gould, "Expenses Plus," *New York Times*, May 3, 1942, sec. 8, p. 10.

59. Ibid.; Jolson quoted in *Variety*, May 21, 1947, 1.

60. Patrick Egan to radio editor, *New York Times*, February 21, 1937, sec. 10, p. 12; Orrin E. Dunlap, Jr., "Radio Hitches Its Programs to the Guest Stars," *New York Times*, April 10, 1938, sec. 10, p. 10.

61. Gould, "Expenses Plus," 10; *Variety*, January 17, 1945, 1; Wilson Brown, "Unwelcome Guest Stars," *Radio Guide* 9 (November 3, 1939): 9.

62. H. Allen Smith, "Phooey to the Duke of Windsor," *Variety*, January 5, 1949, 38; FAS script, January 5, 1947.

63. Allen to Jack Mulchay, n.d., in Joe McCarthy, ed., *Fred Allen's Letters* (Garden City, N.Y.: Doubleday, 1965), 195.

64. Quote from Fred Allen, "A Kind Word for the Comedian," *New York Herald-Tribune*, September 10, 1947, 22. On Lamour, see Allen to H. Allen Smith, "January 22" [1942], in H. Allen Smith Papers, Special Collections, Morris Library, Southern Illinois University–Carbondale. Hereinafter cited as Smith Papers.

65. *Variety*, April 28, 1948, 1.

66. *Variety*, May 17, 1944, 32.

67. "Allen Switching Guest Technique on Programming," *Variety*, November 19, 1947, 27.

68. Allen, *Treadmill to Oblivion*, 220–221.

69. The information on Allen's guests is derived from the program scripts, in Fred Allen Papers, microfilm copies, Manuscripts Division, Library of Congress, Washington, D.C.

70. See the following issues of *Variety*: April 2, 1947, 1; April 9, 1947, 25; April 16, 1947, 27. Abe Burrows, who wrote the "Duffy's Tavern" program, has an account of his preparation for Allen's guest appearance on the show in 1944 in *Honest Abe: Is There Really No Business Like Show Business?* (Boston: Little, Brown, 1980), 82–83.

71. *Variety*, April 3, 1946, 38.

72. *Variety*, January 31, 1945, 17.

73. See the following issues of *Variety*: April 16, 1941, 33; January 24, 1945, 36; November 20, 1946, 50.

74. One of several record and tape anthologies of cuts from Benny and Allen broadcasts is the two-record set "The Radio Fight of the Century: Jack Benny vs. Fred Allen," Radiola Company Release 29 and 30.

75. Allen, *Treadmill to Oblivion*, 53. One of Benny's writers in 1937 wrote later: "None of us even heard the original insult on the Allen show." Bill Morrow, "Eight Years Before the Mast, or The Wreck That Jack Built," in *Off-Mike*, ed. Jerome Lawrence (New York: Duell, Sloan and Pearce, 1944), 30.

76. Allen, *Treadmill to Oblivion*, 63. Special added "Benny Bit" for January 20 and 27, 1937, THT scripts, and the Benny program's script for March 14, 1937, give the flavor of the early feud. In a later chapter, the comedy of feuding is considered.

77. Accounts of the feud include Allen, *Treadmill to Oblivion*, 53–63; Benny's remarks in the Radiola records cited in note 74; Mary Livingstone Benny and Hilliard Marks, with Marcia Borie, *Jack Benny, A Biography* (Garden City, N.Y.: Doubleday, 1978), 79–82, 127, 268; Irving A. Fein, *Jack Benny: An Intimate Biography* (New York: Putnam's 1976), 71–74; Milt Josefsberg, *The Jack Benny Show: The Life and Times of America's Best-Loved Entertainer* (New Rochelle, N.Y.: Arlington House, 1977), 239–246. Each of the last three accounts contains errors of fact.

78. MacDonald, *Don't Touch That Dial!*, 120–121; Josefsberg, *Jack Benny Show*, 97.

79. Jerome Beatty, "'What's His Name?' Charlie Cantor, the Great Mr. Anonymous of Radio," *American Magazine* 136 (July 1943): 37–38.

80. Jack Gould, "They Say the Right Thing at the Wrong Time," *New York Times Magazine*, March 24, 1946, 22.

81. See the following issues of *Variety*: June 30, 1943, 2; July 14, 1943, 66; July 21, 1943, 36; November 24, 1943, 3; December 1, 1943, 24; February 2, 1944, 22; and see "Mighty Allen No Players," *Newsweek* 22 (December 27, 1943): 66.

82. Allen, *Treadmill to Oblivion*, 75–76; see also p. 36.

83. Auerbach, *Funny Men Don't Laugh*, 133.

84. Hutchens, "Fred Allen: Comedian's Comedian," 314; see also Pentecost and Faulkner, "Murder on the Fred Allen Program," 146.

85. Allen, "A Kind Word for the Comedian," 22.

86. Bryan, "Eighty Hours for a Laugh," 106.

87. The first reference is found in many Allen scripts of the early 1940s; the second is in the TST script, October 11, 1942.

88. *Variety*, May 17, 1944, 26.

89. Hutchens, "Fred Allen: Comedian's Comedian," 314.

90. Based on material in folder of Atwell clippings, Billy Rose Collection.

91. Nye, "Gags Flow Swiftly at Fred Allen Show," 10; based on material in folders of Jack Smart and J. Scott Smart clippings, Billy Rose Collection.

92. Biographical sketch of Brown, CBS Biographical Service, July 23, 1945, and other material in folder of Brown clippings, Billy Rose Collection.

93. Based on material in folder of Walter Tetley clippings, Billy Rose Collection.

Chapter 4

1. Merrill Denison cites the first figure in "Radio and the Writer," *Theatre Arts Monthly* 22 (May 1938): 369; the second is from Katharine Seymour and John T. W. Martin, *Practical Radio Writing: The Technique of Writing for Broadcasting Simply and Thoroughly Explained* (London: Longmans, Green, 1938), v. See also Erik Barnouw, *Handbook of Radio Writing: An Outline of Techniques and Markets in Radio Writing in the United States*, rev. ed. (1939; reprint, Boston: Little, Brown, 1947), 3.

2. Erik Barnouw, *Tube of Plenty: The Evolution of American Television* (New York: Oxford University Press, 1975), 103.

3. John Crosby, "Radio and Who Makes It," *Atlantic Monthly* 181 (January 1948): 23; other samples of this commentary include William Orton, "'The Level of Thirteen-Year-Olds,'" *Atlantic Monthly* 147 (January 1931): 1–10; Armstrong Perry, "Weak Spots in the American System of Broadcasting," in "Radio: The Fifth Estate," ed. Herman S. Hettinger, the *Annals* 177

(January 1935): 22–28; Harriet Van Horne, "It Is Later Than Radio Thinks," *Saturday Review* 27 (February 19, 1944): 26–30; Lloyd Free, "What Can Be Done to Improve Radio?" *New York Times Magazine*, August 25, 1946, 9ff.; "The Revolt Against Radio," *Fortune* 35 (March 1947): 101–103ff.; Llewellyn White, "The Shortcomings of Radio," *Atlantic Monthly* 179 (April 1947): 64–70; Robert M. Hutchins, "Radio in the United States: Soap, Toothpaste and Cereal," *Musical America* 70 (August 1950): 20; John Crosby, "Seven Deadly Sins of the Air," *Life* 29 (November 6, 1950): 147–148ff.; Charles A. Siepmann, *Radio's Second Chance* (Boston: Little, Brown, 1946).

4. Quoted in "Revolt Against Radio," 101.

5. Van Horne, "It Is Later Than Radio Thinks," 26.

6. James Farrell, "The Language of Hollywood," *Saturday Review* 27 (August 5, 1944): 29; Thomas H. Uzzell, *Writing as a Career: A Handbook of Literary Vocational Guidance* (New York: Harcourt, Brace, 1938), xi; see also H. William Fitelson, ed., *Theatre Guild on the Air* (New York: Rinehart, 1947), x–xi. Critics of mass media during the 1930s directed much of their ire at motion pictures. Many comments similar to Farrell's, and the experiences from which they grew, can be found in Richard Fine, *Hollywood and the Profession of Authorship, 1928–1940* (Ann Arbor: UMI Research Press, 1985).

7. Farrell, "Language of Hollywood," 32; J. Fred MacDonald, *Don't Touch That Dial! Radio Programming in American Life from 1920 to 1960* (Chicago: Nelson-Hall, 1979), 56. For an early expression of the view that radio would strengthen the fine arts, see Charles D. Isaacson, "Is Radio an Enemy of the Theatre?" *Theatre Magazine* 37 (January 1923): 15.

8. Van Horne, "It Is Later Than Radio Thinks," 28; Denison, "Radio and the Writer," 365–370.

9. Wolfe Kaufman, "Literati Meets Radio, and Vice Versa, and Columbia Makes Air Safe for Poets," *Variety*, April 14, 1937, 38.

10. "Tired Comedy Pulse Is Static," *Variety*, November 6, 1946, 33; "Poverty of Riches," *Variety*, July 10, 1946, 29; Jerome Lawrence, *Off Mike: Radio Writing by the Nation's Top Radio Writers* (New York: Essential Books, distributed by Duell, Sloan and Pearce, 1944), 6; "'cherchez la writer'—fred allen," *Variety*, June 13, 1945, 44.

11. James Whipple, *How to Write for Radio* (New York: Whittlesey House, 1938), 6; see also pp. 410–414.

12. Arch Oboler, "A Dialogue Between You and Oboler," in Lawrence, *Off Mike*, 56.

13. Crosby, "Seven Deadly Sins of the Air," 152.

14. Jack Gould, "Lack of Incentive," *New York Times*, April 14, 1946, sec. 2, p. 7. Jurisdictional squabbling in the late 1930s between the Guild, an affiliate of the Authors League of America, and the American Federation of Radio Artists (AFRA), an AFL union, retarded improvements in the writers' position vis-à-vis management. See "Authors League in Union Dispute," *New York Times*, August 8, 1939, 13. Also a factor was the feeling among some writers, within and outside radio, that unions were for steelworkers but not for artists. "Workers in the arts, unite!" Ernest Boyd wrote bitterly in 1938. "You have nothing to lose but your brains!" Boyd, "The Muses Join the Picket Line," *American Mercury* 45 (December 1938): 409–413. On the growth of broadcast unions, see Gregory Schubert and James E. Lynch, "Broadcasting Unions: Structure and Impact," in *Broadcasting and Bargaining: Labor Relations in Radio and Television*, ed. Allen E. Koenig (Madison: University of Wisconsin Press, 1970), 41–66.

15. Seymour and Martin, *Practical Radio Writing*, 288.

16. Bob Landry, "Take Off Those Handcuffs," *Variety*, January 1, 1935, 85.

17. Paul R. Milton, "Against the Taboos," *New York Times*, December 7, 1947, sec. 2, p. 13.

18. Quoted in Siepmann, *Radio's Second Chance*, 190.

19. True Boardman, "The Original Radio Drama for Money!" in Lawrence, *Off Mike*, 62–63.

20. Lloyd Shearer, "Regarding Gag Writers," *New York Times*, November 12, 1944, sec. 2, p. 7; Lloyd Shearer, "It's the Gag That Gets the 'Boff,'" *New York Times*, October 21, 1945, sec. 6, p. 18; Milt Josefsberg, *The Jack Benny Show: The Life and Times of America's Best-Loved Entertainer* (New Rochelle, N.Y.: Arlington House, 1977), 418; Jack Hellman, "It's the Man Behind the Typewriter Who Gives Comics Laughs out Front," *Variety*, January 8, 1947, 115. The authors of another article quoted $650 as the average weekly salary paid to comedy writers in 1944. See "Gag Writers Wanted," *Newsweek* 24 (November 6, 1944): 91.

21. *Variety*, July 14, 1943, 44; and September 29, 1943, 49.

22. Shearer, "Regarding Gag Writers"; "Gag Writers Wanted," 88, 91–92.

23. "The Listener," "Laughter on the Air," *Atlantic* 171 (June 1943): 119.

24. Crosby, "Radio and Who Makes It," 25.

25. Crosby, "Seven Deadly Sins of the Air," 154.

26. For example, George Rosen, "Don't Look Now, But Your Radio's Static," *Variety*, January 8, 1947, 107.

27. Ernest M. Walker, quoted in *Variety*, April 30, 1947, 42; see also Rosen, "Don't Look Now, But Your Radio's Static"; Shearer, "Regarding Gag Writers"; Eddie Cantor, "What's Wrong with Radio," *Variety*, July 7, 1937, 28.

28. Alice Goldfarb Marquis, "Written on the Wind: The Impact of Radio during the 1930s," *Journal of Contemporary History* 19 (July 1984): 385. For comments on radio's consumption of material, see Albert F. McLean, Jr., *American Vaudeville as Ritual* (Lexington: University of Kentucky Press, 1965), 24; Hellman, "It's the Man Behind the Typewriter Who Gives Comics Laughs out Front"; Orrin E. Dunlap, Jr., "Tricks of Jesters," *New York Times*, February 9, 1936, sec. 10, p. 15; Orrin E. Dunlap, Jr., "Furiously Proceeds Radio's Gag Hunt," *New York Times Magazine*, August 26, 1934, sec. 6, pp. 12, 15; "Veteran Performers Find Radio a Fountain of Youth," *New York Times*, February 4, 1934, sec. 9, p. 11; Carroll Carroll, *None of Your Business: Or My Life with J. Walter Thompson (Confessions of a Radio Writer)* (New York: Cowles, 1970), 29.

29. *Variety*, November 6, 1946, 32.

30. Arnold Auerbach, *Funny Men Don't Laugh* (Garden City, N.Y.: Doubleday, 1965), 126.

31. Wheeler Memoir, Oral History Collection, Butler Library, Columbia University; see also Steve Allen, *The Funny Men* (New York: Simon and Schuster, 1956), 61–62.

32. Fred Allen to H. Allen Smith, July 11, 1940, Smith Papers. As noted, I am retaining Allen's lowercase spelling.

33. On the Peabody, see *New York Times*, April 15, 1945, sec. 2, p. 7; *Variety*, March 21, 1945, 26.

34. Quotes from Shearer, "It's the Gag That Gets the 'Boff'"; "Gag Writers Wanted" (comment by writer Hal Block); Lawrence, *Off Mike*, 34 (comment by writer Don Quinn).

35. For Allen's comments on his first three assistants, see Fred Allen, *Treadmill to Oblivion* (Boston: Little, Brown, 1954), 12–13, 19, 70–71.

36. Allen to H. Allen Smith, "feb. 26," Smith Papers.

37. Hutchens, "Fred Allen: Comedian's Comedian," *Theatre Arts* 26 (May 1942): 314.

38. Orrin E. Dunlap, Jr., "Clowning on the Air Is No Longer a One-Man Show," *New York Times*, January 28, 1940, sec. 9, p. 12.

39. Auerbach, *Funny Men Don't Laugh*, 141–143, 156–157.

40. Ibid., ix.

41. "Comedian's Comedian," *Newsweek* 47 (March 26, 1956): 62.

42. Allen to H. Allen Smith, July 2, 1942, in Joe McCarthy, ed., *Fred Allen's Letters* (Garden City, N.Y.: Doubleday, 1965), 161.

43. Allen to Frank Rosengren, May 5, 1945, in McCarthy, *Letters*, 127; for similar comments, see ibid., 165. "The World's Worst Juggler," *Time*, April 7, 1947, 71; Auerbach, *Funny Men Don't Laugh*, 119, 120, 121, 123, 162, 165; Allen to H. Allen Smith, January 22, [1948?], Smith Papers.

44. Allen to Herman Wouk, August 13, 1954, in McCarthy, *Letters*, 353.

45. Tape recording of the radio program "Conversation" with Clifton Fadiman, March 22, 1956, which includes the Seldes interview; in author's possession.

46. Auerbach, *Funny Men Don't Laugh*, 166.

47. Dwight MacDonald, "A Theory of Mass Culture," in *Mass Culture: The Popular Arts in America*, ed. Bernard Rosenberg and David Manning White (Glencoe, Ill.: Free Press, 1957), 65.

48. Bernard Rosenberg, "Mass Culture Revisited," in *Mass Culture Revisited*, ed. Bernard Rosenberg and David Manning White (New York: Van Nostrand Reinhold, 1971), 11.

49. Russel Nye, *The Unembarrassed Muse: The Popular Arts in America* (New York: Dial Press, 1970), 5. On p. 6, Nye adds: "This does not mean that what the popular artist does is not worth doing, or personally unsatisfying, or aesthetically bad, or commercially cheap."

50. Herbert J. Gans, *Popular Culture and High Culture: An Analysis and Evaluation of Taste* (New York: Basic Books, 1974), 23.

51. David Marc, *Demographic Vistas: Television in American Culture* (Philadelphia: University of Pennsylvania Press, 1984), xv; see also p. 41.

52. For example, Allen to Don Quinn, April 12, 1940, in McCarthy, *Letters*, 230; Allen, "In Defense of Radio?" *New York Herald Tribune*, August 25, 1948, 7.

53. Allen, *Treadmill to Oblivion*, 155.

54. THT script, June 28, 1939. For similar presentations of the comedian's treadmill, see script of "The State of American Humor," broadcast on the series "Living, 1949," January 30, 1949, WNBC, New York, Allen Papers; Allen, "As Thousands Hear," *Variety*, January 2, 1934, 58.

55. Auerbach, *Funny Men Don't Laugh*, 160.

56. Tape of program "Conversation."

57. Allen to Hal Kanter, December 21, 1955, in McCarthy, *Letters*, 334.

58. Milton Wright, *What's Funny—and Why: An Outline of Humor* (New York: Whittlesey House, 1939), chap. 10.

59. The first term is in Wright, 251; the second is in Dunlap, "Furiously Proceeds Radio's Gag Hunt," sec. 6, p. 12. See also Jerome Beatty, "From Gags to Riches," *American Magazine* 121 (March, 1936): 14–15, 169–173.

60. Wright, *What's Funny*, 251–252, 262–263. In a 1947 program, Portland Hoffa recalled that people once threw food at actors. Allen replied: "That's what chased Jack Benny out of vaudeville, y'know . . . when they started to can it." FAS script, October 19, 1947.

61. Auerbach, *Funny Men Don't Laugh*, 106. The "Lou Jacobs" of Auerbach's book was Freedman; see 17–58, 88–107. Carroll, *None of Your Business*, 27–32; Barnouw, *Handbook of Radio Writing*, 12; Aaron Stein, "Gag Man [Freedman] Tries Out His Own Material at the Microphone," *New York Evening Post*, October 18, 1935, Freedman file, Billy Rose Collection; "Sketches by Freedman," *New York Times*, May 10, 1936, sec. 10, p. 2. Walter Blair and Hamlin Hill recall that Mark Twain's Hank Morgan complained about jokes current in King Arthur's Court that he had heard, unchanged, in nineteenth-century Connecticut. See *America's Humor: From Poor Richard to Doonesbury* (New York: Oxford University Press, 1978), 17.

62. Allen to Pat Weaver, August 18, 1936, in McCarthy, *Letters*, 267.

63. Allen to Val Eichen, October 8, 1933, in McCarthy, *Letters*, 285. See, in the same source, Allen to Arnold Rattray, May 15, 1933, 128; and Allen to Jack Mulcahy, n.d., 195.

64. Allen, "As Thousands Hear," *Variety*, January 2, 1934, 58.

65. Allen to H. Allen Smith, "may third" [1941?], Smith Papers.

66. Allen to H. Allen Smith, October 17 [1942], Smith Papers.

67. Allen to H. Allen Smith, May 16 [1947], Smith Papers.

68. SHR script, January 3, 1934; FAS script, October 19, 1947.

69. Allen to H. Allen Smith, November 21, 1940, Smith Papers.

70. Auerbach, *Funny Men Don't Laugh*, 124–125, 152–154; Bryan, "Eighty Hours for a Laugh," 23, 106–108.

71. Allen to H. Allen Smith, May 5, 1942, Smith Papers.

72. Allen to Val Eichen, "Monday" [1933], in McCarthy, *Letters*, 283.

73. THT script, February 8, 1939.

74. THT script, April 20, 1938.

75. Allen to Arnold Rattray, n.d., in McCarthy, *Letters*, 227.

76. Allen to H. Allen Smith, April 12, 1947, Smith Papers.

77. Auerbach, *Funny Men Don't Laugh*, 125–126; see also Allen, *Treadmill to Oblivion*, 239.

78. Allen voiced the latter opinion to columnist Ben Gross, "Looking and Listening: Allen Talks of Radio," undated clipping, Smith Papers. In the year of his greatest Hooperating popularity, Allen wrote: "Any joke an inch off the ground will be over the studio audience's head." "A Kind Word for the Comedian," *New York Herald Tribune*, September 10, 1947, 22.

79. Letter from James G. Rogers, Jr., to W. F. Earls, April 29, 1935, Box 34, folder 51, "Bristol-Myers" [1935], NBC Records. Rogers was with the Benton and Bowles Agency, Earls with NBC.

80. Robert Eichberg, *Radio Stars of Today; or, Behind the Scenes in Broadcasting* (Boston: L. C. Page, 1937), 29.

81. As early as 1944, *Variety* complained about the "almost strictly visual entertainment" of audience-participation programs like Ralph Edwards's "Truth or Consequences." *Variety*, April 19, 1944, 1. On the debate over studio audiences, these sources are helpful: *Variety* issues of October 18, 1932, 47; December 19, 1933, 38; March 13, 1934, 41; October 23, 1940, 3; June 4, 1947, 25; and "Comedians' Verdict Favors an Audience at the Studio," *New York Times*, April 15, 1934, sec. 10, p. 9; "Give Radio Back to Home Listeners, Mounting Squawk," *Variety*, March 27, 1946, 41; Frederic Wakeman, *The Hucksters* (New York: Rinehart, 1946), 209–210, 258; Crosby, "Seven Deadly Sins of the Air," 154–157; Hal Kanter, "The Clucksters," *Variety*, January 8, 1947, 110; Dorothy O'Leary, "Hollywood Audience," *New York Times*, December 15, 1946, sec. 2, p. 11; Mary Jane Higby, *Tune in Tomorrow* (New York: Ace Publishing, 1968), 79–82. Most commentators interested in the origins of the studio audience blame comedians Ed Wynn and Eddie Cantor. See, for example, Sam J. Slate and Joe Cook, *It Sounds Impossible* (New York: Macmillan, 1963), 31, 74–75.

82. THT script, January 12, 1938. For commentary on this program, see "Allen Scathingly Brushes off Comics Who Use Visual Tricks on Ear Shows," *Variety*, January 19, 1938, 35.

83. Quoted in Maurice Zolotow, *No People Like Show People* (New York: Random House, 1947), 267.

84. Quotes from Allen to H. Allen Smith, December 27, 1940, and to Jack Mulcahy, "april 12th," in McCarthy, *Letters*, 149, 193; Allen to Smith, "monday night" [1945?], Smith Papers.

85. Allen to Jack Mulcahy, January 28, 1938, in McCarthy, *Letters*, 200.

86. Quoted in Allen's obituary, *Time* 67 (March 26, 1956): 102.

87. Tape recording of FAS, February 24, 1946.

88. Tape recording of THT, October 7, 1936.

89. TST script, February 4 and 11, 1942, and April 2, 1944. FAS script, May 26, 1946, and May 9, 1948. Harold Lloyd, an expert in visual comedy, wrote: "The easiest laugh in the world is to rob a man of his pants in public." Lloyd, *An American Comedy* (1928; reprint, New York: Dover, 1971), 101. Or, in private: the humorous climax of the classic tale of southwestern humor, T. B. Thorpe's "Big Bear of Arkansas," occurs when Jim Daggett is surprised by the huge bear while squatting in the woods one morning, his pants down around his ankles. The story is available in many collections, including Enid Veron, ed., *Humor in America: An Anthology* (New York: Harcourt Brace Jovanovich, 1976), 119–128.

90. "Follow-Up Comment," *Variety*, June 28, 1939, 38.

91. Hal Block, "You Can't Top a Refrigerator," *Variety*, July 28, 1948, 1; see also Bob Foreman, "What's Happening in Radio?" *Advertising and Selling* 42 (February 1949): 31; Barnouw, *Golden Web*, 286–288.

92. Frank Buxton and Bill Owen, *The Big Broadcast, 1920–1950* (New York: Viking Press, 1972), ix.

93. "Radio II: A $45,000,000 Talent Bill," *Fortune* 17 (May 1938): 122.

94. The following articles describe quiz programs and explore the issues that surrounded them: George Joel, "Quid pro Quiz," *Nation* 151 (November 16, 1940): 474–475; John K. Hutchens, "Who Thought Up the Quiz Show?" *New York Times Magazine*, August 23, 1942, 12, 31; John Lear, "Part-Time Lunatic," *Saturday Evening Post* 218 (August 4, 1945): 14–15ff. (On Ralph Edwards); Henry Pringle, "Wise Guys of the Air," *Saturday Evening Post* 218 (May 11, 1946): 18–19ff. (on "Information

Please"); Maurice Zolotow, "Quiz Queen," *Saturday Evening Post* 219 (July 27, 1946): 18ff.; Don Eddy, "Daffy Dollars: Give-Away Radio Shows," *American Magazine* 142 (December 1946): 38–39; "The Giveaway Craze," *Newsweek* 31 (June 7, 1948): 52; "River of Gold," *Newsweek* 32 (August 2, 1948): 51; Jack Gould, "Jack Benny or Jackpot?" *New York Times Magazine*, August 15, 1948, 16ff.; Ed James, "The Radio Give-Aways," *American Mercury* 67 (October 1948): 430–437.

95. Jane Cobb, "Living and Leisure," *New York Times*, January 5, 1941, sec. 7, p. 15.

96. Gilbert Seldes, *How Dense Is the Mass?" Atlantic* 182 (November 1948): 26.

97. Allen, *Treadmill to Oblivion*, 106.

98. Allen, "In Defense of Radio?"

99. Allen to Maggy O'Flaherty, August 31, 1945, in McCarthy, *Letters*, 239.

100. Allen, *Treadmill to Oblivion*, 218–219.

101. Ibid., 215–216; "Allen Insures Own Radio Fans," *New York Times*, October 4, 1948, 25; Jack Gould, "Fred Comes Back," *New York Times*, October 10, 1948, sec. 2, p. 11.

102. Sources that critically evaluate the audience measurement surveys include Norman Corwin, "Ratings and the Stuffed Banana," *Variety*, January 5, 1949, 97; John Crosby, *Out of the Blue: A Book about Radio and Television* (New York: Simon and Schuster, 1952), 269–271, 281–283; Thomas Whiteside, "Hooperism Clears the Air," *New Republic* 116 (May 5, 1947): 27–30; Jack Gould, "The Curse of Ratings," *New York Times*, February 17, 1946, sec. 2, p. 7; Jack Gould, "How Comic Is Radio Comedy?" *New York Times*, November 21, 1948, sec. 6, p. 64.

103. Allen, quoted in John Garrison, "Is It True Mr. Allen?" *Radio Best* 1 (April 1948), Durante Collection.

104. Allen to H. Allen Smith, n.d. [probably 1941], Smith Papers; see also Allen to Joe Kelly, n.d., in McCarthy, *Letters*, 96.

105. Tape of "Edgar Bergen–Charlie McCarthy Show," November 2, 1947; in author's possession.

106. "A Certain Mr. Allen Rates Raters' Labors as Worthy of Rating," *Variety*, March 27, 1946, 51.

107. Allen, "A Kind Word for the Comedian."

108. FAS script, January 9, 1949; *New York Times*, April 25, 1948, sec. 2, p. 9; "A Certain Mr. Allen Rates Raters' Labors as Worthy of Rating," 51; Allen to Pat Weaver, August 18, 1936, in McCarthy, *Letters*, 267.

Chapter 5

1. Mark Twain, "The Mysterious Stranger," in *The Complete Short Stories of Mark Twain*, ed. Charles Neider (Garden City, N.Y.: International Collectors Library, 1957), 671.

2. Wouk to The Editor, *New York Times*, March 18, 1956, in Joe McCarthy, ed., *Fred Allen's Letters* (Garden City, N.Y: Doubleday, 1965), 358.

3. Useful sources on radio censorship include the following: Henry Adams Bellows, "Is Radio Censored?" *Harper's Magazine* 171 (November 1935): 697–709, by a member of the initial Federal Radio Commission. Harrison B. Summers, ed., *Radio Censorship* (New York: H. W. Wilson, 1939); a reprint edition of this valuable compilation appeared in *History of Broadcasting: Radio to Television* (New York: Arno Press, 1971). Frank J. Kahn, ed., *Documents of American Broadcasting*, rev. ed. (New York: Appleton-Century-Crofts, 1972), contains some key sources on the issues of government regulation and freedom of expression on radio and television. For a pioneer broadcaster's view of censorship in the mid-1930s, see Ted Husing, *Ten Years Before the Mike* (New York: Farrar & Rinehart, 1935), 189–194. For an early discussion of political censorship, see Vita Lauter and Joseph H. Friend, "Radio and the Censors," *Forum and Century* 86 (December 1931): 359–365. For a historian's case study, see David G. Clark, "H. V. Kaltenborn and His Sponsors: Controversial Broadcasting and the Sponsor's Role," *Journal of Broadcasting* 12 (Fall 1968): 309–321.

4. Herman Wouk, *Aurora Dawn* (New York: Simon and Schuster, 1947).

5. Ibid., 169.

6. Ibid., 187.

7. Fred Allen, *Treadmill to Oblivion* (Boston: Little, Brown, 1954), 212; Leo Miller, "What'll Mr. Allen Get Off Tonight?" *Bridgeport Herald*, April 27, 1947, clipping in Durante Collection. *Variety*, January 1, 1947, 21; "Allen To Stay On Despite Censors," *Variety*, February 5, 1947, 1.

8. *Variety*, April 23, 1947, 1.

9. Allen's version of the incident is in his *Treadmill to Oblivion*, 212–214; *New York Times*, April 21, 1947, 29; Harriet Van Horne, "Allen's Joke on Executive Cut Off Air," *New York World-Telegram*, April 21, 1947; "Even Allen Can't Kid the Radio," *New York Post*, April 21, 1947, clippings in Durante Collection; "Little Men Who Were There," *Newsweek* 29 (May 5,

1947]: 63; Jack Gould, "L'Affaire Allen," *New York Times*, April 27, 1947, sec. 2, p. 9. That other comics had experienced difficulties with Menser is indicated in "NBC–Cantor Feud Breaks Out Anew as Censor Menser K.O.'s Besser's Act," *Variety*, June 21, 1944, 2.

10. *Nation* 164 (May 3, 1947): 503; *New York Times*, April 23 and 24, 1947; *Boston Globe*, April 23 and 24 1947; *Detroit Times*, April 24, 1947, clippings in Durante Collection. Letter from Clifford Forester to Niles Trammell, May 7, 1947, Box 115, folder 13, "Trammell: 1947 ACLU," NBC Records.

11. *New York Times*, May 7, 1947, 41.

12. *Des Moines Register*, April 25, 1947, clipping in Durante Collection.

13. *Detroit Times*, April 22, 1947; *PM*, April 22, 1947; *Boston Herald*, April 22, 1947; all clippings in Durante Collection. See also *New York Times*, April 22, 1947, 33.

14. *Variety*, April 23, 1947, 1; Harriet Van Horne, "Sequel to Allen's Gagged Gag," *New York World-Telegram*, April 24, 1947, clipping in Durante Collection.

15. *Variety*, August 6, 1947, 19, and October 29, 1947, 1.

16. Gross's column "Looking and Listening," n.d., clipping in Smith Papers.

17. Judith C. Waller, *Radio, the Fifth Estate* (Boston: Houghton Mifflin, 1946), 57–60; Gilbert Seldes, *The Great Audience* (New York: Viking Press, 1951), 131–132; Christopher H. Sterling and James M. Kittross, *Stay Tuned: A Concise History of American Broadcasting* (Belmont, Calif.: Wadsworth, 1978), 113, 160–161; Theodore Peterson, Jay W. Jensen, and William L. Rivers, *The Mass Media and Modern Society* (New York: Holt, Rinehart and Winston, 1965), 238; Elizabeth J. Heighton and Don R. Cunningham, *Advertising in the Broadest Media* (Belmont, Calif.: Wadsworth, 1976), 11–12; Karl E. Meyer, "Why the Huckster Is No Longer the Heavy," *Saturday Review* 60 (May 14, 1977): 44. For the personal experiences of a radio actress, see Mary Jane Higby, *Tune In Tomorrow* (New York: Ace Publishing, 1968), 36–37, 151, 198–200.

18. Hill's obituaries summarize his career and advertising tactics: see *Time* 48 (September 23, 1946): 84, 86; "Advertising Hill Legends," *Newsweek* 28 (September 23, 1946): 76–78; Frederic Wakeman, *The Hucksters* (New York: Rinehart, 1946). For a general discussion of sponsor interference in programming, and the agencies' resentment, see "Radio Changes but Some Sponsors Still Have the 'Angel' Complex," *Variety*, March 19, 1941, 27.

19. Erik Barnouw, *The Sponsor: Notes on a Modern Potentate* (New York: Oxford University Press, 1978), 33.

20. Quoted in Sam J. Slate and Joe Cook, *It Sounds Impossible* (New York: Macmillan, 1963), 85.

21. Quote from John Crosby, "Radio and Who Makes It," *Atlantic Monthly* 181 (January 1948): 23. Jack Gould, "Matter of Credit," *New York Times*, April 18, 1948, sec. 2, p. 9, is a good discussion of the agencies' role.

22. Wakeman's remarks, spoken on the program "Town Meeting of the Air" in December 1946, are quoted in "The Revolt Against Radio," *Fortune* 35 (March 1947): 102.

23. A. L. Ashby to Edgar Kobak, Interdepartmental Correspondence, March 15, 1935, NBC Records.

24. Bernard B. Smith, "What's Wrong with the Broadcasters?" *Harper's Magazine* 185 (June 1942): 85–86. Stephen Fox, *The Mirror Makers: A History of American Advertising and Its Creators* (New York: Vintage Books, 1984), 161, 211, discusses network–agency conflict; Roland Marchand, *Advertising the American Dream: Making Way for Modernity, 1920–1940* (Berkeley: University of California Press, 1985), 39–41, discusses ad agency–client conflict in a print advertising setting.

25. A good example of its affiliates pressuring NBC to control its comedians' "double entendre, innuendo and off-color humor" occurred in 1942. See *New York Times*, March 18, 1942, 25; *Variety*, March 18, 1942, 35.

26. *New York Times*, April 11, 1937, sec. 11, p. 12.

27. Russell Lynes, *The Lively Audience: A Social History of the Visual and Performing Arts in America, 1890–1950* (New York: Harper & Row, 1985), 290. For comments on censorship of material for vaudeville's family audience, see John E. DiMeglio, *Vaudeville, U.S.A.* (Bowling Green, Ohio: Bowling Green University Popular Press, 1973), 195–197. All the good movie histories discuss censorship of that medium, but see especially Garth Jowett, *Film, the Democratic Art* (Boston: Little, Brown, 1976), 108–259. Jowett's appendices include the 1930 Production Code and other attempts to set industry standards.

28. *New York Times*, December 18, 1937, 13; *Variety*, December 22, 1937, 26, and March 9, 1938, 1.

29. Earl Sparling, "Radio Gets the Jitters," *American Magazine*, March 1939, excerpted in Summers, *Radio Censorship*, 262.

30. Others recognized the broadcasters' fear of the FCC: for example, John K. Hutchens, "You Can't Say That," *New York Times*, November 21, 1943, sec. 2, p. 9. During World War II, the

government presence became even more real, as Washington imposed an effective system of censorship on broadcasters. Sherman H. Dryer, *Radio in Wartime* (New York: Greenberg, 1942), 369–382, contains the "Code of Wartime Practices for American Broadcasters" issued by the Office of Censorship.

31. Quote from memo, Janet MacRorie to Frank E. Mason, July 25, 1938, Box 93, NBC Records.

32. First quote from the remarks of Wayne L. Randall at a meeting to review proposed program standards, transcript dated August 18, 1938; second quote from typed notes from a similar meeting, dated August 23, 1938, both documents in Box 93, NBC Records.

33. Draft, Program Standards of the National Broadcasting Company, p. 5, Box 93, NBC Records.

34. Transcript of August 18, 1938, meeting, Box 93, NBC Records.

35. Draft, Program Standards, 5–6.

36. Ibid., 6.

37. Ibid., 9.

38. Ibid., 11–12.

39. Ibid., 7– 8.

40. Transcript of August 18, 1938, meeting, Box 93, NBC Records.

41. John Crosby, *Out of the Blue: A Book about Radio and Television* (New York: Simon and Schuster, 1952), 272, from his column of July 29, 1946, "Censorship on the Air."

42. John Crosby, "Seven Deadly Sins of the Air," *Life* 29 (November 6, 1950): 157; see also Dryer, *Radio in Wartime*, 53, 61; Jack Gould, "Mr. Allen's Comeback," *New York Times*, October 14, 1945, sec. 2, p. 5.

43. Peter Artzt, "Move Over Fred Allen," *Advertising and Selling* 40 (June 1947): 41.

44. Don Quinn, "An Open Letter to Fred Allen," *Variety*, May 21, 1947, 26.

45. Allen, quoted in Orrin E. Dunlap, Jr., "Radio Clowns at Wits' End for New Jokes," *New York Times*, June 23, 1935, sec. 9, p. 10. Allen, *Treadmill to Oblivion*, 8–9.

46. Memo, Dorothy Kemble to Ken R. Dyke, May 11, 1938, Box 59, folder 28, "Bristol-Myers" (1938), NBC Records.

47. Transcript of August 18, 1938 meeting, Box 93, NBC Records.

48. Memo, Kemble to Dyke, May 11, 1938.

49. Memo, Eugene M. Hoge to Eugene J. Grant, March 30,

1938; memo, I. E. Showerman to E. M. Hoge, April 6, 1938; memo, E. M. Hoge to I. E. Showerman, April 12, 1938, all in Box 59, folder 28, "Bristol-Myers" (1938), NBC Records. For Jack Benny's problems with plugs for commercial products, see Milt Josefsberg, *The Jack Benny Show: The Life and Times of America's Best-Loved Entertainer* (New Rochelle, N.Y.: Arlington House, 1977), 105–106.

50. Memo, I. E. Showerman to E. R. Hitz, February 25, 1938, Box 59, folder 28, "Bristol-Myers" (1938), NBC Records.

51. Allen to Val Eichen [1933], in McCarthy, *Letters*, 283; memo, V. J. Gilcher to John F. Royal, May 2, 1940, Box 74, folder 90, "Bristol-Myers" (1940), NBC Records.

52. Memo, Jack Van Nostrand to several NBC officials, January 13, 1939, Box 66, folder 55, NBC Records.

53. Memo, Janet MacRorie to I. E. Showerman, January 11, 1938, Box 59, folder 28, "Bristol-Myers" (1938), NBC Records; on MacRorie, see Ruth Knight, *Stand By For the Ladies: The Distaff Side of Radio* (New York: Coward-McCann, 1939), 49–52. Also see Orrin E. Dunlap, Jr., "Radio's 'Etiquette Censor' Sits Behind the Microphone," *New York Times*, November 5, 1939, sec. 9, p. 12; and Janet MacRorie, "Taste on the Air," *Education* 60 (June 1940): 622–626.

54. Memo, Janet MacRorie to John F. Royal, February 2, 1938, Box 59, folder 28, "Bristol-Myers" (1938), NBC Records.

55. John K. Hutchens, "Fred Allen: Comedian's Comedian," *Theatre Arts* 26 (May 1942): 313.

56. Memo, I. E. Showerman to Janet MacRorie, December 19, 1938, Box 59, folder 28, "Bristol-Myers" (1938), NBC Records.

57. Arnold Auerbach, *Funny Men Don't Laugh* (Garden City, N.Y.: Doubleday, 1965), 143.

58. Ibid., 122, 124, 144–146, 148–154. Most of the feature magazine articles on Allen discussed his private life and work routine. Examples are Al Hirshfield, "Fred Allen: A Grim Success Story," *New York Times Magazine*, July 2, 1944, 18, 53; J. Bryan III, "Eighty Hours for a Laugh," *Saturday Evening Post* 214 (October 4, 1941): 22–23, 109, 110.

59. This account draws on the following memos: Dorothy Kemble to Ken R. Dyke, May 3, 1938; Edward R. Hitz to I. E. Showerman, December 16, 1938; I. E. Showerman to Janet MacRorie, December 19, 1938; all in Box 59, folder 28, "Bristol-Myers" (1938), NBC Records. For the 1946 incident, see *Variety*, January 1, 1947, 21.

60. Memo, Janet MacRorie to I. E. Showerman, December 20, 1938, Box 59, folder 28, "Bristol-Myers" (1938), NBC Records.

61. Auerbach, *Funny Men Don't Laugh*, 150.

62. John Lear, "You Can't Say That on the Air," *Saturday Evening Post*, July 12, 1947, 23; Durante Collection.

63. See the following issues of *Variety*: February 20, 1943, 31; May 29, 1934, 31; November 6, 1946, 31.

64. Allen to Joe Kelly, n.d., in McCarthy, *Letters*, 98.

65. Crosby, "Radio in Review," July 31, 1946, clipping in Durante Collection; memo, Janet MacRorie to John F. Royal, December 27, 1938, Box 59, folder 28, "Bristol-Myers" (1938), NBC Records.

66. Cited in Sparling, "Radio Gets the Jitters," 264–265.

67. Memo, Dorothy Kemble to William Burke Miller, April 13, 1938, Box 59, folder 28, "Bristol-Myers" (1938), NBC Records.

68. Allen to Bob Welch, October 6, 1942, and to Pat Weaver, n.d., in McCarthy, *Letters*, 258, 272. See also Crosby, "Radio in Review," July 29, 1946, clipping in Durante Collection.

69. Allen to Jack Mulcahy, April 12 [1938 or 1939, probably], in McCarthy, *Letters*, 192–193.

70. FAS script, December 6 and 13, 1939, quote from latter; Allen, *Treadmill to Oblivion*, 41–42.

71. *Time* 35 (February 5, 1940): 44; Allen to New York Stock Exchange, n.d., in McCarthy, *Letters*, 24. Memos, Niles Trammell to Janet MacRorie, March 7, 1940; Janet MacRorie to John F. Royal, February 26, 1940; A. L. Ashby to John F. Royal, February 20, 1940; Bertha Brainard to I. E. Showerman, January 22, 1940; all in Box 74, folder 90, "Bristol-Myers" (1940), NBC Records.

72. *Variety*, May 22, 1935, 37; memo, John F. Royal to Janet MacRorie, May 14, 1935, Box 34, folder 51, "Bristol-Myers" (1935), NBC Records.

73. Allen to Joe Kelly, February 8, 1940, in McCarthy, *Letters*, 106.

74. Allen, *Treadmill to Oblivion*, 181, for Strogonoff; letter, A. L. Ashby to Abraham J. Feitelberg, June 30, 1937, Box 52, folder 24, "Bristol-Myers" (1937), NBC Records.

75. Letters, R. P. Myers to Carlos Franco, July 22, 1938, and Tom H. Buckley to Edgard Kobak, July 15, 1938, Box 59, folder 28, "Bristol-Myers" (1938), NBC Records.

76. Sidney Reznick, "It's Funny, but—" *New York Times Magazine*, May 13, 1945, 23, for the anemia incident; Sid Haster

to Bristol-Myers, January 19, 1939, and George L. Reimer to National Broadcasting Co., January 19, 1939, Box 66, folder 55, "Bristol-Myers" (1939), NBC Records.

77. On occasion he used it with the studio audience in the prebroadcast warm-up: memo, John F. Royal to Frank E. Mullen, March 11, 1946, Box 115, folder 6, "Trammell: 1946 Miscellaneous," NBC Records.

78. *New York World-Telegram*, December 23, 1937, clipping in Fred Allen clipping file, Billy Rose Collection.

79. Letter, A. L. Ashby to T. J. Slowie, December 14, 1939, Box 66, folder 55, "Bristol-Myers" (1939); and Lenox R. Lohr to Rev. George C. Koehler, October 14, 1938, Box 59, folder 28, "Bristol- Myers" (1938), NBC Records.

80. *Variety*, September 11, 1934, 41, reported communist dissatisfaction with Allen; see letter, Emil M. Scholz to Bristol-Myers, April 9, 1934, Box 24, folder 24, "Bristol-Myers" (1934), NBC Records, for the strike.

81. *Variety*, May 8, 1946, 29, on breakfast shows; letter, John E. McMillan to Niles Trammell, June 4, 1940, Box 74, folder 90, "Bristol-Myers" (1940), NBC Records.

82. Allen to H. Allen Smith, December 20, 1940, Smith Papers.

83. *Variety*, March 13, 1940, 1, reports the two jokes; *Variety*, September 11, 1940, 1, reports the networks' caution.

84. Anonymous review of Allen's program, "Sal Hepatica Revue," *Variety*, January 9, 1934, 32.

85. Ruth Brindze, *Not to be Broadcast: The Truth about the Radio* (New York: Vanguard Press, 1937), 192.

86. THT script, May 8, 1935.

87. THT script, November 16, 1938.

88. THT script, June 10, 1936.

89. THT script, November 23, 1938; FAS script, February 7, 1940; TST script, April 2, 1944; FAS script, January 26, 1947.

90. THT script, February 20, 1935.

Chapter 6

1. Lawrence W. Levine, "American Culture and the Great Depression," *Yale Review* 74 (Winter 1985): 221.

2. S. J. Perelman, "The Great Sourpuss; or, Should Auld Acquaintance Be Exhumed?" *Holiday* 12 (December 1952): 95, 97–98, 101, 102. Arthur Frank Wertheim links radio comedy and

Depression conditions in his "Relieving Social Tensions: Radio Comedy and the Great Depression," *Journal of Popular Culture* 10 (Winter 1976): 501–519; see also J. Fred MacDonald, *Don't Touch That Dial! Radio Programming in American Life, 1920–1960* (Chicago: Nelson-Hall, 1979), 94, 113–114.

3. John K. Hutchens defined a radio comedy formula as "a pattern that will have a comfortable familiarity about it, something to which you can look forward with assurance from week to week." Hutchens, "The Funny Fellows," *New York Times*, October 11, 1942, sec. 8, p. 10.

4. The verdict was not unanimous, but many contemporary literary critics and cultural arbiters decided that radio had little to do, in its origins or contributions, with "real" American humor. "Let us, for decency's sake," wrote Bernard DeVoto in 1937, "say nothing of the radio skit—after all, there has always been feloniously bad humor." DeVoto, "The Lineage of Eustace Tilley" [review of Walter Blair's *Native American Humor*], reprinted in *Critical Essays on American Humor*, ed. William Bedford Clark and W. Craig Turner (Boston: G. K. Hall, 1984), 75. More careful students of the media disagree. The historian Daniel Czitrom deprecates the idea that the commercial values of advertisers and broadcasters shaped all programming and that the "media have . . . manufactured content out of thin air. Historically, the raw materials for 'media fare,' as well as its creators, have been drawn from an assortment of cultural milieus." He writes of "the media's reliances on older cultural forms adapted to new technologies." Czitrom, "Dialectical Tensions in the American Media Past and Present," in *Popular Culture in America*, ed. Paul Buhle (Minneapolis: University of Minnesota Press, 1987), 14. That radio comedy illustrates a sharing across often artificial categories such as "media" and "art," or "mass culture" and "high culture," is a concept central to this book.

5. "The end of the nineteenth century did not, of course, abruptly halt the flow of humor in the older traditions." Walter Blair added this statement and a subsequent discussion of persisting traditions to the revision of his *Native American Humor* (1987; reprint, San Francisco: Chandler, 1960), 162. In the reissue of another book, Blair notes that "both media [sound movies and radio] were very cordial to oral storytellers. So several who'd developed skills in burlesque, vaudeville, and stage revues became fantastically popular performers on screens, on airwaves, or (as a rule) on both." Blair cites W. C. Fields, Jack Pearl (as Baron Munchausen), and Jim Jordan (as Fibber McGee). Blair, *Tall-Tale*

America: A Legendary History of Our Humorous Heroes (1944; reprint, Chicago: University of Chicago Press, 1987), 262. See also Walter Blair, "'A Man's Voice Speaking': A Continuum in American Humor," in *Veins of Humor*, ed. Harry Levin, Harvard English Studies no. 3 (Cambridge: Harvard University Press, 1972), 185–204.

6. Quotes from *Variety*'s reviews of two Allen programs, January 9, 1934, 32, and March 9, 1938, 32.

7. Arlen J. Hansen, "Entropy and Transformation: Two Types of American Humor," *American Scholar* 43 (Summer 1974): 412, 421. "Exaggeration is as much a part of our national inheritance as are democracy and our capacity for Dream." Sanford Pinsker, "On or about December 1910: When Human Character—and American Humor—Changed," in Clark and Turner, *Critical Essays on American Humor*, 188; see also the editors' "Introduction," 2.

8. Douglas Gilbert, *American Vaudeville: Its Life and Times* (1940; reprint, New York: Dover, 1968), 251; see also p. 263 on Allen.

9. Benny described his radio persona in Orrin E. Dunlap, Jr., "Comedian Rides the Radio in the Saddle of Reality," *New York Times*, April 28, 1940, sec. 9, p. 12. Allen once called Benny "the first comedian in radio to realize you could get big laughs by ridiculing yourself instead of your stooges." Quoted in Milt Josefsberg, *The Jack Benny Show: The Life and Times of America's Best-Loved Entertainer* (New Rochelle, N.Y.: Arlington House, 1977), 60; see also Arthur Frank Wertheim, *Radio Comedy* (New York: Oxford University Press, 1979), chap. 7, "The Fall Guy."

10. Tapes of the "Jack Benny Program," December 7, 1947, and "Fibber McGee and Molly," December 23, 1941.

11. THT script, September 26, 1934.

12. THT script, February 16, 1938.

13. FAS script, May 26, 1946.

14. SBR script, September 22, 1933.

15. THT script, January 27, 1937.

16. THT script, June 8, 1938.

17. TST script, December 20, 1942.

18. Gilbert Seldes, *The Great Audience* (New York: Viking Press, 1951), 124–125.

19. LBC script, January 22, 1933.

20. HOS script, May 23, 1934, quoted; also SBR script, August 25, 1933.

21. THT script, June 9, 1937.

22. HOS script, April 18, 1934.

23. THT script, March 22, 1939.

24. THT script, May 15, 1935.

25. Shirley Louise Staples, "From 'Barney's Courtship' to Burns and Allen: Male–Female Comedy Teams in American Vaudeville, 1865–1932," doctoral dissertation, Tufts University, 1981, 325. See also Wertheim, *Radio Comedy*, chap. 9, "Scatterbrains," on Jane and Goodman Ace ("Easy Aces") and George Burns and Gracie Allen.

26. The latter phrase is Allen's in letter to Joe Kelly, March 20, 1933, in Joe McCarthy, ed., *Fred Allen's Letters* (Garden City, N.Y.: Doubleday, 1965), 92; for characterizations of Portland's radio persona, see Hugh Pentecost and Virginia Faulkner, "Murder on the Fred Allen Program," *American Magazine* 135 (July 1944): 145; Arnold M. Auerbach, *Funny Men Don't Laugh* (Garden City, N.Y.: Doubleday, 1965), 132.

27. THT script, February 23, 1938.

28. SHR script, January 24, 1934.

29. HOS script, March 21, 1934.

30. TST script, November 29, 1942.

31. THT script, March 4, 1936.

32. Gilbert Highet, *The Anatomy of Satire* (Princeton: Princeton University Press, 1962), 69. Highet defines parody "as imitation which, through distortion and exaggeration, evokes amusement, derision, and sometimes scorn." Ibid.

33. Sources that illuminate our tradition of parody include Robert C. Toll, *Blacking Up: The Minstrel Show in Nineteenth-Century America* (New York: Oxford University Press, 1974), 93–96 (parodies of *Uncle Tom's Cabin*); David Grimsted, *Melodrama Unveiled: American Theater and Culture, 1800–1850* (Chicago: University of Chicago Press, 1968), 235–240; Walter Blair, "Burlesques in Nineteenth-Century American Humor," *American Literature* 2 (November 1930): 236–247; Constance Rourke, *American Humor: A Study of the National Character* (1931; reprint, Garden City, N.Y.; Doubleday Anchor, 1953), 101–110.

34. Lawrence W. Levine, "William Shakespeare and the American People: A Study in Cultural Transformation," *American Historical Review* 89 (February 1984): 34; see also Ray B. Browne, "Shakespeare in American Vaudeville and Negro Minstrelsy," *American Quarterly* 12 (Fall 1960): 374–391.

35. Nathaniel Benchley, "Introduction," in *Twentieth Century Parody, American and British* (New York: Harcourt, Brace, 1960), xiv.

36. Earl F. Bargainner, "W. S. Gilbert and American Musical Theatre," *Journal of Popular Culture* 12 (Winter 1978): 448; see also pp. 446–447.

37. FAS script, November 25, 1945. Allen repeated the skit on April 14, 1946. Durocher was a frequent guest on Allen's programs. For commentary on the "Brooklyn Pinafore," see the following issues of *Variety*: November 28, 1945, 30; March 6, 1946, 37; May 18, 1949, 30. On November 23, 1947, Allen presented the "Football Pinafore," and on May 15, 1949, a "Television Pinafore."

38. TST script, March 19, 1941.

39. TST script, April 23, 1944.

40. TST script, May 20, 1942, 30. Allen wrote to H. Allen Smith: "the charlie chan estate it [*sic*] attempting to shake us down and will settle for $3000. we killed charlie chan in a sketch a couple of years ago. what harm was done, i don't know but since warner oland departed this life the chan pickings have been slim and apparently the derr bigger widow grabs at any chance to catch a fleeting dollar." Allen to h.a., nov. 9th [1942], Smith Papers.

41. TST script, February 13, 1944.

42. THT script, January 9, 1935.

43. TST script, February 13, 1944.

44. *New York Sun*, May 1, 1937, clipping in Allen clipping file, Billy Rose Collection.

45. TST scripts, March 8, 1942, and February 11, 1942.

46. MacDonald, *Don't Touch That Dial!*, 157–159.

47. THT script, June 5, 1935.

48. THT script, October 9, 1935.

49. THT script, January 1, 1936.

50. THT script, April 21, 1937; TST script, June 6, 1943.

51. THT script, December 14, 1938.

52. THT script, May 17, 1939.

53. TST script, December 25, 1940.

54. TST script, April 9, 1944.

55. THT script, October 7, 1936.

56. THT script, April 21, 1937.

57. THT script, November 23, 1938.

58. TST script, January 24, 1943.

59. Citing radio feuds as an example, Lawrence W. Levine

has noted the flowering of "ritual insult" during the 1930s. "The practice of ritual insult was a perfect channel for anger which was either unfocused or which could not be aimed at its appropriate target. It is not coincidence that during the Great Depression, when the American people had a substantial amount of anger of this sort, ritual insult flourished in popular humor." Levine, *Black Culture and Black Consciousness: Afro-American Folk Thought from Slavery to Freedom* (New York: Oxford University Press, 1977), 356. Levine does not acknowledge that insulting also has roots in conventionalized white commercial amusement. Of successful radio ad-libbers, John K. Hutchens wrote: "In the exacting school of audience response they learned the type of humor that is most immediately effective, which is, in a word, the insult." Hutchens, "The Tricky Ad Lib," *New York Times Magazine*, May 24, 1942, 29. In 1938 *Variety* criticized a recent Benny–Allen radio appearance. "Toward the end the gagging degenerated to mere bandying of comic name-calling. It was faintly Gus Sun." The Gus Sun Circuit connected a string of smalltime vaudeville theaters; the ritual insult was a vaudeville convention. *Variety*, March 30, 1938, 34.

60. Five years earlier, however, *Variety* recognized that "Allen's program abounds in 'inside stuff' references to show business." *Variety*, January 27, 1937, 31.

61. John Crosby's column in the *New York Herald-Tribune*, entitled "The Mechanical Joke," January 3, 1951, appeared in his *Out of the Blue: A Book about Radio and Television* (New York: Simon and Schuster, 1952), 54–56.

62. Edwin O'Connor, "No Laughing Matter," *Atlantic Monthly* 178 (September 1946): 130; for examples of celebrity humor, see FAS scripts, March 9, 1947 (Milton Berle, guest), and May 11, 1947 (Bing Crosby, guest).

63. FAS script, October 18, 1939.

64. TST script, December 10, 1941.

65. THT scripts, January 26, 1938, and February 1, 1939.

66. TST script, November 5, 1941.

67. TST script, February 25, 1942.

68. THT script, January 2, 1935.

69. THT script, March 6, 1935.

70. THT script, May 18, 1938, for "House"; TST script, May 7, 1941. Benny parodied Allen's show on his broadcast of April 5, 1936, to cite one example.

71. TST script, February 1, 1939.

72. TST script, January 16, 1944.

73. Both quotes from script of "Jack Benny Program," March 14, 1937; copy in Allen Papers.

74. TST script, November 20, 1940.

75. TST script, December 18, 1940.

76. THT script, March 15, 1939.

77. FAS script, December 9, 1945.

78. TST script, December 18, 1940.

79. Tape recording of FAS, March 20, 1940.

80. Joseph Boskin, *Humor and Social Change in Twentieth-Century America* (Boston: Trustees of the Public Library of the City of Boston, 1979), 14.

81. Albert F. McLean, *American Vaudeville as Ritual* (Lexington: University of Kentucky Press, 1965), 119.

82. Robert C. Toll, *On with the Show: The First Century of Show Business in America* (New York: Oxford University Press, 1976), 95; elsewhere Toll quotes minstrel headliner Lew Dockstader in 1916: "The pun and the conundrum were mighty popular with our grandfathers. They screamed over both." Toll, *Blacking-Up*, 54; see also Rourke, *American Humor*, 106.

83. Norris W. Yates, *Robert Benchley* (New York: Twayne, 1968), 24; Norris W. Yates, *The American Humorist: Conscience of the Twentieth Century* (Ames: Iowa State University Press, 1964), 341, 343.

84. Walter Blair and Hamlin Hill, *America's Humor: From Poor Richard to Doonesbury* (New York: Oxford University Press, 1978), 277, 280–281, 285–286, 288–289, 291.

85. Andrew Bergman, *We're in the Money: Depression America and Its Films* (New York: New York University Press, 1971), 31.

86. TST script, November 6, 1940.

87. THT script, May 13, 1936.

88. THT script, March 31, 1937. On lawyers, see THT script, April 28, 1937.

89. The first quote is from *Chicago Sunday Tribune*, October 23, 1932, sec. 7, p. 4; the second is from LBC script, April 16, 1933.

90. LBC scripts, October 23 and December 4, 1932.

91. TST script, May 14, 1944; see also TST scripts, March 8, 1942, and March 7, 1943.

92. TST script, January 3, 1943.

93. TST script, May 3, 1942.

94. TST script, December 27, 1942.

95. TST script, January 2, 1944.

96. LBC script, October 30, 1932.

97. LBC script, December 11, 1932.

98. Fred Allen, *Treadmill to Oblivion* (Boston: Little, Brown, 1954), 16–17.

99. Orrin E. Dunlap, Jr., "Radio Artists Seek 'Tags' of Identification on the Air," *New York Times*, February 18, 1934, sec. 9, p. 11.

Chapter 7

1. Joe Morella, Edward Z. Epstein, and Eleanor Clark, *The Amazing Careers of Bob Hope: From Gags to Riches* (New Rochelle, N.Y.: Arlington House, 1973), 85.

2. Louis D. Rubin, Jr., "Introduction: 'The Great American Joke,'" in *The Comic Imagination in American Literature*, ed. Louis D. Rubin, Jr. (New Brunswick: Rutgers University Press, 1973), 4.

3. Louis Kronenberger, "The American Sense of Humor," in *Humor in America, an Anthology*, ed. Enid Veron (New York: Harcourt Brace Jovanovich, 1976), 269.

4. Kenneth Rexroth, "The Decline of American Humor," *Nation* 74 (April 1957): 375.

5. For example: "American Humor: Hardly a Laughing Matter," *Time*, March 4, 1966, 46–47. Phyllis Battelle, "Serious Mind Lay Behind Fred Allen's Quips," *New York Journal-American*, March 20, 1956, in Allen clipping file, Billy Rose Collection. Battelle quotes Herman Wouk at the time of Allen's death: "He was the greatest satirical wit in America in our time." Edwin O'Connor placed Allen in the company of Ring Lardner and Finley Peter Dunne, rather than with such radio personalities as Hildegarde and Red Skelton, in his "No Laughing Matter," *Atlantic Monthly* 178 (September 1946): 131.

6. Gilbert Highet, *The Anatomy of Satire* (Princeton: Princeton University Press, 1962), 233 and 156; see also pp. 3, 5, 16–17.

7. Quoted in Kathy Peiss, *Cheap Amusements: Working Women and Leisure in Turn-of-the-Century New York* (Philadelphia: Temple University Press, 1986), 157.

8. John K. Hutchens, "Fred Allen, Comedian's Comedian," *Theatre Arts* 26 (May 1942): 308.

9. Aaron Stein, "Court Room Broadcasting," *New York Evening Post*, October 25, 1934, in Allen clippings, Billy Rose Collection. John K. Hutchens claimed that Allen was the first to

ridicule radio, a claim that is impossible to confirm. Hutchens, "Comedian's Comedian," 308.

10. These sources are among those that trace and analyze this major transformation in American humor: Norris W. Yates, *The American Humorist: Conscience of the Twentieth Century* (Ames: Iowa State University Press, 1964); Norris W. Yates, *Robert Benchley* (New York: Twayne, 1968); Veron, *Humor in America*, 201, 249; Walter Blair and Hamlin Hill, *America's Humor: From Poor Richard to Doonesbury* (New York: Oxford University Press, 1978), 388–459; Hamlin Hill, "Modern American Humor: The Janus Laugh," *College English* 25 (December 1963): 170–176; Lawrence E. Mintz, "American Humour and the Spirit of the Times," in *It's a Funny Thing, Humor*, ed. Antony J. Chapman and Hugh C. Foot (Oxford, England: Pergamon Press, 1977), 17–21; Lawrence E. Mintz, "American Humor in the 1920s," *Thalia: Studies in Literary Humor* 4, no. 1 (Spring and Summer 1981): 26–32. See also the important essay by Nancy Walker, "'Fragile and Dumb': The 'Little Woman' in Women's Humor, 1900–1940," *Thalia: Studies in Literary Humor* 5, no. 2 (Fall and Winter 1982–1983): 24–29.

11. Fred Allen, "Gargantua Has the Last Laugh," *New York Times Magazine*, April 1, 1945, 14; Allen also used Gargantua to reveal human discontent in TST script, April 19, 1942, and in FAS script, April 21, 1946, which contains the poem "Gargantua's Soliloquy."

12. THT script, June 24, 1936.

13. THT script, May 18, 1938.

14. THT script, October 12, 1938.

15. TST script, November 6, 1940.

16. TST script, January 8, 1941. For other portraits of "little man" figures, see TST scripts, January 22 and April 23, 1941, and June 14, 1942.

17. TST script, December 6, 1942.

18. TST script, December 27, 1942.

19. TST script, February 28, 1943.

20. THT script, March 16, 1938.

21. TST script, January 1, 1941.

22. For Melchior, TST script, December 12, 1943, and FAS script, February 2, 1947; for Spaulding, TST script, January 2, 1944.

23. FAS script, January 13, 1946.

24. LBC script, February 12, 1933.

25. CBS press release, November 1, 1943, Program Information Division, CBS Inc., 51 West 52nd St., New York, N.Y.

26. SBR script, August 18, 1933.

27. THT script, July 11, 1934.

28. THT script, October 3, 1934.

29. Fred Allen, *Treadmill to Oblivion* (Boston: Little, Brown, 1954), 210–211.

30. Allen to H. Allen Smith, April 1, 1941, Smith Papers.

31. Allen to Smith, August 15, 1941, Smith Papers.

32. Allen to "h.a." [Smith], "october 7" [1942?], Smith Papers.

33. "The Executive," printed in Joe McCarthy, ed., *Fred Allen's Letters* (Garden City, N.Y.: Doubleday, 1965), 145–146.

34. LBC script, October 30, 1932.

35. THT script, April 22, 1936.

36. HOS script, April 4, 1934.

37. FAS script, October 18, 1939.

38. THT script, April 22, 1936.

39. THT script, March 29, 1939.

40. SBR script, September 8, 1933.

41. THT script, December 1, 1937.

42. THT script, April 19, 1939.

43. THT script, June 1, 1938.

44. THT script, December 19, 1934.

45. THT script, December 15, 1937.

46. FAS script, January 13, 1946.

47. One of Allen's burlesques of Tin Pan Alley is in THT script, June 8, 1938.

48. TST script, December 17, 1941.

49. THT script, May 5, 1937.

50. THT script, March 16, 1938.

51. For example, Allen, *Treadmill to Oblivion*, 239–240; a half-hour presentation entitled "The State of American Humor," with Allen and Ben Grauer, broadcast on the program "Living 1949" (NBC), January 30, 1949. Fred Allen, "As Thousands Hear," *Variety*, January 2, 1934, 58; Fred Allen, "A Kind Word for the Comedian," *Variety*, September 17, 1947, 2.

52. THT script, October 7, 1936.

53. SBR scripts, August 4, 1933, and October 13, 1933; THT scripts, May 20, 1936, and October 19, 1938; TST script, February 4, 1942.

54. THT script, April 10, 1935.

55. Allen, quoted in an unidentified newspaper clipping, Allen clipping file, Billy Rose Collection.

56. FAS script, October 11, 1939.

57. TST script, February 12, 1941.

58. TST script, April 9, 1941.

59. FAS script, December 13, 1939.

60. THT script, April 20, 1938.

61. THT script, December 4, 1938.

62. TST script, May 31, 1942; a similar bit, more accessible to readers, is in Max Wylie, ed., *Best Broadcasts of 1940–41* (New York: Whittlesey House, 1942), 80–88.

63. TST script, December 26, 1943.

64. THT script, April 12, 1939.

65. TST script, October 4, 1942. Allen presented other good soap opera parodies; see FAS script, May 29, 1940, and TST script, January 14, 1942.

66. On the "eagle show" of March 20, 1940, lost in the furor over the bird, Allen did a skit spoofing the quiz "Pot of Gold."

67. TST script, February 12, 1941.

68. Alan Havig, "Frederic Wakeman's 'The Hucksters' and the Postwar Debate over Commercial Radio," *Journal of Broadcasting* 28, no. 2 (Spring 1984): 187–199.

69. FAS script, October 13, 1946. See the review of this show in *Variety*, October 16, 1946, 40.

70. Wylie, *Best Broadcasts of 1940–41*.

71. Max Wylie, ed., *Best Broadcasts of 1939–40* (New York: Whittlesey House, 1940), 156–165.

72. TST script, February 12, 1941.

73. TST script, January 3, 1943.

74. TST script, March 21, 1943.

75. THT script, September 19, 1934.

76. FAS script, May 5, 1946.

77. TST script, March 26, 1941.

78. THT script, January 11, 1939.

79. THT script, April 22, 1936.

80. THT script, May 5, 1937.

81. HOS script, June 20, 1934.

82. THT script, November 21, 1934.

83. These and other themes form the substance of Alan Havig, "Fred Allen and Hollywood," *Journal of Popular Film and Television* 7, no. 3 (1979): 273–291.

84. "Allen in Wonderland, In Which a Comedian Recounts His First Impressions of Hollywood," *Brooklyn Daily Eagle*, November 24, 1935, Allen clipping file, Billy Rose Collection.

85. For example, see THT script, March 2, 1938.

86. The following record Allen's disenchantment with the

film capital as his knowledge of the place grew: "All in from Hollywood," *New York Times*, October 27, 1935; H. Allen Smith, "Fred Allen Feels Out of Place in Midst of Hollywood Antics," *New York World-Telegram*, July 6, 1940; Thornton Delehanty, "Fred Allen on the Perils of Picture-Making," *New York Herald-Tribune*, October 8, 1944; all in Allen clipping file, Billy Rose Collection. Also see Fred Allen, "a fable," *Variety*, January 5, 1949, 12.

87. THT script, June 22, 1938.

88. THT scripts, July 18, 1934, and May 19, 1937.

89. THT script, November 4, 1936.

90. THT script, April 6, 1938.

91. HOS script, April 4, 1934.

92. FAS script, October 18, 1939.

93. FAS script, June 19, 1940.

94. Ibid.

95. THT script, May 11, 1938.

96. FAS script, November 15, 1939.

97. THT script, July 18, 1934.

98. THT script, October 31, 1934.

Chapter 8

1. HOS script, March 21, 1934.

2. HOS script, April 18, 1934; THT script, February 20, 1935.

3. HOS script, March 21, 1934.

4. TST script, December 6, 1942.

5. TST script, May 7, 1944.

6. TST script, December 19, 1943.

7. Jack Gould, "Programs and People," *New York Times*, October 13, 1946, sec. 2, p. 9.

8. William Moyes, "Behind the Mike," *Portland Oregonian*, October 22, 1946, clipping in Durante Collection. See also Llewellyn White, "The Shortcomings of Radio," *Atlantic Monthly* 179 (April 1947): 67. The 1946–1947 season was the Alley's third year because of Allen's absence from radio's 1944–1945 season.

9. Arthur Frank Wertheim, *Radio Comedy* (New York: Oxford University Press, 1979), 261, 263–271, and chap. 15, "Allen's Alley." Wertheim's fine chapter on Allen's shows of the 1940s mistakenly entitles them "Allen's Alley" (p. 335). For an earlier discussion of the Alley, see Jim Harmon, *The Great Radio Come-*

dians (Garden City, N.Y.: Doubleday, 1970), 168–174. Allen's own retrospective look, which includes exerpts from scripts, is in Fred Allen, *Treadmill to Oblivion* (Boston: Little, Brown, 1954), 179–210.

10. For example, this recent article focuses on those four: Maurice Zolotow, "Unforgettable Fred Allen," *Reader's Digest*, October 1987, 56; Wertheim, *Radio Comedy*, 339.

11. TST scripts, January 17 and 24, February 28, and June 13, 1943.

12. Norris W. Yates, *The American Humorist: Conscience of the Twentieth Century* (Ames: Iowa State University Press, 1964).

13. TST script, March 12, 1944.

14. FAS script, November 3, 1946.

15. TST script, May 7, 1944.

16. TST script, June 4, 1944.

17. Paul Antoine Distler, "Ethnic Comedy in Vaudeville and Burlesque," in *American Popular Entertainment*, ed. Myron Matlaw (Westport, Conn.: Greenwood Press, 1979), 36. Distler notes the persistence of "the dialect gag" through the twentieth century.

18. Final draft, "Program Standards of the National Broadcasting Company," July 1938, Box 93, NBC Records.

19. "Mrs. Nussbaum is a rich characterization in the first place, to be sure, but it is executed with faultless timing and a magnificent sense of appreciation. Miss [Minerva] Pious is providing a comic cameo that shouldn't be missed." Jack Gould, "Mr. Allen's Comeback," *New York Times*, October 14, 1945, sec. 2, p. 5.

20. Richard Lamparski's interview with Minerva Pious, n.d.; audiotape in author's possession.

21. Letter, Max Wilk to Niles Trammel, November 17, 1948, Box 115, folder 28, "Trammel: 1948 Fred Allen," NBC Records.

22. Jerome Lawrence, ed., *Off Mike: Radio Writing by the Nation's Top Radio Writers* (New York: Duell, Sloan and Pearce, 1944), 194. In 1952, one humorist said "good riddance" to the Jew of stage comedy. See Sam Levenson, "The Dialect Comedian Should Vanish," *Commentary* 14 (August 1952): 168–170.

23. Henry Popkin, "The Vanishing Jew of Our Popular Culture," *Commentary*, July 1952, 49. Gene Shalit included samples of dialect comedy in his recent anthology of American humor, with the comment that "good-hearted ethnic humor in America

has largely vanished. Too bad for America." Gene Shalit, *Laughing Matters: A Celebration of American Humor* (Garden City, N.Y.: Doubleday, 1987), xxviii.

24. Sources that discuss ethnic comedy in vaudeville include these fine dissertations: Robert William Snyder, "The Voice of the City: Vaudeville and the Formation of Mass Culture in New York Neighborhoods, 1880–1930," doctoral dissertation, New York University, 1986, 180–190; Shirley Louise Staples, "From 'Barney's Courtship' to Burns and Allen: Male–Female Comedy Teams in American Vaudeville, 1865–1932," doctoral dissertation, Tufts University, 1981, 59–76, 89–103, 164–184. One student of the Irish stereotype wrote in 1949 that "Fred Allen has lifted his Irishman [Ajax Cassidy] almost bodily from the vaudeville stage." Arthur Robert Williams, "The Irishman in American Humor: From 1647 to the Present," doctoral dissertation, Cornell University, 1949, 133. Ethnic humor is prevalent in folklore and jokelore. Levine, for example, finds that "the Irishman remained a central butt of black humor throughout the twentieth century." Lawrence W. Levine, *Black Culture and Black Consciousness: Afro-American Folk Thought from Slavery to Freedom* (New York: Oxford University Press, 1977), 301. On the use of dialect in literature, see Walter Blair and Raven I. McDavid, Jr., eds., *The Mirth of a Nation: America's Great Dialect Humor* (Minneapolis: University of Minnesota Press, 1983).

25. See Jack Gould, "They Say the Right Thing at the Wrong Time," *New York Times Magazine*, March 24, 1946, 61; and Norbert Muhlen, "Radio: Political Threat or Promise?" *Commentary* 3 (March 1947): 206.

26. FAS script, March 23, 1947. The comic Jew of twentieth-century media entertainment, as Altman observes, was "largely a creation of Jews themselves." Sig Altman, *The Comic Image of the Jew: Explorations of a Pop Culture Phenomenon* (Rutherford, N.J.: Farleigh Dickinson University Press, 1971), 15. On Pious, see Judy Dupy, "Name Your Mighty Allen Accent, And It's Minerva Pious," *PM*, February 25, 1942, 23.

27. From FAS scripts, October 7 and 28, 1945, December 2, 1945, and January 20, 1946.

28. FAS script, November 18, 1945.

29. TST script, March 14, 1943; FAS scripts, May 5, 1946, and April 13, 1947.

30. The statement is Robert C. Toll's in his *Blacking Up: The Minstrel Show in Nineteenth-Century America* (New York: Oxford University Press, 1974), 14. On Mose, see also Walter

Blair and Hamlin Hill, *America's Humor: From Poor Richard to Doonesbury* (New York: Oxford University Press, 1978), 147; and Constance Rourke, *American Humor: A Study of the National Character* (Garden City, N.Y.: Doubleday Anchor, 1953), 115–118.

31. FAS script, October 26, 1947.

32. FAS script, May 18, 1947.

33. FAS script, October 6, 1946.

34. HOS script, June 20, 1934.

35. THT script, November 21, 1935.

36. TST script, January 3, 1943.

37. TST script, February 4, 1942.

38. FAS script, November 2, 1947.

39. SBR script, August 4, 1933.

40. FAS script, November 10, 1946.

41. FAS script, December 22, 1946.

42. FAS script, November 17, 1946.

43. TST script, April 4, 1943.

44. Blair and Hill, *America's Humor*, 128–129; Enid Veron, ed., *Humor in America: An Anthology* (New York: Harcourt Brace Jovanovich, 1976), 109.

45. FAS script, January 6, 1946.

46. FAS script, January 27, 1946.

47. FAS script, November 10, 1946.

48. FAS script, March 9, 1947.

49. FAS script, January 12, 1947, for the Booth remark. "Claghorn, the Dixie Foghorn," an editorial in the *Richmond Times-Dispatch*, probably written by Virginius Dabney, commented: "We 'southrons' . . . have to go around protesting that we aren't all raucous nitwits and foghorns like Senator Claghorn." The editorial is in B. A. Botkin, *A Treasury of Southern Folklore* (New York: Crown, 1949), 305.

50. David E. E. Sloan, ed., *The Literary Humor of the Urban Northeast, 1830–1890* (Baton Rouge: Louisiana State University Press, 1983).

51. See, for example, THT script, May 25, 1938, and FAS script, October 21, 1945.

52. The first reference is in *Variety*, December 28, 1938, 32; the second is in Jean Walker, "Fred Allen Makes High Art of the Funnyman Business," *Daily Worker*, October 4, 1941, Allen clipping file, Billy Rose Collection. New York City, of course, has placed its distinctive imprint on much that the entertainment industry and mass media have produced, as is suggested in

these sources: Roland Marchand, *Advertising the American Dream: Making Way for Modernity, 1920–1940* (Berkeley: University of California Press, 1985), 36–37 (on how the city distorted the perceptions of ad agency professionals); Benjamin McArthur, *Actors and American Culture, 1880–1920* (Philadelphia: Temple University Press, 1984) ("in the late nineteenth century New York asserted itself as America's cultural arbiter by becoming the packager and dispenser of the arts for the nation"— p. 8); Thomas Grant, "Mythologising Manhattan: The *New Yorker*'s New York," *American Studies* 28 (Spring 1987): 31–46; Robert A. M. Stern, Gregory Gilmartin, and Thomas Mellins, *New York 1930* (New York: Rizzoli International Publications, 1987), 48–89 (on the city as depicted in twentieth-century painting, photography, moving pictures, and song).

53. For criticism of the Hollywood bias, see Jack Gould, "How Comic Is Radio Comedy?" *New York Times*, November 21, 1948, sec. 6, p. 22; Edwin O'Connor, "No Laughing Matter," *Atlantic Monthly* 178 (September 1946): 130, 132. See *Variety*, September 3, 1947, 22, for lists of the comedy programs broadcast from New York (6 of them) and Hollywood (28 of them). On Hollywood's growth as a radio production center, see the following issues of *Variety*: October 16, 1946, 28; November 13, 1946, 24; February 12, 1947, 24; February 26, 1947, 33; March 5, 1947, 27; November 17, 1948, 25; and see *Business Week*, November 6, 1937, 27.

54. Allen to Auerbach, "nov. 21st" [1944?], Arnold M. Auerbach Collection, Archive of Contemporary History, University of Wyoming, Laramie. For a similar comment, see *Variety*, December 27, 1944, 1.

55. See Veron, *Humor in America*, 63–65; Blair and Hill, *America's Humor*, 66–73, 176–177; Rourke, *American Humor*, chap. 1; Walter Blair, *Native American Humor* (1937; reprint, San Francisco: Chandler, 1960), 45; Toll, *Blacking Up*, 13–14; Louise M. Eich, "The Stage Yankee," *Quarterly Journal of Speech* 27 (February 1941): 16–25.

56. *New York Times*, October 23, 1981, B9.

57. Both quotes from FAS script, May 16, 1948.

58. FAS script, October 6, 1946.

59. FAS script, January 6, 1946.

60. FAS script, December 1, 1946.

61. FAS script, December 8, 1946.

62. FAS script, February 24, 1946.

63. FAS script, November 14, 1948.

64. FAS script, May 2, 1948.

65. FAS script, April 27, 1947.

66. FAS script, December 14, 1947.

67. FAS script, June 16, 1946.

68. FAS script, October 13, 1946.

69. FAS script, December 28, 1947.

70. FAS script, March 16, 1947.

71. FAS script, May 8, 1947.

72. Richard M. Dorson, *Jonathan Draws the Longbow* (Cambridge: Harvard University Press, 1946), 70: "Preeminently the comic [Yankee] figure was a fool, an ignorant countryman, baffled by urban ways, befuddled by modern machinery, legitimate game for dupes and hoaxes. The industrial age had passed him by; mechanical contrivances caused Jonathan surprises and grief."

73. FAS script, May 8, 1947.

74. FAS script, December 2, 1945.

75. FAS script, February 10, 1946.

76. FAS script, April 14, 1946.

77. FAS script, October 19, 1947.

78. FAS script, March 20, 1949.

79. Stephen J. Whitfield, "Richard Nixon as a Comic Figure," *American Quarterly* 37 (Spring 1985): 114: "Beginning in the 1960s, satire could become more direct, more savage, and more explicitly cruel, without fear of censorship, stigma, or punishment." Norris W. Yates notes that during World War I, "humorous writers in America tended to avoid the crucial issues and to pick around on the fringes of the war for their subject matter." Allen, especially during World War II, did the same. Norris W. Yates, *Robert Benchley* (New York: Twayne, 1968), 47.

80. In THT scripts, November 9 and 23, 1938, and May 10, 1939. Nineteenth-century humorists satirized the exaggerated public oratory of their time. See Barnett Baskerville, "Nineteenth Century Burlesque of Oratory," *American Quarterly* 20 (Winter 1968): 726–743. Senator Robert A. Taft, at midcentury, defended the dignity of the U.S. Senate against the comic ridicule of mass entertainment, including Allen's Senator Claghorn. *Variety*, February 18, 1948, 1.

81. TST script, February 6, 1944.

82. FAS script, February 22, 1948.

83. FAS script, October 31, 1948.

84. TST script, April 2, 1944.

85. THT script, November 2, 1938.

86. FAS script, April 17, 1949.
87. FAS script, October 13, 1946.
88. TST script, October 4, 1942.
89. TST script, May 14, 1944.
90. FAS script, June 27, 1948.
91. Telegrams, Gosden and Correll to Franklin D. Roosevelt, March 5, 1933; Stephen Early to Gosden and Correll, March 6, 1933; Correll and Gosden to Stephen Early, October 11, 1937; Early to Correll and Gosden, October 11, 1937; all in President's Personal File 3795, Franklin D. Roosevelt Presidential Library, Hyde Park, New York.
92. FAS script, October 4, 1939.
93. TST script, January 9, 1944.
94. FAS script, December 14, 1947.
95. FAS script, January 25, 1948.
96. FAS script, November 7, 1948.
97. THT script, November 25, 1936.
98. THT script, February 19, 1936.
99. The skit appeared, for example, in THT script, December 22, 1937, and FAS script, December 22, 1946.
100. THT script, November 2, 1938.
101. FAS script, November 24, 1946.
102. FAS script, January 9, 1949.
103. TST script, November 1, 1942.
104. TST script, March 21, 1943.
105. TST script, January 2, 1944.
106. TST script, January 3, 1943.
107. FAS script, December 7, 1947.
108. FAS script, November 14, 1948.
109. FAS script, January 23, 1949.
110. FAS script, October 3, 1948.
111. FAS script, October 26, 1947.
112. FAS script, November 2, 1947.

Chapter 9

1. Critics recognized the failure: see Jack Gould, "Radio and TV in Review," *New York Times*, September 25, 1950, 42; Jack Gould, "Mr. Allen on Video," *New York Times*, October 1, 1950, sec. 2, p. 11.
2. Allen to Alton Cook, July 3, 1950, in Joe McCarthy, ed., *Fred Allen's Letters* (Garden City, N.Y.: Doubleday, 1965), 141.
3. John Crosby, "Unemployed Actor," December 5, 1949,

in his collection of columns, *Out of the Blue: A Book about Radio and Television* (New York: Simon and Schuster, 1952), 33.

4. Allen to "dear allen," july 6 [1953], Smith Papers.

5. Groucho Marx to Fred Allen, September 4, 1953, and Allen to Marx, August 21, 1956, in Groucho Marx, ed., *The Groucho Letters: Letters to and from Groucho Marx* (New York: Manor Books, 1967), 90–91. For other assessments, see Philip Hamburger, "Television," *New Yorker* 29 (September 5, 1953): 74; "Oh, Mr. Al-len," *Newsweek* 42 (August 31, 1953), 58.

6. Frank DeBlois, "Fred Allen's Last Interview," *TV Guide*, April 21, 1956, 5–7. My thanks to Professor J. Fred MacDonald of Northeastern Illinois University for calling this article to my attention.

7. Steve Allen, *The Funny Men* (New York: Simon and Schuster, 1956), 150.

8. R. W. Emerson, secundus [Neibhur], "Television's Peril To Culture," *American Scholar* 19 (Spring 1950): 138. My thanks to Charles C. Brown for calling this article to my attention.

9. Crosby, "Unemployed Actor," 33.

10. Fred Allen, "the moderate life of a moderator," *Theatre Arts* 37 (October 1953): 25.

11. Ibid.

Index

All fictional characters, such as Ajax Cassidy and Archie Bunker, are indexed by given rather than surname, and characters without first names, such as Mr. Moto or Mrs. Mulligan, are indexed by title.

AMERICAN CIVILIZATION

A series edited by Allen F. Davis